Why Can't We All Just Get Along...

Shout Less. Listen More.

Iain Dale

HarperCollins*Publishers*

HarperCollins*Publishers*
1 London Bridge Street
London SE1 9GF

www.harpercollins.co.uk

HarperCollins*Publishers*
1st Floor, Watermarque Building, Ringsend Road
Dublin 4, Ireland

First published by HarperCollins*Publishers* 2020
This edition published 2021

13 5 7 9 10 8 6 4 2

© Iain Dale 2020, 2021

Iain Dale asserts the moral right to be
identified as the author of this work

A catalogue record of this book is
available from the British Library

ISBN 978-0-00-837913-1

Printed and bound in Great Britain by
CPI Group (UK) Ltd, Croydon

MIX
Paper from
responsible sources
FSC™ C007454

This book is produced from independently certified FSC™ paper
to ensure responsible forest management.

For more information visit: www.harpercollins.co.uk/green

'Now that every word is taken down and that the speaker knows that he is addressing not a private club, but a gathering that may embrace the whole nation … he must walk delicately and measure his paces; he cannot frisk and frolic in the flowery meads of rhetoric; he dare not "let himself go".'

Lord Curzon, The Rede Lecture, University of Cambridge, 6 November 1913

'Over the past two decades, national political and civil discourse has been characterized by "Truth Decay", defined as a set of four interrelated trends: an increasing disagreement about facts and analytical interpretations of facts and data; a blurring of the line between opinion and fact; an increase in the relative volume, and resulting influence, of opinion and personal experience over fact; and lowered trust in formerly respected sources of factual information.'

World Economic Forum, 2018

Contents

Part Three: ISSUES

Prologue

Publication date of the hardback edition of this book was set for 28 May 2020. The publicity plan was in place. I was booked to appear at thirty or so different literary and political events during May, June and July. I was pumped. Ready for action. *Why Can't We All Just Get Along ...* was set to be the publishing sensation of the summer. OK, I exaggerate to make a point, but what could possibly have gone wrong? As Harold Macmillan would have said, 'Events, dear boy, events.' Or coronavirus, to be more precise.

In some ways the timing could not have been better, because the rows in the media and among some politicians have brilliantly illustrated many of the points I make in the following pages.

Nuance is a word you will read a lot over the coming 300 pages. In the debate about coronavirus it hardly featured. On social media some reckoned that Boris Johnson deliberately engineered policies to ensure tens of thousands of older people would die, which, given that it was the older generation who largely voted him into power, is a bit of a counter-intuitive view to hold. Others clearly regarded him as the nation's saviour, and how dare anyone question any aspect of the government's response. It was yet another example of how social media divides and rules without seemingly caring a jot about the consequences for our public discourse.

There's little doubt that the coronavirus crisis has deepened the disconnect between the media and the general public. Part of this growing mistrust came from the daily press conferences, where a succession of journalists have seemed to delight in asking 'gotcha' questions; challenging the minister on duty to apologise for this, that or the other; or enquiring whether they were 'ashamed' of failures to deliver on promises. To the public, these questions were designed to generate headlines for the journalists themselves (or their organisation) rather than to scrutinise government actions or tease out more information and/or an explanation of policy.

There was little nuance or context. When health secretary Matt Hancock announced a target of 100,000 Covid-19 tests per day by 30 April, this target was gold-plated by the media into a pledge, from which he would not be allowed to resile.

I genuinely think it would have been impossible for Winston Churchill to have fought the Second World War with a twenty-four-hour news media in full cry. I saw a tweet featuring a suggestion of how a lobby journalist in 1940 might have posed a question at Churchill's daily press briefing …

Winston, under your leadership we're out of Europe, which the BBC fought against. Immigrant workers are staying away. The army has no PPE and ran away at Dunkirk. Hospitals are underfunded. We have no allies in Europe. You failed to stop bombers attacking London.

The shops are empty, the economy is devastated and you missed an opportunity to escape from a German-led Europe. Why do you not surrender and resign after your failures?

Many a true word spoken in jest.

When it fell to me to announce live on air that Boris Johnson had been taken into intensive care, I saw both the best and the worst of human nature. I received a lot of texts and tweets from diehard Labour voters and political opponents saying they wished the Prime Minister well; some were even moved to tears by the news. Others, however, saw fit to tweet their delight. Boris Derangement Syndrome took on a whole new form, as evidenced by thousands of despicable tweets that expressed the hope he would suffer as much as possible and even die.

This is not to excuse government. The daily press conferences were a mistake. There was an imperative to say something new, yet often there was little new to say. Tired mantras were repeated day after day. 'We made the right decision at the right time.' 'We're straining every sinew.' 'I'd like to pay tribute to …' 'We mustn't forget that behind every death is an individual story.' It seemed to many that the politicians lacked basic human empathy and automatically reverted to robotic answers.

While I certainly blame the media for getting it wrong in this crisis, politicians cannot escape blame either.

All the issues raised here are examined in great detail in this book, and although it was intensely irritating for its publication to be delayed, in a way the messages contained in it are even more relevant than when I started writing it in 2019. How we answer these questions will determine the kind and quality of media and public discourse we'll be getting in the future.

It's all summed up in something I tweeted on 23 April 2020, which was seen by 1.6 million people.

> Every journalist/columnist/commentator (including me) in the broadcast and print media needs to look at themselves in the mirror and answer this question: how have I contributed to the fact that I am less trusted than the people I am supposed to hold to account? Discuss.

On the bright side, the country coming together each Thursday evening at 8 p.m. to applaud the NHS and key workers has been heart-warming to witness. When it first happened, I interviewed the then Labour Shadow Chancellor, John McDonnell, immediately afterwards. He had been out on his street clapping away and I had been watching it on my TV screen. We both became a bit emotional and turned into blubbering wrecks.

While the response to coronavirus has engendered some pretty big divisions, the whole lockdown process, which we've now gone through three times, has allowed people time to reflect on their life priorities and to rekindle old friendships, albeit virtually, and has encouraged neighbourliness and a more real sense of community spirit. Political enmities have often been cast aside in the national interest. The collective sense of national grief over the tens of thousands who have fallen victim to coronavirus has proved to me that the answer to the question posed in the title of this book is that, yes, we can get along if we really put our minds to it.

The Decline in Public Discourse

'So you're a shock jock, then?' is a question people often put to me when I say I work on a speech radio station. No. I'm not. I'm the very antithesis of a so-called 'shock jock', or at least I like to think I am. I am always up for a robust debate, but instead of causing division and hatred, I like to think I try to bring people together and give people a platform to argue a case I might not agree with, but I respect. Hence the title of this book.

Over the years, I have grown hugely frustrated and a little bit angry about the decline in the way we talk to and debate with each other. It doesn't have to be this way, if only we could all exercise a little self-restraint and recognise the importance of politeness and mutual respect. It sounds so simple, doesn't it? It really is. We don't need to return to the days of deference, but it's within us all to behave better both online and offline. I include myself in that.

How did we get here? Why has the internet, and social media in particular, exacerbated this growing trend towards rudeness and hatred? Those are two questions I want to explore in this book, as well as search for some answers.

This is not an intellectual book, mainly because I am not an intellectual and don't pretend to be one. It's written from experience and it's written from the heart. It is about how we communicate with each other, but it's also a book that uses my life experiences to illustrate the themes I address. It's not an autobiography, but it is autobiographical.

I've divided the book into three sections – broadly, media, politics and issues. In some chapters I've adapted previous pieces of writing that I've done over the years and incorporated them into the narrative here.

Rather fittingly, the inspiration for this book was a tweet. It was just before Christmas in 2018, and I said this.

> FYI I'm very happy to engage in polite debate on any
> issue. I probably respond more than most. However, if
> you call me a c**t, use profane language or insult me for
> no reason, I will mute/block you. No questions asked.
> You'd never dare say it to my face so don't do it here.

I can't remember what someone said to provoke that tweet but it was no doubt one of the usual insults I get from random strangers on social media on a daily basis. Someone at the *Mail on Sunday* noticed and asked if I would write an article for their New Year's edition on the state of public discourse. And that's how I spent Boxing Day 2018. I wrote that so far as political discourse was concerned, 2018 plumbed poisonous new depths of anger and abuse.

It was more than a year to forget. To borrow from a now familiar Brexit mantra, politics seemed to crash over a cliff and into the waves of intolerance.

It was a year that saw our then prime minister, Theresa May, told to 'bring her own noose' by one Tory MP, another warning that 'the moment is coming when the knife gets heated, stuck in her front and twisted – she'll be dead soon'. It was a year when Boris Johnson mocked Muslim women who wore burkas for 'looking like letter-boxes' or 'bank robbers'.

And there was the sight of Labour MP Luciana Berger arriving at her party's conference with a police escort for her own protection after being targeted by the sort of vile anti-Semitic abuse we thought had been consigned to history.

Yet what we heard and saw in public was mild compared with what went on behind the scenes – the private abuse our politicians reserved for each other and the sort of thing I've encountered all too frequently as a political pundit and broadcaster on television and radio.

Take the time I sat with a Remain-supporting minister in a TV studio, ahead of broadcast. As we chatted, he was spitting blood about the 'fucking lunatic Brexiteers', saying how he would personally ensure a special place in hell for them. Minutes later he was serenely explaining to the interviewer that the country must come together, while he and his colleagues were working in tandem to provide a united government.

The noted liberal historian Simon Schama seemed to have caught a bad case of Brexit Derangement Syndrome when, on the weekend following Boris Johnson becoming prime minister, he thought it appropriate to call him 'fatso' in a tweet objecting to a perfectly normal journalistic metaphor about the cabinet being put on a war footing:

> Can someone please stand up and start shouting (it wont
> [sic] be the weasel Corbyn) 'YOU ARE NOT
> CHURCHILL, fatso, and the EU is not the Third Reich.
> You do not have a war cabinet because THERE IS NO
> WAR. How DARE you invoke the sacrifices of those
> [who] fought one!'

It is difficult to imagine the great historians of the past indulging in such public venom. Would A. J. P. Taylor have deigned to insult Harold Macmillan in such a way? Would Thomas Babington Macaulay, perhaps Britain's greatest nineteenth-century historian, have called Lord Palmerston a 'bedswerver' (a nineteenth-century word for 'adulterer')? Had Twitter existed in 1920, would G. M. Trevelyan have shouted to Lloyd George that he was a RANDY OLD GOAT?! Doubtful.

Brexit Derangement Syndrome (BDS), more recently replaced by Boris Derangement Syndrome, has driven normally sane people round the bend. Sufferers are obsessed by only one thing and lose all sense of perspective. Their normal calm empirical analysis and assessment is trumped by cries of righteous and illogical outrage.

Scroll forward to New Year's Day 2020 and little seemed to have changed. Well, in Australia at any rate. Australian Green Party senator Mehreen Faruqi tweeted that Prime Minister Scott Morrison should 'just fuck off' over his refusal to provide more funds for firefighters to combat the terrible bush fires. An ABC journalist told a Twitter correspondent to 'go fuck yourself' and a Tasmanian Labor MP told a tweeter to 'get a life, you loser'. All in a day's politics …

Was it ever thus? To a degree, perhaps, but things are getting worse. The coarsening of public life has taken on a frightening new momentum – and it seems that people can no longer exchange opposing views without questioning their opponent's parentage.

I gently chided the Labour candidate Faiza Shaheen for her tweet decrying Iain Duncan Smith's knighthood in the New Year's Honours List. I suggested that instead of ranting about how evil he was, it might have been more polite and deft for her to congratulate him, while still making clear her opposition to his policies. I didn't expect to be thanked for my troubles, but even a grizzled old hack like me was quite shocked at the response. For two days afterwards I could barely look at my Twitter feed. It was infested with the hard-Left spitting their bile at me. All I had done was dole out some well-meant advice, from one electoral loser to another. Coming across as a bad loser is never a good look.

Yes, for all its undoubted benefits, social media is a big part of the problem. A minor disagreement can spiral out of control into a vituperative slanging match within seconds, and frequently does so.

Take the mild-mannered Labour MP for Bermondsey, Neil Coyle. Piers Morgan had made a comment about murdered Labour MP Jo Cox on early morning television. Responding immediately, Coyle tweeted this:

> It's early doors Piers but I say this hand on heart: go fuck yourself. You're a waste of space, air and skin. Trying to use Jo against us whilst encouraging the fascists is shocking even for a scrote like you. You make me sick.

The tweet was later deleted and an apology issued.

The anonymity, spontaneity and instant nature of social media – especially Twitter – encourages people to say things and behave in a way they wouldn't dream of doing in normal life. I know. I've been guilty of it myself on too many occasions.

As one of my followers put it: 'On the radio, Iain Dale is nice, nice, nice. On Twitter he can be an absolute beast.' And I could do nothing except admit that she was right.

Twitter has become a hateful place, an absolute sewer, and if I didn't work as a pundit and commentator, I'd happily remove myself from its clutches. Upset the Cybernats (somewhat vicious online supporters of the Scottish National Party), the Corbynistas, adherents of Leave.eu or the pro-Europe #FBPE (Follow Back, Pro EU) cult and you enter a living Twitter-hell for days on end.

Just look at the response from Corbynites to anyone who was concerned that anti-Semitism was being tolerated in the Labour Party. Or imagine the reaction you'll get from the so-called Cybernats if you dare to criticise Nicola Sturgeon.

As the columnist Suzanne Moore tweeted after a particularly bruising encounter with trans activists: 'One thing Twitter has ruined for ever is the fantasy that Left-wing people are nice. What a bunch of b*******, spewing out nastiness …' That's not to say things are any better on the Right. They're not.

Yet social media is not the sole cause of the problem – far from it. The problems are both wider and deeper. Political conversation itself is now, to be frank, debased. Political debate has become a binary world, with everything in black and white. Shades of grey have been driven out.

What, for example, should we make of those such as Labour's Laura Pidcock, who proudly declared that she couldn't possibly be friends with a Conservative? It was perhaps karma that she went on to lose her North West Durham seat in the December 2019 general election.

She, like a growing number of us, appears to live in an echo chamber, determined to reinforce existing views. God forbid that we should question our own side.

If you're on the Left, you think Channel 4 News is the most balanced news programme on TV.

If you're on the Right, you probably believe the BBC to be a hotbed of liberal Lefties. Whatever happened to research, to careful questioning, to open-minded debate. To nuance.

If we're not willing to engage with people who hold different views, how on earth can we challenge ourselves – or those in power?

It was one of my 2019 New Year's resolutions to play my own small part and aim at a little more civility in political exchanges, whether on Twitter or elsewhere. I told my (then) 125,000 followers that I would mute or block anyone who insulted me using four-letter words.

It's not that I'm a snowflake, but that sort of abuse is plain wrong. Most people wouldn't dream of calling me something obscene to my face, so why should I let them do so on Twitter?

Even children are now brought up to hate. Hate him, hate her, hate Manchester United, hate the Tories, hate the EU.

How much is the 'B' word responsible for this change in climate, for making foul-mouthed rants seem somehow normal? Has Brexit helped unleash and legitimise argument by insult?

It's clear that the referendum and ongoing argument have opened a Pandora's box of anger and rage. Yet that cannot be an excuse for descending into common abuse.

For example, as a Brexiteer, I believe Britain will be better off outside the EU. At the same time, I cannot prove it and must acknowledge the fact.

We need a sort of collective resolution – on the part of those in power and from the nation in general – to grow up. Yet, somehow, I doubt we'll get it.

It surely comes to something when it was left to Her Majesty the Queen to ask the nation, politely, to behave with more civility, which she did in her 2018 Christmas message. 'Even with the most deeply held differences, treating the other person with respect and as a fellow human being is always a good first step towards greater understanding.'

Despite this toxic political debate, there is massive demand for live political discussion and debates all around the country.

In the summer of 2019 I hosted a run of 24 shows at the Edinburgh Festival Fringe. I was also invited to Panmure House in Edinburgh, the home of Adam Smith, to take part in a panel with economist and comedian Dominic Frisby and Heather McGregor from Heriot-Watt University, who made it her mission to restore Panmure House to its former glory. We were each deputed to give our favourite Adam Smith quote and explain our reasons. This is the quote I chose:

> There is no art which one government sooner learns of another than that of draining money from the pockets of the people.

A fascinating discussion on the merits and demerits of taxation ensued, and although I'm by no means an economic expert, I felt I more than held my own. Towards the end, the subject of Brexit came up and I explained why I thought Brexit offered many opportunities as well as posed some economic threats, and why we ought to talk more about the economic opportunities rather than just concentrate on the threats as most of the media loves to do. I said I thought that there were huge opportunities for British manufacturing to revive, which provoked a man in the front row to laugh derisively. I asked him why he was laughing, but instead of engaging me in argument he said: 'Ninety per cent of what you have said is shit.' There was a collective intake of breath from the one hundred people in the audience.

I told him he was incredibly rude, as did several members of the audience. A lady then asked a question about the decline of public discourse. I replied that it comes to something when someone thinks it is acceptable to come to an august building like Panmure House and be so rude to a guest speaker's face. Still, at least he gave me some material to start this book with!

As children we are taught to respect our so-called 'elders and betters' and indulge in the centuries-long tradition of deference. We repress our natural instincts to speak our minds and instead often caveat or give nuance to our real thoughts and views. At least that's what used to happen.

The internet has seen the erosion of deference to such an extent that within a generation we'll be able to see its dead corpse twitching. The decline of deference has mirrored the rise of division and provocation, on display every day in the worlds of politics and the media. Some will say t'was ever thus, but they lack perspective.

As the age of deference disappears, we appear to be regressing to the ways we treated each other in bygone ages, not just in politics but in much of the rest of society. The themes of most of Hogarth's cartoons could equally comprise the subject matter of modern-day political cartoonists like Martin Rowson and Steve Bell.

It is good that the internet has given the voiceless a voice. The existence of social media and the invention of blogging have been great advertisements for the advancement of democracy in that they enable people to participate in the debate in ways they couldn't have done before. But all advances bring dangers, whether it is in the fields of technology, medicine, media or business. It is how we respond to these potential dangers that determines whether they turn out to be good for society or not.

In the end, we can regulate the internet all we like – assuming it's even possible to do so without international buy-in – but it's human nature that is in question here. We like to believe that as humans we are fundamentally good and motivated by the best of intentions. The trouble with the internet is that it gives equal opportunity to those with malign intentions and whose aim is to cause disharmony and conflict. Such people are difficult to edit out of the conversation because their voices tend to drown out the peacemakers.

This has been at the core of political philosophy down the centuries. Are human beings fundamentally 'good' or fundamentally flawed? The French philosopher Rousseau was a prime advocate of the view that all of us are born innocent and if we became bad it is because society made us so. If we all existed in a Nirvana-type land we would all develop into thoroughly nice, well-meaning, rounded members of society without a rude word spoken between us.

Rousseau saw hurt feelings and contempt as intrinsically bad characteristics. He believed that there should be no place for criticism, judgement, blame and comparison with others. In effect, he believed that human beings are by nature without sin and therefore society is entirely responsible if these same human beings veer off the path of righteousness.

Thomas Hobbes, the English philosopher who pre-existed Rousseau by a century or more, took the opposite point of view. He believed that human beings were programmed to relentlessly pursue their own self-interest, to pursue pleasure and avoid pain. Human nature was defined by the permanent conflict between fear and hope. Instead of Rousseau's world where the land flows with the milk of human kindness, in the slightly dystopian world of Hobbes' we all live in perpetual fear and suspicion of one another. The contract that society arrives at to sustain itself is largely formed out of fear, and is then enforced by fear. Roll forward 350 years and you can see this at work in any modern-day election campaign.

Look at the way we have been programmed to fear people from different backgrounds, social classes, sexualities and races, and Hobbes must be looking down in wonderment at his own foresight. However, it is possible to argue that this world of conflict and fear is being eroded as the generations change or die out. Racial and religious stereotypes are gradually disappearing because it is easier for us to meet and get to know people from different backgrounds. Travel, the media and the internet all facilitate this. Even in the last 20 years, in modern Western liberal democracies attitudes towards gay people have been transformed. The opposite may be true in parts of eastern Europe and Africa, but the trend is there for all to see.

Just as human nature evolves, so does the language we use. The shame of using certain swear-words in modern-day discourse seems to be on the wane. Our discussion of sex-related issues is on the increase. Twenty years ago the regulators would get involved if a woman's breast was seen on our TV screens before 9 p.m. Today they seem completely unconcerned by programmes such as Channel 4's *Naked Attraction*, which revels in sending people on dates after they have seen their potential partner stark naked. It seems to me a game-show panel that doesn't feature one or more comedians using the work 'fuck' at least once is considered a rarity. It surely can't be too long before our TV shows feature full naked sex, including penetration, and there are no bars on what people say at all. TV executives will argue it's the only way to compete with audiences on the internet, and given the decline in TV viewing, you can see their point.

As we know, on the internet, anything goes. Reaction is instant. Nuance goes out the window. The need to express a view with little time for any considered thought is imperative. Rationality is trumped by shoutiness. Someone who inadvertently says something mistakenly is immediately dubbed a liar. Anyone who questions the wisdom of open borders must be a racist. Express a view a tad to the right of Tony Blair and you automatically become a fascist. Agree with nationalising the water industry? You must be a communist.

I am regularly called a fascist by people who clearly have no understanding of what the word actually means. This is how Wikipedia defines a 'fascist' philosophy:

Fascism is a form of far-right, authoritarian ultranationalism characterized by dictatorial power, forcible suppression of opposition, and strong regimentation of society and of the economy … Fascists believe that liberal democracy is obsolete and regard the complete mobilization of society under a totalitarian one-party state as necessary to prepare a nation for armed conflict and to respond effectively to economic difficulties.

I believe in none of those things. In fact, I am the antithesis of a fascist, given that I believe in a small state, the primacy of free markets, civil liberties, liberal democracy and racial equality, and I reject utterly any violence pursued in the furtherance of political objectives. No matter, the haters will always hate. It is perhaps just as well my skin grows thicker with each passing year. But should it have to?

There are people who fight against the sewer of abuse that exists on Twitter. The Guido Fawkes website launched an initiative called Positive Twitter Day in 2012 with the aim of encouraging people to engage in only positive exchanges. 'Wouldn't it be nice to encourage each other to be nice and civil in our tweets?' the site says. It has involved mental health charities and even Twitter itself is now supporting the day. What a pity #PositiveTwitterDay is only in place for one day – the last Friday in August.

Kerry-Anne Mendoza is the editor of the far-Left website The Canary. Seven days before #PositiveTwitterDay in 2019 she tweeted this.

You can fuck all the way off. Then, just when you think you've fucked off as much as it's possible to fuck off, I'm gonna need you to dig deep and fuck off a little bit more.

One suspects Ms Mendoza is the type of person who ought to observe #PositiveTwitterDay.

This sort of language is, however, nothing new, as Nick Robinson noted, writing in *The Spectator*:

Robust discourse long pre-dates the Johnson, Trump and even Twitter eras as I have been reminded as I savour *Tombland*, the latest in C.J. Sansom's magnificent *Shardlake* series. It brings alive the story of the 1549 uprising of the people against the elite in the Kett rebellion. Gentlemen and their briefly liberated serfs exchange splendid insults. My favourites are 'you dozzled spunk-stain' and 'you bezzled puttock'.

I must remember those two insults for my next Twitter spat. They might have slightly more impact than my new insult of choice – muppet. The language may stay the same, with one or two modifications, but the ability of people to broadcast this disrespect or abuse has increased exponentially.

PART ONE

MEDIA

Chapter 1

Our Love/Hate Relationship with Social Media

'From the streets of Cairo and the Arab Spring,
to Occupy Wall Street, from the busy political
calendar to the aftermath of the tsunami in Japan,
social media was not only sharing the
news but driving it.'

Dan Rather

If you're under 35 years of age you will have no recollection of a time without the internet, let alone social media. You probably can't believe that mobile phones weren't 'a thing' before the early 1990s. The height of modern technology then was possession of a fax machine and a Sky dish. Before 1989, Britain only had four TV channels. Before the mid-1980s, computers barely existed for most of the population.

Nowadays, most of us rely on technology to exist. We spend hours every day glued to our smart phones, which aren't just used for phone-calls but to communicate with other people by email, text, Facebook, Twitter, WhatsApp,

Snapchat or goodness knows what else. We share intimate aspects of our lives with perfect strangers. We have an online brand that we spend hours carefully nurturing and curating.

I first encountered a computer at university. I was studying German and Linguistics at the University of East Anglia. It was 1983 and as part of my Teaching English as a Foreign Language module I had to do a seminar in Computer Assisted Language Learning. Our task was to create lessons using BBC Basic, a computer language that might as well have been Swahili, so far as I was concerned. I had never had a very mathematical brain, and computer coding was beyond me. In the end I had to go to see my course tutor and ask that instead of computer coding a lesson, could I write an extra essay. Luckily, he agreed. And to think, 20 years later I would be regarded as an internet innovator. Hilarious. But I'm getting ahead of myself.

Two years later I went to work for an MP in the House of Commons. I'm not going to lie, I was a glorified secretary. Nowadays, I'd award myself the title of chief of staff. I was the only staff. My employer, Norwich North MP Patrick Thompson, had an Apricot word-processing computer and a Brother printer. Virtually all of my contemporaries had to make do with typewriters. I learned how to do mail merging and we were one of the first to trial primitive forms of direct mail.

In my next job at the British Ports Association I also introduced computerisation into an organisation that seemed to have operated in the same way for decades. I built a database (once I'd worked out what the word meant) of press contacts and politicians.

In the early 1990s at the transport-related public affairs company The Waterfront Partnership I remember saying one day to my colleague David Young, 'Dave, I read an article about something called email. Can you look into it and set it up for us please?'

A year or two later I had my own personal computer and was arranging dates – OK, less dates, more one-night stands – on Compuserve forums. Twenty-five years later I am still with my partner, who was the ex of one of my hook-ups.

I have related my computer history because for people of my generation it has completely revolutionised how we communicate with other people. For younger generations it's changed nothing. It's what they've always known. I learned in my Linguistics class at university that the optimum age to learn a language is seven years old. Young brains are also best able to absorb and comprehend new technology. Give your iPhone to a youngster to install and they'll do it far more quickly than you could. That's just the way things are.

So there I was, visiting a friend in Washington, DC in the spring of 2002, and he asked me if I had a blog. Er, no, I said, I didn't, adding: 'What's a blog?' His answer proved to be a revelation and it was one that in time was to change my life. Within ten minutes he had created a blog for me and off I went.

Up until then, unless you were a technical geek, it was quite cumbersome to update a website. Usually someone else had to do it for you. But blogs meant that you could update your own website in seconds, and tell the world what you were thinking in real time. But so what? I instantly understood what a blog could do, not just for me, but more generally. Different people use blogs in different ways, but essentially they are a hugely democratising force: blogging gives everyone a chance to have their say.

Up until the advent of blogging, Mrs Miggins from 32 Acacia Avenue, Scunthorpe, would have had precious little chance to make her views known. She might get a letter published in the local paper, possibly even a national one on the odd occasion. She could phone in to a radio show, but that was about it. With a blog, Mrs Miggins could have her say whenever she wanted. Now, she might not have attracted the hugest of audiences, but in a sense, that didn't matter. No one sets out to blog with the aim of competing with the mainstream media. But the truth is that blogging started to eat a wedge into mainstream media influence. So much so that, having once viewed it as a pastime for sad geeks who tapped away at their keyboards in their bedrooms while wearing stripy pyjamas, mainstream media journalists started to embrace it – not just in politics, but across the gamut of journalism.

I decided early on that I wanted to make mine a very human blog. I wanted to write about my life, my experiences and my emotions, as well as providing political commentary and the odd dose of humour. It was a mix people seemed to like, and I always got a massive reaction whenever I wrote about anything in my personal life. I wrote about my dog dying. I wrote about delivering a eulogy at a funeral for the first time. I shared my feelings on my football team, West Ham, reaching the FA Cup final, only for their hopes to be dashed in the last minute. I wrote about my family, death, love and my civil partnership.

Writing a blog inevitably means becoming a bit of a hate figure, and writing about politics doubles your chances. I managed to make a lot of enemies along the way, but also a lot of friends and fans. Even now, people come up to me and tell me how much they miss the old incarnation of my blog.

The blog started as a personal diary, with little political content. Unfortunately, the original blog got deleted. In October 2003 I was selected as a Conservative candidate to fight the North Norfolk seat at the next general election. I decided to use my blog as an innovative way to have a dialogue with the electorate. Judging by the landslide result against me, it wasn't a success! I then took a break from blogging for six months while I worked as chief of staff to David Davis during his leadership campaign. So my story really starts at the end of 2005 when I restarted the blog. It instantly attracted a sizeable readership due to a number of political news stories I broke on the blog. And it was the John Prescott affair with his Private Secretary, Tracey Temple, and Charles Kennedy's toppling as Lib Dem leader, that really catapulted it into becoming a must-read in the Westminster Village.

At its peak, the blog was attracting 20,000 readers a day, and more than 150,000 unique users a month. Compared to national newspapers that's not huge, but the circulation of the *New Statesman* was around 20,000 and *The Spectator* 70,000 so, in its niche, the blog did rather well. I never sought to monetise it, even though I could have. For me it was more of a marketing tool.

Blogs are a spin doctor's worst nightmare come true. It would be understandable if political parties regarded them as uncontrolled, uncontrollable and sometimes downright troublesome. But if they did, they would be missing a huge opportunity to market their message without the filter of mainstream media reportage and comment. The political party that can harness social media, it is said, is the one that will prevail. Or maybe not. At the 2019 general election there is little doubt that Labour won the internet war. Their Facebook campaigns were more heavily viewed, and liked, and they had an army of Twitter users only too willing to do their bidding – most of whom seemed to have fewer than 20 followers. So successful were they that they even convinced me by polling day that we were heading for a hung parliament. If we ever needed proof that Twitter is not at all representative of the general public, this was it. Perhaps there's a lesson to learn here when we discuss the coarseness of the language deployed on Twitter in later chapters.

Political party memberships are also not representative of the public at large, not least in age profile. Membership in all parties had been on the decline, in part because parties had no idea how to communicate with members. Mailshots are expensive, monthly magazines far too costly and, despite spending large amounts of money on websites, none of the parties had ever really 'got' interactivity. Party websites continued to speak 'at' people rather than to them, let alone with them. Even nowadays they haven't learned how to have a conversation with people. In its heyday my blog would get more traffic than the official Tory Party and Labour Party websites. Guido Fawkes probably still does.

The trouble is most politicians see all the dangerous downsides of social media and blogging. They are seen by many as threats rather than opportunities. Some MPs, such as Lib Dem Lynne Featherstone, Labour's Tom Watson and Tory Ed Vaizey, 'got it' right from the off, but even in 2020 the majority of politicians only do the bare minimum on social media. They have websites because everyone does.

They're on Twitter, but view the medium with suspicion and a degree of terror.

Writing the blog became a bit of a responsibility. People expected me to write at least five or six new blog posts every day. Fifty per cent of the people who read the blog returned three or more times every day. Their appetite demanded ever more content. I loved the interaction but, in the end, maintaining my prolific output proved too much. In September 2010 I achieved a lifetime's ambition and was hired by LBC Radio to present their weeknight evening show. But I also had a day job running Biteback Publishing and *Total Politics* magazine. Effectively I was doing two full-time jobs, five days a week, and then also trying to write five stories a day on the blog. Something had to give. I knew that my writing was suffering and I wasn't providing the readers with what they had been used to. So I took the decision to close down the blog. When I announced it in December 2010, it was the nearest thing I can think of to witnessing my own death. It even made the *Today* programme.

I could also see that blogging – at least as I had been doing it for the previous few years – was about to change. Once the mainstream media decided to start their own blogs, people like me couldn't compete. In all honesty, I had also fallen out of love with blogging.

Blogging has been (or maybe was?) an immense force for good. It has uncovered major stories and held the media and politicians to account in a way that two decades ago would have been unthinkable. It's given thousands of ordinary voters a voice.

Back in 2010, I could see that Twitter was about to eclipse blogging in terms of popularity. What I hadn't bargained for was that Twitter paved the way to far higher levels of abuse and vituperation.

Blogging was a relatively spontaneous medium compared to how long it takes a newspaper article or broadcast report to be seen by the general public, but with the advent of Twitter, blogging became somewhat clunky and slow. A blogpost could be written in a few minutes. A reactive tweet took a matter of seconds.

I registered my Twitter name early on – in May 2007, but initially I couldn't quite see the point of it. I remember taking part in a panel with someone who literally tweeted every two minutes of his life. Who on earth would be interested in that, I thought. *Times* journalist Rachel Sylvester seemed to agree, quoting psychologist Oliver James to prove her point:

> Twittering stems from a lack of identity. It's a constant
> update of who you are, what you are, where you are.
> Nobody would Twitter if they had a strong sense of
> identity.

Sylvester argued that everyone who tweets must have something missing in their lives. She may be right about some, but it's also what MSM journalists used to say about blogging, which many of them chose to ignore or were forced to take up. She also maintained that 'Twitter is reality TV without the pictures'. There is a small amount of truth in that, especially when you look at those who tweet obsessively. It was for that reason that I was a comparatively late developer on Twitter.

But having decided how I wanted to use it, and that I wouldn't do it too often, I grew to enjoy it – at least until the last three or four years. For me, it complemented the blog brand and strengthened the feeling of community I tried to engender within the blog. When I joined LBC I used it to augment the marketing of my radio show and to drag in new listeners. That's my prime aim nowadays.

Some people use Twitter purely as a broadcast mechanism. Some use it to describe their everyday lives, as if we should be interested in what time they go to bed, or put out the cat. I try to stick to tweeting about things I think – and I emphasise, the word, think – might be of interest either to my followers or blog readers. It's mainly about events I am going to, media programmes I may be appearing on (it saves a blogpost), giving a bit of (hopefully insightful) political commentary, or saying something that I think might be vaguely funny. It's as simple as that. Those who want to can dub it 'narcissistic' all they want, but is it any more narcissistic than writing a blog or a newspaper column in the belief that people might be interested in what you say? I don't think so.

I still think that Twitter and Facebook are offering something positive in our public discourse. Friendships are formed, friendships are renewed. Last year I was sorting through some boxes from my time working in Germany in the 1980s and came across a diary date with a friend who was a teaching assistant in Hamburg at the time. All I knew was that his name was Ray. I tweeted this information and thanks to the research ability of some of my Twitter followers Ray and I were direct messaging each other within half an hour.

We soak up the information both platforms offer. We relish the spontaneity and instantaneousness. If there's a breaking news story during my radio show, I rely on Twitter to tell me what's going on. Yes, you have to curate it carefully and only rely on trusted sources, but I bring my listeners the news far more quickly that the BBC ever can with their cumbersome verification procedures.

In real breaking news situations Twitter can, as a presenter, be your best friend, During the London riots and the Egyptian revolution I was able to report things to my listeners more speedily than if I had relied on the normal news sources – Reuters, AP, PA, etc. But as well as being your best friend, Twitter can be your worst enemy. At around 6.15 p.m. on 23 April 2013 I noticed a tweet from the AP feed that read:

> BREAKING: Two explosions in the White House. Barack Obama said to be injured.

Wow. Big story. If it were true. I looked at my Sky News screen. Nothing. I couldn't see any other tweet referring to it. I have a general rule of thumb that I won't announce anything on air unless I have double sourced it on Twitter, from two proper sources – not just random Twitter accounts. Boy was I tempted though. But a sixth sense kicked in and told me to bide my time. I clicked onto the AP feed and it looked fine. But there was something that set alarm bells ringing. Thank goodness, because a couple of minutes later I saw a tweet that explained the AP feed had been hacked.

So I wasn't taken in, but the American stock market was. It plummeted in the minute after that tweet was sent. Wall Street turned out to be more gullible than me. There's a message there somewhere!

I don't pretend to be a journalist in the conventional sense of the word, but there are obviously journalistic aspects to what I do, and there are journalistic ethics, routines and conventions that I follow. When my blog was at its height of popularity, I'd break quite a few stories, and I got a kick out of being first to do so. It happened several times. But there was always the fear that you'd be scooped by someone else if you didn't press SEND pretty damn quickly. Obviously, that has its dangers, in that if you do it too quickly you might not quite have checked it out properly and thus stand to get a lot of egg on your face.

Only once have I been caught out, when I failed to realise a Twitter account wasn't actually the *Daily Mail*'s official one, but a fake. A listener pointed it out and I apologised immediately. That's what you should always do.

I've been at the centre of a few Twitter storms in my time, mainly of my own making. As I relate in Chapter 6, when I was filmed in a sort of scuffle with an anti-nuclear protester on Brighton seafront during the Labour Party Conference, the incident was amplified on Twitter to the extent that I couldn't look at it for several days. But that was seven years ago. If that happened in 2021 I have absolutely no doubt that the social media storm engendered would result in me being fired from my job. LBC stuck by me in 2013, but large companies nowadays tend to give in to the Twitterati at the first sign of trouble on social media. The veteran ITN newscaster Alastair Stewart would certainly pay testament to that. In January 2020 he was summarily sacked from the job he had held for 40 years after a somewhat unseemly spat with a political activist. Stewart had quoted Shakespeare at him, and the quoted passage ended with the word 'ape'. The activist was mixed race and highlighted the use of the word. Even though the word 'ape' was being used to indicate mimicry and Stewart had also previously used the quote to a Caucasian correspondent, it didn't matter to the Twitter mob. They got their man.

Politicians get it more than most on social media. Look at how many female Labour MPs were treated when they dared to stand up for British Jews who were under attack from some anti-Semitic Labour activists. But the abuse is directed at politicians from all parties and both genders.

I received an email not long ago from someone who clearly had a lot of time on their hands.

> Dear Iain, has anyone ever remarked that your eyes are almost identical to the eyes of a wild rat. I first noticed this when I saw you on Sky News with Jacqui Smith.
>
> Regards, C

Try as I might, I can't work out the mentality of someone who would actually spend time typing an email like that and then actually sending it. What did they hope to achieve? I've always thought I had rather nice eyes!

It's not just the political world that is affected by rudeness and horribleness on social media. A friend of mine, Deborah Slattery, who now lives in Spain, decided to join a Cat Lovers Facebook group hosted in America. A rather harmless thing to do you might think, where thousands of people share and comment online over cat pictures. You'd be wrong.

Deborah came across a picture of a black-and-white cat whose owner had shaved its fur to make it look like a poodle replete with a pompom at the end of its tail. You could see its body skin. She left a fairly innocuous comment to the effect that she didn't like what the owner had done and felt that it had made a fool out of her cat. The response was immediate. 'How dare you, you fucking bitch.' Worse was to come. Another woman said. 'You are obviously not a cat lover; how dare you make such judgmental remarks? I hope you die of cancer. In fact I hope you die a slow painful death from cancer you bitch!!'

A further commenter expressed the hope that Deborah's own cats would die. The next day her cat, Sushi, was shot. She died a few weeks later.

In early 2020 a 25-year-old former Tory activist, Joshua Spencer, was jailed for online threats of violence towards the senior Labour MP Yvette Cooper. He had sent messages claiming to have paid 'crackheads' £100 to beat her up and warned her that 'if you make peaceful revolution difficult you make a violent one inevitable'. He got nine weeks for his troubles.

The trouble is that violent threats don't necessarily stay online. The threats are real.

Chapter 2

When Opposites Collide

'A conversation in which the two parties have
different beliefs should never begin with the
intention of converting the other party to your own
beliefs. Every worthwhile conversation's goal should
be to understand the other person's opinions and
help them understand your own.'

Emily Eskowich

Politicians of all colours will be used to hearing two things
when they go canvassing. They'll knock on the door of 32
Acacia Avenue and will be greeted by Mrs Miggins, who
will berate them and accuse them of being all the same.
She will question why she should bother to vote given
there's no real choice. Then she will slam the door, feeling
a warm afterglow of giving a politician what for. The
politician then moves on to number 34 and speaks to Mr
Bloggs, who opens the door and explains that he thinks it
would be wonderful if politicians could put all their
interests aside in the national interest. 'Why can't you all

just get along?' he asks plaintively, not actually expecting a real answer.

These two views of the world are both perfectly understandable, and widely held. But they are mutually exclusive. While politicians will take every opportunity to be all things to all people, essentially they come in two breeds. Breed number 1 is the ideologically pure politician who is totally sure of his/her own views and creed, and won't brook any kind of compromise. It's a game of them and us. There's a right and wrong, with few shades of grey.

Breed number 2 despises confrontation and recognises that the minority have a right to be represented, and politics is the art of compromise.

Breed 1 and Breed 2 do not understand each other. They therefore question each other's motives, and in a world of hung parliaments stalemate ensues, often followed by a degree of personal acrimony and vituperation. Look at how MPs on both sides of the Brexit debate have acted in recent years, not just towards their political opponents, but towards each other too, even if they were ostensibly supposed to be taking the same party whip.

For many it's deeply personal. Some Labour backbenchers loathed their leader, Jeremy Corbyn and they didn't bother to hide it. There was similar acrimony on the Tory benches where some Remainers had no reservation about talking to the media in the most lurid terms about their leader, Boris Johnson.

Television and radio shows delight in putting opposites up against each other to create a row. It was ever thus in some ways but the priority of producers nowadays is to achieve a moment that can go viral on Facebook or YouTube and grab a page lead in the next day's newspapers.

All this is entirely understandable, but rather than enhancing the quality of public debate, it damages it.

I like to think that I've rarely gone down that road, and if I have there has been a good reason for it.

Each week I record an hour-long podcast with former Labour Home Secretary Jacqui Smith. It's called 'For the Many'. We gave it that title because we want it to appeal to people across the political spectrum. How do we do that? By being civil to each other and not deliberately having a row. In more than 250 episodes I don't think we have ever raised our voices or shouted down the other. We talk about the political events of the week and try to interpret them for our audience, which is not just full of political geeks. People listen to us while cooking the dinner, working out in the gym or walking the dog. We do it with a light touch and provide a few laughs along the way.

Arguing respectfully and with humour is surely better than an hour of ding-dongs in which there may be a lot of drama but not a lot of nuance. And that's why we have one of the highest rated UK political podcasts. Indeed, you look at some of the other good ones, such as Nick Robinson's Political Thinking or Matt Forde's Political Party or Paul Brand's Acting Prime Minister, and you can see they have two things in common. They are at least 30 minutes in length and they are conversational. There is no battle of wills. No presenter trying to be the story rather than the person they are interviewing. If only more political TV and radio programmes had this approach.

Back in May 2017 I became part of a new weekly political discussion show on CNN International called *CNNTalk*. The format was very simple. One presenter, Max Foster, plus a panel of three – me, former Labour adviser Ayesha

Hazarika, and economist and *Telegraph* columnist Liam Halligan. We would discuss one subject for half an hour. The chemistry between us was instant. Max knew when to intervene or just let us get on with it. He is a presenter who doesn't think it's all about him. Yes, from time to time we could have some feisty arguments, but because they didn't happen every show, the audience realised they were genuine disagreements when they happened. After a while CNN asked if we'd do the show twice a week, then three times, and then it went daily. The audience loved it, and CNN HQ loved it. The theme of the show often revolved around Donald Trump's latest antics, Brexit, terrorism, gun control or sometimes something more esoteric, such as whether 3D printers could make replica guns. We would never know the subject until three hours before it went on air, and there were many times when I walked into the studio wondering what on earth I could say, given I knew very little about what we were to talk about. What it taught me was that I can actually speak about any subject and sound authoritative and calm. I was like the proverbial swan – calm on the surface but feet paddling away under water.

It was a real sadness to us all when, after two years, the show was canned, for no other reason than CNN decided to go in a different direction.

Compare *CNNTalk* with the BBC's *Question Time* and they are like chalk and cheese. One is all about calm, rational debate and hopefully informing its audience. The other used to have the same aims, yet currently has become a bearpit of political arm wrestling, and not just among the panellists – the audience now readily participate too. When the show started in September 1979 under the chairmanship of Sir Robin Day, there were four panellists.

Nowadays there are five or sometimes six, which means each panellist has to compete for the stage. In the early years each participant would speak when they were asked to. They treated each other with respect. Today it is very different, with many panellists often being openly contemptuous of the others. The word 'liar' is thrown around with impunity. Other insults are commonplace. The audience thinks nothing of totally disrespecting the guests or even each other.

I've appeared on the programme twice, with very contrasting experiences. In April 2018 I made my debut. I was half excited and half filled with dread. Why dread? Well, quite a few people have made complete arses of themselves on *Question Time*, in a way that's more difficult to do on its radio equivalent, *Any Questions?* There's that constant fear of gulping like a goldfish when you get a question that completely throws you. Or you have a row with another panellist and come off worst. However, I talk for three hours every day about subjects I may know very little about or am not interested in personally, so over the years you develop an ability and a confidence to talk reasonably fluently about anything that's put to you. But you do have to have some self-knowledge. For instance, although I could be reasonably confident of doing OK on *Question Time*, I would certainly not have the confidence to do a show like *Have I Got News for You*. I've learned over the years that although I am capable of being funny, I'm not half as funny as I like to think I am!

My first appearance was in Chesterfield. The other panellists were Vince Cable, Liz Truss, Emily Thornberry and *Guardian* columnist Nesrine Malik. It was also Nesrine's first time.

I arrived around 6 p.m. and there then followed an hour of chit-chat, briefing from the producers and make-up. David Dimbleby swept into the room at around 7.50 and made a great effort to sit down and talk to Nesrine and I individually. He was incredibly charming, put us at our ease and encouraged us to interact with the audience and the other panellists, and not to be shy to interject.

'Do you know the questions in advance?' is the second most frequent question I've had and I can categorically say no. However, let's face it, you have to be a bit of a dunce if you can't predict the subject areas of at least two or three questions.

By the time we were called to go into the auditorium I had exactly the same feeling as I always have before *Any Questions?* I become a nervous wreck, convinced that I am totally underprepared and won't have a thought in my head to express when David Dimbleby calls on me.

Some panellists go on stage with no notes, others have reams. Nesrine didn't have any notes, which I rather admired. I just took on small cue cards with five bullet points on each subject. I also had a newspaper article that I would have used against Vince Cable had Brexit come up. But it didn't. The notes were a safety valve. In the end I didn't look at them very often. Someone I know who was on *Question Time* recently looked over at his fellow panellists' notes and saw that virtually every potential answer on every conceivable subject was more or less scripted.

And so the time came. We all stood in the wings waiting to be called in by David Dimbleby. I was first, as I was seated on the far side of the stage. I walked in and smiled at the audience before taking my seat. All the others then took theirs. Emily Thornberry got a very loud cheer, which made me think it would be a very pro-Labour audience. In fact, it was a very fair audience and devoid of some of the usual frothing-at-the-mouthers that there have been on the programme in recent years. The whole set is much smaller and more intimate than it seems when watching on TV. You're much closer to the audience than the TV pictures show.

The warm-up question was a complete surprise. 'Was the Derbyshire Chief Constable right to order the Police Male Voice Choir to change its name and include women?' I always think the thing to do in a warm-up question is to make the audience laugh, which I tried to do, although I now can't remember what I said. In fact, to be honest, the audience members gave far better responses than any of the panel. Anyway, with that, we were off. David Dimbleby pressed his stop-watch, turned to face the camera and introduced the panel.

I didn't go in with any pre-prepared lines because I think it rarely ever works. One bit of advice Piers Morgan gave me in advance was to make sure you give a direct answer to the question. He reckoned too many people skirt around the original question, forget what it was within thirty seconds, and then go on a tour of the whole subject. It was good advice and I think I did answer every question directly.

The biggest dilemma is to know when to interrupt another panellist. On a debut show you don't want to be too much of a shrinking violet, but then again you don't want to appear too dominating. I know from previous experience of being on a panel that I always come off the stage thinking I didn't have enough of a say, and yet when I watch it back I've probably spoken more than anyone else.

Sometimes less is more. If you ramble, you know you'll be cut off. I adopted a policy of only interrupting when I really had something to say.

I'm long enough in the tooth to know when I've performed well on a programme and when I haven't. I knew when I came off stage I'd done better than I thought I would, so I was quite content.

On my second appearance, in September 2019, it was all rather different. David Dimbleby had retired and Fiona Bruce had taken over the presenter's role. It was the first show of the programme's autumn run, and the government and country were in a meltdown over the prospect of a no-deal Brexit. Unusually it was broadcast live, which meant I could present my evening radio show, then get a cab over to the venue in Westminster. I arrived just a few minutes before we went on stage for the warm-up question, so didn't have a lot of time to chat to the five, yes five, other panellists. Again Emily Thornberry, Labour's Shadow Foreign Secretary, was on the show, along with government minister Kwasi Kwarteng, the SNP Westminster leader Ian Blackford, Liberal Democrat MP Layla Moran and Brexit Party MEP Richard Tice.

In 15 years of political TV punditry it had never occurred to me to walk out of a show, live on air. But it nearly happened on this show. The thought flitted through my mind as yet again the other panellists talked over each other and I was barely allowed to get a sentence out without being interrupted.

As SNP Westminster leader Ian Blackford interrupted me for the third time, after I had barely uttered a word, I threw up my hands and blustered: 'What on earth is the point of debating if this is what you're going to do?'

Don't get me wrong, interrupting is all part of the cut and thrust of political debate. It has its place, but we all know the rules of the game. With the exception of the Liberal Democrat Layla Moran, all of the other panellists took interrupting to an extreme, which made large parts of the programme unwatchable.

In the three days following the show I received around four hundred emails, and gained an extra ten thousand Twitter followers. There had been widespread outrage at the lamentable standard of debate on the show, and how it was handled.

The truth is that *Question Time* is not alone in suffering from this. On this and other shows, politicians think it is quite acceptable to call each other 'liars' on TV, and Emily Thornberry did this within half a minute in her first answer.

There are ways of calling out mendacious politicians without actually calling them 'liars'. Fiona Bruce didn't see fit to pick her up on that, yet did challenge Tory MP Kwasi Kwarteng later in the show, asking him: 'Are you calling Emily dishonest?'

Question Time has become a bear pit where the audience behaves in a way it would never have done ten years ago. I'm not seeking to hark back to an age of deference, but the bear-baiting and insults that go from audience to panel and back are rendering such programmes almost unwatchable for many.

I well remember the golden days of the show when the likes of Dr David Starkey, Clare Short, Shirley Williams and Norman Tebbit would debate robustly but with respect for each other and the rules of the show. Perhaps we need to take a leaf out of the Norwegian political TV show *Einig*, where panellists are obliged to be polite to each other, not interrupt, and to listen and then engage. It could happen here if we had a broadcaster brave enough to embrace the format. The recently retired BBC Director General Lord Hall made a speech in early 2020 in which he said: 'I'm a great believer in the long-form political interview where you can explore at length, not in soundbites, the real policy decisions that politicians are making.' He's right.

In some ways I can't blame the *Question Time* audience for being angry. They have been let down by a generation of politicians, most of whom don't even acknowledge the fact.

Over the last few years Brexiteers have rightly complained about the imbalance of panels on political TV shows like *Newsnight*, *Politics Live* and *Question Time*. I once refused to appear on a panel to discuss Brexit when I was outnumbered three to one. It's not that I can't look after myself, but producers who think it is OK to put together a panel like that shouldn't be in the job.

Because of the political events of the week, it was clear that Brexit would dominate the show, so the *Question Time* producers decided to have a panel of three Brexit supporters and three Remainers. But with six panellists rather than the usual five, it was clear that everyone would struggle to make themselves heard.

In retrospect it would have been better to go with four panellists and allow a more meaningful debate to take place. But it could still have worked with six panellists had each of the panellists played the game. Instead, it became the Emily Thornberry show. However, it was me who was upbraided for having the temerity to try to engage with an audience member, and was reprimanded by Fiona Bruce with a curt: 'This is not the Iain Dale show.'

She was dead right. I spoke for precisely 4 minutes 33 seconds in a total of eight interventions, whereas Emily Thornberry spoke for 10 minutes 34 seconds in 15 interventions, two of which were more than two minutes long.

The Brexiteers on the panel spoke for a total of 15 minutes 22 seconds, while the Remainers spoke for 23 minutes 48 seconds. The audience got 7 minutes 46 seconds, of which Brexit-supporting audience members spoke for all of 2 minutes 34 seconds.

Having said all that, while Richard Tice, the Brexit Party MEP, and I spoke the least of all the six panellists, only speaking when you have something to say can have its merits. I deliberately tried not to take part in the orgy of talking over other people. I may not have always succeeded but at least I made the effort.

I would suggest that the *Question Time* producers go back to having only four panellists from time to time. I suspect the audience would prefer it and there would be a little more light shed on issues, and perhaps a little less heat. They would probably respond: 'Nice idea, but it wouldn't make great TV.'

In decades, or even centuries gone by, crowds of tens of thousands would gather to listen to the politicians of the day make grand speeches, even if they couldn't actually hear a word that was said. In the pre-microphone age, word was passed to the back of the audience explaining what the speaker was saying. As the radio and television age progressed, the appetite for live political debate switched from the church hall to the radio set in the corner of the living room or, later, to the 'gogglebox'.

Five months after that *Question Time* appearance, on my regular Friday morning slot on *Good Morning Britain*, I didn't just think about walking out, I actually did it. Normally, I'm on each week with Jacqui Smith to talk about the political stories of the day. On this occasion she was on holiday, so they told me that left-wing economics commentator Grace Blakeley was to be my partner for the day. I like Grace, and after she came on my radio show for the first time I promoted her with producers of several leading TV shows. Ten minutes before we were due on air, we were told we were to be joined by Radio 5 Live presenter Nihal Arthanayake. I'd never met him before but knew him by reputation as someone who had to feign impartiality, because he is a definite man of the Left. Presenters Ben Shephard and Kate Garraway started by asking Grace about the tragic case of the mentally ill 18-year-old who threw a six-year-old off a sixth-floor balcony at the Tate Modern. She spoke for about a minute, with no interruption from me, blaming the whole thing on austerity and government cuts. I regarded this as preposterous and spent a whole nine seconds saying so. I was then interrupted by both of them, who wouldn't let me continue. It's a typical tactic of the Left. Shut down the debate and don't let the other person speak. I made repeated attempts to continue, but I was in the middle and it was a pincer movement from both sides. The presenters didn't intervene, so I decided to calmly take off my microphone, stand up and leave. I had no interest in another ten minutes of being shouted down by two people who weren't interested in debating or even listening to another viewpoint. Social media went into meltdown. Initially it was 90 to 10 in my favour, but as time progressed, it split down tribal lines. If you were on the Left, I acted childishly, spat out my dummy and had no counter to Grace's wonderful arguments. If you were on the Right, I was completely justified in doing what I did and the other two were a disgrace for closing me down. The argument continued for days afterwards. I made my peace with Grace over direct messages on Twitter, but Nihal launched into a barrage of unprofessional tweets seeking to undermine me. It said more about him than it did about me. The whole thing was an object lesson in why these panel debates aren't worth having unless the participants can bring themselves to acknowledge that there may be another point of view. It's why Jacqui Smith and I are popular on that show and on our podcast, because we can disagree without falling out. There is a real appetite for respectful debate nowadays, in a way that maybe there wasn't in years gone by.

As the end of the twentieth century drew near, even at election time, it was difficult to attract an audience to hear a politician sell their electoral wares. I remember in the 1983 general election organising a public meeting for the revered electors of Norwich North to hear a speech from Peter Walker, then a senior cabinet minister in Margaret Thatcher's cabinet. The meeting was attended by a grand total of seven men and a dog, and the dog had only walked in because it was trying to find its owner.

In my own election campaign in North Norfolk in 2005, three public meetings were organised by local churches and community groups across the constituency, in Wells-next-the-Sea, Fakenham and North Walsham. Out of an electorate of more than eighty thousand voters only about three hundred and fifty of them could be bothered to venture out on a spring evening to hear the candidates debating with each other. If memory serves me correctly, they were actually rather constructive and polite debates, but I doubt they changed very many people's minds given that most of those attending each debate were allied to one political party or another.

However, things appear to be changing.

I first noticed this when the then Conservative MP Ann Widdecombe and I toured the country's regional theatres with our 'In Conversation' show, *An Audience with Ann Widdecombe*. We 'played' around sixty or seventy venues in front of good-sized audiences. They had each paid around £15 to come and hear La Widdecombe's words of wisdom. I remember her remarking at the time that the secret to reviving the old-style political public meeting was to charge people to attend. She may have been joking, but her words turned out to be prophetic.

As an aside, on the first occasion I appeared on Radio 4's *Any Questions?* programme, I was wracked with nerves and the host, Jonathan Dimbleby, finished introducing me by saying that I host the theatre show 'A Night with Ann Widdecombe'. He mischievously looked at me and asked: 'Is that a whole night?' I rolled with the audience laughter and replied: 'That's for me to know and you to guess ... A gentleman never tells.' Cue more audience laughter. We were on our way and having got an audience reaction my nerves had gone. It was a good way for Jonathan to put me at my ease.

A new generation has grown up thirsting for information and political insight. They don't see political parties as the only vehicles to make their views known. The age of the pressure group and interest group has arrived, and they exert far more influence on this generation than tribalistic political parties. That's not to say political parties have become irrelevant, but they no longer enjoy the salience, relevance or impact that they once did. The problem for political parties has always been that they have very little to offer their members, apart from the chance to part with more money and the occasional opportunity to meet a political luminary. Given the increasing influence of the central party on local constituency parties, they often don't even have a free hand in choosing their parliamentary candidates nowadays.

It is estimated by the House of Commons Library that only 1.7 per cent of the electorate belongs to a political party. Having said that, back in 2013 the figure was only 0.8 per cent. Since then, with the exception of UKIP, all political parties have increased their membership, with Labour seeing a rise from under 200,000 to a peak of nearly 600,000 in 2020. The Liberal Democrats have nearly tripled their membership in recent years, while the Conservatives have bounced back from a low of 124,000 a few years ago to nearly 200,000 at the time of writing.

Why has this happened? In part it is due to the two crises that have hit the United Kingdom over the last decade – the financial crash and Brexit. In times of crises, political tribes circle the wagons and people who had drifted away often return to the fold. Or in the case of the Labour Party, the election of Jeremy Corbyn as leader inspired the previously disparate groups on the far Left to join, and in some sense take over, the party. The Brexit Party attracted more than a hundred thousand registered supporters within weeks of being formed – all people who saw it as a vehicle to achieve more than a BRINO: Brexit in Name Only.

So the rise in party membership is partly about 'circling the wagons' and partly about being genuinely inspired, but there's also a third, rather more negative reason, and that's the fact that our politics is becoming increasingly polarised. On both sides of the political divide, people are on the defensive, so they retreat into their own political silos. They're right, and everyone else is wrong, and never the twain shall meet.

But those who are not aligned to one cause or another often feel ignored as they struggle to come to terms with the events that are affecting them. They don't trust the representatives of political parties to be honest, so they look elsewhere for their current-affairs appetites to be sated.

That in part explains the rise of the live political event, whether they be at literary festivals, regional theatres, big London venues or the Edinburgh Festival Fringe. These events tend to be conducted in a polite and respectful tone, free of the normal Westminster argy-bargy. They're designed to be more discursive and enlightening and to enable those attending to leave the event feeling better informed than they were when they arrived. How many people can genuinely say that at the end of most TV political debates they have learned anything at all? The analysts often concentrate on the body language displayed by the participants rather than what they actually said.

In early 2019 Conservative backbencher and arch Eurosceptic Jacob Rees-Mogg sold out the 2,000-seater London Palladium. The *Spectator* panel debates between commentators and politicians regularly sell more than one thousand tickets. Intelligence Squared, which was formed in 2002, host Oxford Union-style debates and so popular have they been that the format has been licensed all over the world. In London they can attract audiences of up to two and half thousand, and they also broadcast most of their events on Facebook or YouTube and then release them as podcasts.

Literary festivals are now often populated with politicians or political commentators, even when they don't have books to flog. The kind of people who attend these festivals are invariably politically interested and on the liberal left. The festivals tend to be somewhat unimaginative in who they invite and concentrate on 'people like them', who often preach to a rather tepid echo chamber. They're the sort of events at which the *Guardian*'s Polly Toynbee goes down a storm, but where Rod Liddle or Douglas Murray would cause a riot – that's if they were ever invited in the first place.

Conservative MP George Freeman launched a new Politics Festival in 2016, which was immediately dubbed Glastonbury for Politicos. It was initially invite-only and aimed at people on the Right who were interested in new ideas and new thinking. By 2019 it had widened its remit and was open to anyone. Judging from the guest list, which included former Labour ministers and self-confessed communist Ash Sarkar, it has become a very big tent indeed.

Having observed the increasing popularity of live political events, be they debates or interviews, I decided to try my own hand at it. In the summer of 2018, my agent introduced me to James Seabright, one of the leading promoters at the Edinburgh Festival Fringe. We agreed we'd do an initial run of nine shows called 'Iain Dale All Talk' and James booked us in at one of the Fringe's best venues, the Gilded Balloon. Nine shows rapidly turned into 12 and then 24. My guest line-up included politicians like Nicola Sturgeon, John McDonnell, Sadiq Khan, Jo Swinson and Nicholas Soames as well as media personalities such as

Kate Adie, Yasmin Alibhai-Brown, Kirsty Wark and Christiane Amanpour.

I did my own 'flyering' on the streets of Edinburgh and was amazed at the number of people who told me they were booking tickets and thought I'd got a great line-up.

I remember one chap coming up to me before a show brandishing the show flyer. 'Are all these people really coming?' he asked in disbelief. 'Of course,' I replied. 'What, you mean Sadiq Khan is actually coming to Edinburgh – you mean the real Sadiq Khan?' 'Yes, I replied.' He walked away and then immediately came back. 'How on earth do you get all these people?' he asked. 'I have a good contacts book,' I retorted. He seemed satisfied with that.

I reflected on this and decided that he reacted in this way because he thought that highfalutin politicians didn't generally mix in his circles. In Edinburgh you see them up close and personal, and that was the whole point.

I wasn't intending to do hard-hitting political interviews. I wanted to have a proper conversation and find out what makes them tick. Judging from the audience reaction, I think that was the right approach. They kept telling me that I had enabled them to see a side of the politicians they rarely ever glimpsed in the routine forensic and combative interviews they saw on TV or listened to on the radio. Word spread so far that I kept being asked if I would release recordings of each show so that people who weren't able to go to Edinburgh could listen to them. Hence the Iain Dale All Talk podcast was born.

And I enjoyed the whole experience so much I hope to make it an annual event.

The interest in politics and current affairs is higher than it has ever been, and not just in the UK. Despite the sometimes appalling state of our discourse in the political field, more and more young people appear to be taking part in the conversation. The question remains, however, whether they will go one step further and progress from having an active interest to becoming active participants. That is why everyone active as a political thought leader, or politician, has a responsibility to moderate their language, avoid deliberately divisive rhetoric on public platforms and thereby encourage people to believe that pursuing an active interest in politics is a noble thing to do. The media has a responsibility here too, especially the social media companies. People need to know what the consequences are if they step beyond the borders of acceptable behaviour.

As you read this, you're probably thinking 'some hope' or 'fat chance' or words to that effect. I have to remain optimistic about the possibility of this happening, albeit over a protracted period of time, otherwise I'd have to conclude that there is little hope for our liberal democracy.

Chapter 3

The Art of the Political Interview

'You often see politicians who try to put on a
different persona; they think they should be more
jolly or serious. Invariably, the persona they
choose is worse than their own.'

Sir David Frost

The art of the political interview has changed a lot over the
years. I remember seeing an audio clip of an interview with
Clement Attlee in 1951. 'Is there anything else you'd like to
say about the coming election?' asked the ever-so-eager
interviewer. 'No,' replied Mr Attlee. 'Thank you very much,
prime minister,' declared the grateful interviewer.

Political interviews in those days were not about holding
politicians to account, they were there to enable politicians
to tell the electorate whatever they felt like at the time.
There was no scrutiny, no controversy and certainly no
rudeness. How times have changed.

I won't go through the entire history of political interviewing, but surely everyone can agree that the point of an

interview is to elicit information to enable the viewer or listener to understand and learn more than they had known before. It can also be about exposing hypocrisy, duplicity or falsehoods.

I have never gone into an interview thinking to myself, 'I'm going to do you over.' I don't go into an interview chasing a headline, even though in big interviews I know there's pressure on me to deliver one. Many current-day interviewers appear to believe that unless they've generated a headline they've failed, especially in the eyes of their employers or editors. All too often the interview becomes more about the interviewer than the interviewee. The interview becomes more of a spectator sport than an interview.

In these days of flea-like attention spans and social media, 30-, 60- or 90-second clips go viral within minutes if an interviewer has made an interviewee squirm. Lurid headlines are attached that often bear little relation to what actually happened in the interview. The 'gotcha' moment is everything.

You'll never come across a clip on a media website where the broadcaster's own interviewer is made to look like a prize chump by the person they're interviewing, but it often happens. Why? Because generally the politician knows more about a subject than the interviewer does, no matter how well they brief themselves.

I remember doing an interview on Radio 5 Live once, when I turned the question back on the presenter, who clearly knew nothing about the subject under discussion and was just reading from a list of questions prepared by her producer. I simply said: 'Why do you ask that?' Answer came there none. Just ten seconds of radio silence and the faint sound of gulping goldfishes. It's always been a source of mystery to me why politicians just sit there and take it. Why don't they fight back?

Politicians are conditioned to go into interviews expecting a gladiatorial contest, especially if the interviewer is presenting on a high-profile news or current affairs programme. Invariably, these interviews last three or four minutes, but rarely more than ten. The politician, whatever their party allegiance, will be briefed by their advisers beforehand and will want to make two main points. These points will be made regardless of the question asked. There will be soundbites that have been pre-learned, and that will be used in each interview undertaken by the politician – and there could be as many as a dozen interviews one after the other. So the challenge for the interviewer in these circumstances is to pre-empt the soundbite or allow it to be said once and then move on. If the interviewee just keeps repeating the soundbite in different ways, the interviewer becomes tetchy and the interview becomes confrontational, at which point the interviewee gets defensive and clams up. And the poor listener or viewer gets nothing out of the exchange whatsoever.

The interviewer seems to interrupt every few seconds before the politician has had a chance to utter five words. It drove Ann Widdecombe to ask the *Today* programme's John Humphrys if he was paid per interruption. It was clearly a joke, but it's easy to understand why she asked the question.

In a sense, a game is being played out, but it's become an unedifying one, in which everyone loses. The pressure on the interviewer to catch out the politician and get a news line conflicts with the pressure on the politician to sell whatever line they've been deputed to trot out by their spin doctors or party HQ.

The trouble is that editors and producers don't believe that their audience will tolerate interviews that last longer than a few minutes. Cram as much in. Variety is the spice of life. Pace, pace, pace. It's not just in news interviews that this attitude is prevalent. It's happening all over the media and the internet. We're told that if you put an interview clip on Facebook, make sure it's no more than 90 seconds long. Any answer on a panel show that is longer than 45 seconds is likely to be interrupted by the host.

It is rare on radio or television to find any programme that interviews a politician for more than 15 minutes. Gone are the days when cabinet ministers would subject themselves to an hour-long grilling by the likes of Sir Robin Day, Brian Walden or Jonathan Dimbleby. The fact that they don't do it any longer is not down to them, it's due to the broadcasters. The longest interview any politician does on any BBC programme is 15 to 18 minutes on the *Andrew Marr Show* or *Today* programme. Even on the BBC News Channel or Sky News, long-form interviews are by and large a thing of the past.

The BBC cancelled Andrew Neil's *Straight Talk* show in 2013, where a single politician would be grilled for half an hour. Stephen Sackur's *HARDtalk* on the News Channel is the only programme where a single politician is questioned for half an hour – but this show only interviews non-UK politicians and personalities. It can't be because of cost, because a half an hour one-on-one interview is about the cheapest form of television there is. It can only be because editors have come to the conclusion either that the best way to inform their viewers is through short, sharp interviews, or that they prefer their current affairs content to be akin to a blood sport. Heat has become more important than light.

On my radio show I've tried to fight back against this trend. Yes, I do a fast-paced Newshour each evening with short interviews, but I also regularly conduct 30- or 60-minute interviews with politicians. They enjoy them. I enjoy them, and most importantly the audience enjoys them. The reason they work is that I don't treat them as interviews in the conventional sense. To me they are conversations. Why do I differentiate in this way? Because in my view people tend to reveal far more in conversations than they do in confrontational set-tos. Perhaps it's because they don't regard me as a normal interviewer, but as someone who hails from the same political background as they do. I don't mean that in a party-political way, but I grew up living and breathing party politics. I stood as a candidate. They know this, and even if they come from a different party to the one I used to support, they know I understand their jobs, their lives and their motivations more than someone who has been a political journalist since they were knee-high to a grasshopper. Not being a trained journalist, broadcaster or interviewer has its compensations sometimes.

I do not approach long-form interviews in a conventional way. I don't spend hours preparing for them. I caused consternation on the faces of Andrew Marr and Rachel Sylvester from *The Times* when I was asked by Amol Rajan on Radio 4's *Media Show* how I prepared for interviews. I decided to tell the truth and admit that I generally don't do much preparation at all. For big interviews I might write down four or five subject areas to cover, but experience has told me that if I have a list of questions in front of me, I will ask them, but the effect is somewhat stultifying. Self-knowledge is a wonderful thing and I know I perform best when I freestyle.

I'm always happy for my producer to suggest questions in my ear or on the screen in front of me, but that's it. The look on Andrew Marr's face was a picture. He went on to explain that he not only spends a long time preparing questions, but he also war-games the interviews with his producers. They try to anticipate the likely answers and then tailor the follow-up questions accordingly. It clearly works for Andrew, but it's something I would be hopeless at. Some of my best interviews have been ones where I have done no preparations whatsoever. That approach works for me. It wouldn't for others.

It's a high-risk strategy because sometimes I've got near to the end of an interview and a little voice in my head has told me I've got nothing out of it. And then, as if by magic, I ask another question, and bingo! The interviewee commits some news.

But there are times when a bit of strategic preparation is necessary. A week before the Brexit referendum in June 2016 I did a 30-minute interview with the Chancellor of the Exchequer, George Osborne. It was the longest radio interview he had ever done. I knew I had to be rather more forensic than my normal style.

George Osborne has a habit of recognising when an interviewer is about to intervene or interrupt. His voice becomes a little louder and he makes sure he gets out what he had intended to say. He's actually quite easy to interact with and I rather like interviewing him.

But I got a massive news line out of him. I asked him what preparations the Treasury had made for a Leave decision in the referendum, given the polls were showing the two sides neck and neck. He told me that the Treasury has done absolutely no planning for a Brexit scenario. There were no civil servants involved in contingency planning. Breathtaking. And totally irresponsible for someone in his position, as I lost no time in telling him. It's an interview I remind him of from time to time.

Perhaps the biggest interviews I have ever done were with Theresa May and Boris Johnson. Both interviews received blanket media coverage, but for different reasons.

At the beginning of October 2017 Theresa May made her annual speech to her party conference in Manchester. I was not in the hall, but instead commentating on it for CNN in the hall next door. Midway through the speech I realised that everything had fallen silent. It turned out that a stand-up comedian had gone onto the stage and handed Theresa May a P45. A few minutes later a couple of letters from the conference backdrop slogan fell off. And to top it all, the prime minister had lost her voice, and at times could barely speak. But she soldiered on and eventually her nightmare came to an end.

For several months I had been trying to persuade Number Ten to do a phone-in in the LBC studio. Much to my astonishment, they agreed to do it the week following May's disastrous conference speech. She was the first prime minister since Tony Blair to do a radio phone-in outside an election period. These things always carry a slight risk for a politician because they can never be sure they won't be tripped up by a member of the public. Interviewers can be tame beasts compared to Jill in Sidcup.

We took several calls and I thought she dealt with most of the questions very well, including one from a

Conservative who told her that the only way of defeating Jeremy Corbyn was for her to stand down. Not an easy one for any politician to navigate.

But it was Brexit that produced the headlines. An Italian lady phoned in to ask about EU citizens' rights post-Brexit and mentioned a possible second referendum. I then asked May the same question I'd asked Jeremy Hunt a week earlier: if there was a new referendum now, how would she vote? She simply refused to answer the question. Five times. She prevaricated, she obfuscated, she said she didn't answer hypothetical questions. I said to her that she was leading a government that was implementing Brexit, so surely she thought it was a good idea and could therefore say she would vote Leave in another referendum. I got a death stare. I then said, well, if her health secretary could answer the question, why couldn't she? Answer came there none.

Some people thought I shouldn't have asked her such a question – I must have known I wouldn't get a straight answer. Others seem to think it was the most brilliant question an interviewer has ever asked. It wasn't. I honestly thought she would follow Jeremy Hunt's lead and say that, knowing what she knows now, she would vote for Brexit.

The clip was played out on every single news programme ad nauseum over the ensuing 24 hours. Andrew Neil on *This Week* called it 'The Iain Dale Question'. I suppose one positive emerged from it: no one could ever again accuse me of being a Tory patsy interviewer.

She and her team were less than pleased. I never interviewed her again.

I first interviewed Boris Johnson in early 2007, on the day he announced he was running to be Mayor of London.

He came into the 18 Doughty Street studio, accompanied by his two press officers, Katie Perrior and Jo Tanner. He was his usual ebullient self, and we were slated to do a 30-minute interview. We sat down and I kicked off by asking what I thought was an ice-breaker, softball question. It proved to be rather more difficult for Boris than it should have been. This was the question: 'What would be the first thing you would do on day one of a Boris Johnson mayoralty.' Remember that look of horror on Theresa May's face? Well, Boris invented it. He looked terrified. 'Well, er, yes, er, I think, well, yes, er, good question, I think, well I think, yes, hmmm.' At that point I fleetingly considered starting the interview all over again. But then I thought, if he can't answer such a simple question, he ought not to be running for mayor. The rest of the interview went off unremarkably.

The next time I interviewed him he'd been Mayor of London for three years. If he hadn't been across the detail of London-related policy in 2007, he certainly was now.

During my twelve years on LBC I've interviewed Boris many times, but not so much in the last few years. I don't mind admitting he would be in my top five people I find most difficult to interview. If he's on the phone it's almost impossible to interrupt him. If he's live in the studio he never looks you in the eye, which also makes it difficult to interrupt. You have to win his trust. It's almost as if he assumes your intention is to do him in, so you have to waste valuable minutes asking him questions that he thinks are perfectly reasonable, and then he starts to open up a bit.

In June 2019 I was asked by Brandon Lewis, the chairman of the Conservative Party, if I would compère a series of hustings that the two finalists (who turned out to be

Boris Johnson and Jeremy Hunt) in the race for the Tory Party leadership would be doing all over the country. In the end I agreed to host 10 of the 16 events. The first was in Birmingham. It proved to be rather more exciting than I had anticipated.

The previous evening the *Guardian* had broken a story that the police had been called to the flat in south London that Boris shared with his girlfriend Carrie Symonds. There had, apparently, been a 'domestic', which their neighbours had helpfully recorded on their phone and then called the police. What actually transpired is still a matter of conjecture, but it was a story that led in all the Saturday morning newspapers and news bulletins.

I travelled up to Birmingham with Brandon Lewis. 'You do know I'll have to ask Boris about this, don't you?' I told him as we whizzed up the M1. 'And if I do ask him about it, the audience will boo me.' When we got to the venue, I popped my head around the doors of both green rooms to say hello to the two candidates and their teams. Boris approached me, hand outstretched, and we indulged in some small talk. He then looked me in the eye and said, 'You're not going to mention this stuff in the papers, are you?' 'Of course I am,' I said. 'I won't labour the point, but you must understand I will have to ask about it.'

I then assumed he would mention it in his five-minute speech before my interview section began. I was wrong. He didn't. So I approached the subject immediately.

'Why were the police called to your house last night?' To applause from the audience, our aspiring prime minister said: 'I don't think they want to hear about that kind of thing. I think they want to hear about my plans for this country and my party.' He started to ramble on about red buses. My third attempt was brief and to the point: 'Just answer it – it's a very simple question. If the police are called to your home, it makes it everyone's business.' Boris replied: 'People are entitled to ask about my determination and my character. When I make a promise in politics, I keep that promise and I deliver.' I tried again: 'Does a person's private life have any bearing on their ability to be prime minister.' Totally avoiding the question, Boris said: 'I have the determination and the courage to deliver.'

When the booing started I resisted the temptation to burst out laughing. I had a job to do and I was damn well going to do it. Had I not done I would have been a journalistic laughing stock, and rightly so.

In the write-ups afterwards the atmosphere was described as 'Trumpian'. It was nothing of the sort. Had this happened in 1985 they would still have booed. Their tribal leader was under attack and they were going to circle the Tory wagons around him. I got that. In other circumstances, and had I been among them, I may well have joined in.

After the fifth time of asking I decided to give up. To go on would have been gratuitous. He clearly thought that if he gave an inch and offered any detail, it would have been open season for the rest of the media, and events proved him correct. To this day we don't know any more about what actually happened than we did then.

I hadn't realised the whole thing was being broadcast live on Sky News and the BBC. The rest of the interview and Q&A passed off without incident.

Afterwards, I genuinely had no feel for whether I had done the right thing. The old imposter syndrome came back. What would Andrew Neil have done, I asked myself.

Would Nick Robinson have got any more out of him than I did?

Meanwhile, Boris and his team had already left. I was told later that Boris hadn't realised that I was chairing another nine of the hustings, and when he was told he blurted out: 'But he hates me!' Not at all. I've always liked him, but in the aftermath of the events he'd been through over the previous 48 hours I didn't blame him at all for not relishing another nine rounds with me.

I then switched on my iPhone and it went mad with text after text from members of the political lobby. They all thought I had done a brilliant job, which was a relief. Quite a few Tory MPs also got in touch telling me that I should have no regrets. If ever I suffered from imposter syndrome about my interviewing – and I did – then this experience ought to have extinguished it. Yet though I know that Boris Johnson's team understood I had to pursue the question, I don't expect ever to interview him again.

It happens more and more often that politicians will blacklist a particular interviewer, especially if they have had a single bad experience. The fact that we have such a diverse media means that politicians can pick and choose who they want to be interviewed by. Donald Trump only does interviews with people who are sympathetic to him. He did a 30-minute interview with Nigel Farage, not because he thought Nigel Farage was going to be a good interviewer, but because he didn't expect to be challenged. It was a tremendous scoop for LBC, and the fact that it lasted for half an hour had BBC and Sky journalists foaming at the mouth with jealousy. Farage got stick for some softball questions, but his critics didn't like to acknowledge that he got several great news lines out of the interview.

LBC employs me at least in part because they know I am good at attracting big-name politicians to the station. As a presenter, I am a producer's dream because I help them do their job by using my contacts book wherever possible. They keep asking me to text a minister's Special Adviser because their own texts are routinely ignored. I don't mind getting my hands dirty. I will do anything I can to land the guest I want. I've never quite understood why some of my colleagues seem to think it's somebody else's job.

But the game has to be played. I want the interviewee to agree to be interviewed by me again. If you know that you'll never ever interview someone again, there is a risk you might be rather more aggressive and forensic than you would otherwise have been, but what's the point in being gratuitously insulting or just plain rude. Yes, you may get some headlines out of it, but if it affects your ability to book guests in the future, is this really the best strategy?

I make a point of treating all my interviewees the same. At least I try to. Because people know my past political allegiances, they automatically believe I will be softer on right-of-centre politicians. Those very same politicians don't seem to agree. Indeed, one of my best friends, Brandon Lewis, maintains that he finds me the most difficult person to be interviewed by. David Davis, another good friend of 30 years' standing, has also said he gets no special favours from me. A Green Party press officer was looking at one of my interviews with Davis in order to prepare her leader Siân Berry for an interview with me. She said to my producer: 'Does Iain not like David Davis – he was very robust with him?' I had to laugh.

I've only once had a complaint from a Labour MP about how I conducted an interview, when I pulled her up for the untruths she was telling about the consequences of a 'no-deal' Brexit. I told her she was being totally irresponsible and unnecessarily scaring people. She told my producer she'd never be interviewed by me again. My initial response was to shrug my shoulders, but in the end I concluded that the failure was mine. If an interview goes wrong, it's rarely the politician's fault, it's usually the interviewer's.

Most politicians are adults. They know when they're on a sticky wicket but they usually play the game, even if they know it's inevitable they will come off worst. Others? Not so much. Let me give you too contrasting examples.

There are some politicians who, no matter how hard you try, are always going to stick to a script that has been drilled into them by a party spin doctor. They'll trot out the usual well-worn phrases until you as the interviewer, to say nothing of the listener, are quite prepared to slit your wrists to put yourself out of your misery.

I've known Conservative politician Priti Patel for 20 years and interviewed her on several occasions. But each time it's the same: 'long-term economic plan', 'hard-working people' and countless other pre-approved soundbites.

In September 2015 she was put up by Conservative HQ to react to the election of Jeremy Corbyn as Labour Party leader. I thought it might be different. Silly me. Right from the off she was in full soundbite mode. 'Puts the security of our country in danger.' 'A danger to hard-working people.' And so it went on. She repeated each soundbite at least four times, just to make sure. I could have asked her how her summer holidays had been and she would have told me that Jeremy Corbyn would put the security of hard-working people's summer holidays in danger. I soon lost the will to live and asked why she hadn't seen fit to actually congratulate

Corbyn on his massive win. 'It's not for me to do that, I'm here to talk about the danger of his …' blah blah blah. I reminded her that it might be considered good manners. Off she went again. It was as if she had been programmed to say something and couldn't possibly deviate from it without getting a bollocking from Number Ten.

In the end she came across as rude and a bit of a clone. When you meet Priti Patel, most people are charmed. She's funny, has a wicked twinkle in her eye and is very entertaining. But put a microphone in front of her and she becomes a robot politician. And that's why she is often put up for these interviews. They know she can stick to a line without deviation or hesitation but with guaranteed repetition. At the time, I counted her a friend. But I'm afraid that when I am doing my job, friendship is left at the studio door. It took three and a half years for her to agree to do another interview with me.

Contrast this with an interview I did around the same time with Conservative MP Rob Halfon. I can't recall what he was coming on to talk about, but whatever it was he didn't seem very well briefed. I'm afraid I gave him a very hard time. Later that evening my phone rang, and it was him. I momentarily wondered whether to answer it, but in the end I did, albeit with a slight sense of foreboding. Rob is one of those few people in politics who everybody likes. No one has a bad word to say about him. 'I just want to thank you,' he said. 'You taught me a valuable lesson earlier.' 'I did?' I queried. 'Yes, it taught me I need to be properly briefed,' he said, laughing.

And that's exactly how to react. He proved himself to be a political adult, in contrast to Priti Patel's rather childish behaviour.

It happens rarely, but sometimes an interviewer gets so frustrated by a politician's inability to answer a question that they curtail the interview. That occurred recently when Richard Madeley, who fancies himself as a political interviewer, interviewed the then Defence Secretary, Gavin Williamson, on *Good Morning Britain*. Williamson was at a wildlife park with elephants and giraffes walking behind him. Madeley was being quite aggressive and interrupted Williamson repeatedly, but Williamson held his ground. It was in the aftermath of the Salisbury poisonings, Williamson having rather clumsily said he wished the Russians would shut up and go away. Madeley, quite reasonably, wanted to know if the Defence Secretary regretted his words. Four times he put the question, four times Williamson avoided answering it. In the end Madeley brought the interview to an end by saying: 'Interview terminated, because you won't answer the question.' Fair enough you might think, but, as I told Madeley live on his show the next day when he was preening himself over the press coverage the incident had attracted, I regard it as a failure of the interviewer if an interview is terminated. He looked daggers at me and then wouldn't speak to me for the rest of the paper review, instead directing every question to my colleague Jacqui Smith.

A myth has grown up that Jeremy Paxman, one of the country's greatest ever political inquisitors, adopted the maxim that 'when a politician tells you something in confidence, always ask yourself why is this lying bastard lying to me'. It wasn't Paxman who said that – although everyone thinks he did – it was *Times* correspondent Louis Heren.

Do I think that everybody you talk to is lying! No I do
not. Only a moron would think that. But I do think you
should approach any spokesman for a vested interest with
a degree of scepticism, asking 'why are you saying this'
and 'is it likely to be true?' Yes of course I do.

As an aside, Jeremy Paxman is far from the snarling
rottweiler he is painted as. I suspect it's a reputation he
revelled in, but I remember the first time I was interviewed
on *Newsnight* and I was quaking in my boots, he could not
have been nicer. He came into the green room beforehand
and put me at my ease, and after it was all over he walked
me through the corridors of TV Centre and out to my car.
That's normally left to a junior producer. I've never forgotten it.

Nowadays interviewers come under huge pressure to
deliver the soundbite from their guest that will make headlines across the rest of the media. Back in 2009 Andrew
Marr astonished Gordon Brown by asking if he was taking
'prescription painkillers and pills' to help him cope with
the pressures of the job of prime minister. This followed
weeks of rumours that Brown was in a state of depression.
It was quite a moment. Labour spin doctors were understandably furious – even more so when Marr admitted it
wasn't a spontaneous question, but one that had been
planned and war-gamed with his long-term editor, Barney
Jones.

In the summer of 2019 Robert Peston similarly caught
Tory leadership contender Jeremy Hunt unawares by
suddenly asking him about his baby sister who had
drowned in a bath when he was two years of age. Peston
was criticised for broaching the subject and admitted his

questioning could have been described as 'clumsy' or even 'wrong'. He had prewarned Hunt and his team that he knew about the incident and would bring it up in the interview.

When interviewing anyone about a sensitive personal issue, it is incredibly difficult to know how to approach it. In the end you have to banish all thoughts of embarrassment and potential awkwardness from your mind and do your job. It's fine to empathise and show compassion, and each situation is different and needs a unique approach.

All this offers further proof, if it were needed, that interviewing is not a science, it is an art. It's also about the interviewer listening as well as speaking.

Chapter 4

Thanks for your call, what would you like to say?

'You have the voice of John Major crossed
with a sleeping pill.'

LBC listener to me

It's hardly an original way to start a chapter on radio by
saying that it's a much more intimate medium than television. It just is. And that's why, given the choice of presenting on the radio or on television, radio wins every time.
You build a personal, even intimate, relationship with the
listener to the point where they regard you as a friend.

Right from the start I have shared things about my life
with my listeners and been encouraged to do so. Why?
Because it enables the listener to get to know me and come
to trust me. I've never been afraid to emote on the radio
because I know it's exactly how many in my audience will
be feeling. Keeping it real, though, is the most important
thing a radio presenter can do. I once knew a presenter
who had created an entirely fake persona because he felt
that if he were to be himself he would be too unlikeable.

People see through that. Shock jocks are in a permanent stage of rage. Sure, I can rage along with the best of them, but if you do it every day and are a one-trick pony it becomes a bit of a tired act.

I always respect the fact that someone has had the guts to pick up the phone to talk to me. The least I can do is be polite and allow them to speak. On the odd occasion, if someone says something particularly stupid or nonsensical, I might well become more aggressive in my response, but the point is that I do it so rarely that people's ears prick up when I do start getting a bit antsy.

Presenters who bully and ridicule caller after caller soon find that they attract a particular kind of audience. It's one that thinks the sun shines out of their rears and agrees with every word they say, and delights in anyone thinking otherwise being 'taken down' by the oh so clever presenter.

Yes, it's nice to have people ringing in to agree with you, but it can make for bloody boring radio. I revel in people ringing in to disagree with me, and we can have a good canter round the course and part as friends. That's how it should be. Yes, I've 'lost it' with the odd caller, where I have a right old rant at them. It's happened with racist or homophobic callers on occasion, and Brexit has provoked the odd fulmination on my part, but in ten years on the radio, I'd say it might happen on average once a month. Or maybe I'm kidding myself that I'm much more polite than I really am. My listeners can be the judges.

One of my favourite callers is Sean, from Consett. He's an out-and-out leftie, thinks the Tories are all evil and I love him. He always works himself up into a complete frenzy and we have a spirited but good-natured discussion. And then once he's exploded, we part as friends. Just as it should be. He once spat out Margaret Thatcher's name, so I interrupted and told him she was my political heroine. 'Heroine? Heroine?' he exclaimed. 'You must be on bloody heroin to think that!'

If I hadn't opened Politico's Bookstore in 1997, I doubt whether I'd be on the radio now. One day, one of our regular customers, Jo Phillips – Paddy Ashdown's former spin doctor, and then producer of Radio 5 Live's *Sunday Service* – came into the shop and asked if I fancied co-presenting *Sunday Service*, deputising for journalist Andrew Pierce, who presented alongside Fi Glover and former Gordon Brown spinner Charlie Whelan. I thought all my Christmases had come at once. I became Andrew Pierce's deputy for three years and presented the show around twenty times. It had long been my favourite show on the radio and now I was interviewing, commenting, indulging in political humour and banter with Fi Glover, my favourite radio presenter.

Perhaps my proudest moment was coming up with a sports quiz for newly appointed Sports Minister Richard Caborn. We gave him no advance warning, and from memory he scored one out of ten. It made all the papers the next day. My big mistake was to let others take the credit for it.

I then presented a monthly books show on the late lamented Oneword Radio and spent 18 months presenting on Britain's first internet TV station, 18 Doughty Street.

And then I met Tommy Boyd. Tommy was a name from my childhood. He made his name as the presenter of *Magpie*, a kids' programme on ITV, but then moved into speech radio, where he became a huge success. He rang me up one day in early 2009 and told me he was launching an internet talk radio station called Play Talk. He told me that whoever he talked to about recruiting presenters, the conversation always came back to me.

We broadcast from a studio in a barn near Arundel on a Friday night. It was just me, a microphone and the listeners. I think I only did five or six programmes and a nine-hour local-election-night marathon, but it was enough for me to confirm in my own mind that I absolutely loved radio phone-ins and could hold my own as a presenter. Tommy was hugely encouraging and assured me when Play Radio went tits up after only a few weeks that I had a big future in radio.

In August that year, only a few weeks after the demise of Play Talk, my friend Yasmin Alibhai-Brown, the author and commentator, told me she had secured an audition at LBC. I had appeared on LBC quite a bit in the past, starting with Gyles Brandreth's Sunday afternoon arts show in 1999. Indeed, his show provided me with my first presenting opportunity when we swapped roles so I could host him taking part in his 'Stairway to Heaven' feature – a sort of *Desert Island Discs* for those who have just died. I was also a regular pundit on Sandy Toksvig's lunchtime show during the Iraq war.

I was excited for Yasmin but wanted to do my own audition, so I emailed the station's Managing Editor, Jonathan Richards, explaining who I was, and that Yasmin and I would be a brilliant double act, having done a lot of Sky News paper reviews together. We gelled. We disagreed on everything but got on personally like a house on fire. Anyway, he suggested we come in to do a joint audition. We spent 40 minutes in a tiny studio doing a mock show.

To be honest I wasn't sure that it went very well. Something must have sparked though, for three weeks later I was asked to present that day's evening show. The usual presenter, Petrie Hosken, was ill, so I had little time to prepare. But it was just me. Not Yasmin. #awkward.

Before I knew it, it was time to go into the studio. One and a half minutes to get my papers sorted out and off we went. No script. Talk about being thrown in at the deep end. In three hours we talked about the future of the Lib Dems, then had a panel of politicians and ended up by talking about assisted suicide.

And then it was all over. I have to say I thoroughly enjoyed it. I felt totally at home. A professional radio presenter friend of mine tweeted me afterwards and said: 'That was the most laid-back debut I've ever heard. You're a natural.'

Nothing happened then for some time, as they were clearly waiting to see if I would get a parliamentary seat for the 2010 election. In February I did a couple more shows, then I asked the LBC programme director Jonathan Richards if I could put some ideas to him for an election night programme. I did, he liked my proposal and I hosted a six-hour programme with Gaby Hinsliff from the *Observer*, which most regarded as a minor triumph.

I had then covered virtually every show in the schedule apart from the overnight slot. And in August I had four weeks sitting on for Petrie Hosken again, which is when I really came into my own. Jonathan Richards then offered me the evening show on a contract because Petrie was moving to the afternoons.

I knew that I was far from the finished article as a radio presenter, but I genuinely felt I could become quite good at it. That's not meant to sound arrogant. Most things in my life I have had to learn. I've always had to work hard to keep up with others, but for the first time in my career I was doing something I felt completely at home with. I sat in front of that microphone and thought to myself, 'I know I can be good at this.' Three years later I won the Radio Presenter of the Year award, a feat I repeated in 2016.

There's nothing quite like presenting a live radio show for three hours. One minute you're doing a routine phone-in on whether HS2 should be cancelled, the next you're having to cope with breaking news of a terror attack. It's happened to me on several occasions. And that's when you really earn your money as a presenter. You sink or swim.

At this point I should maybe point out that I have no formal training as a journalist or indeed as a broadcaster. I revel, though, in handling breaking news. My first experience was covering the Arab Spring events in the spring of 2011. The thrill of crossing to Cairo to speak to an Egyptian filmmaker on the top of a hotel giving us live commentary on the events in Tahrir Square will never leave me.

But it was on 22 May 2013 that I came off air and thought to myself, maybe for the first time, I really can do this. It was only a couple of months since I had been promoted to present LBC's *Drive* show.

Sometime after 3 p.m. our Classic FM newsreader came over to my producer Matt Harris and said there was an ongoing incident in Woolwich. It looked as if someone had been killed with a machete or samurai sword and that armed police had shot the two people behind the attack. Eavesdropping, it was clear to me that this was a story that would dominate my four-hour drivetime show. At that point it had never entered my head that it could be a terror incident. As details started to come in, I tweeted asking for witnesses to phone our newsroom – frankly it was more in hope than expectation, but at around a quarter to four I noticed Matt was deep in conversation with someone on the phone. As the clock edged toward 4 p.m. I wondered what on earth he could be talking about, seeing as we needed to head down to the studio. It soon became clear. 'Do a short intro telling people what we know – then get into the call quickly. James was there. He saw your tweet. He can tell us everything.'

And indeed he did. James was actually only a few yards away and witnessed the whole horrific attack. I've done some emotional interviews in my time, but this was different. My role was to listen and encourage him to explain what went on. Yes, it was graphic and, yes, at one point I thought to myself: should we be giving so much gory detail at ten past four in the afternoon when children could be listening while being driven home from school? But equally, I thought: people need to know exactly what happened here. As it went on, I thought to myself: 'He's still in shock.' It was gripping listening, and in some ways very upsetting. I suspect I wasn't alone in trying to hold my emotions in check. And for once I succeeded.

It was clear to me that this was far worse than we had ever contemplated. Just keep calm. Stick to what we know and don't say anything unnecessarily provocative.

I decided to give our Muslim listeners an opportunity to tell me their reaction to what had happened. If I were a Muslim, my heart would have sunk and I'd have been thinking: 'Here we go again.' We had a lot of calls, most of which I couldn't get to, but they all had the same message. Not in our name.

By this time, the *Daily Mail* was using our interview with James, and Sky News flashed up a giant LBC logo as they replayed part of it. I was being deluged with texts and tweets from other journalists asking for James's number. I'm afraid I had to say that he was in no condition to do more interviews, especially as I had finished my interview by telling him I thought he could do with talking to someone who could counsel him properly. It was the responsible thing to do, I thought.

That interview won me a Sony Silver Award for interview of the year. I must admit I felt a complete fraud. It wasn't about me; it was about James. I should also point out that once I realised James was in shock, I called an end to the interview and asked him to stay on the line to speak to my producer Laura. You have a duty of care in cases like this and, luckily, I didn't need anyone to tell me that. Laura spoke to James several times over the next 24 hours. He was being hounded by other members of the media who wanted their own interviews with him. Journalists were banging on his door at 2 a.m. and putting notes through his letterbox. He felt harassed and bullied. Laura kept in touch with him and gave him all the advice she could.

A year later we invited him back on the show on the anniversary of the attack. He came into the studio and told us how the whole incident had affected him and his family. His marriage came under pressure as his wife found it difficult to process what she had witnessed. They moved from the area as they couldn't bear driving past the scene each day. I expressed the hope that they'd managed to get away on holiday, but his employer wouldn't give him any leave. I found myself offering him and his family a week in my house in Norfolk. We've stayed in touch by direct message from time to time on Twitter ever since.

The relationship between a presenter and producer is a unique one. It's one of trust, respect and total, utter disrespect from time to time. If there's a good relationship, magical radio can be the result. It there isn't, it's usually the listener that suffers. A good producer makes you a far better presenter than you really are. They know when to stop me going off on a particular tangent, and when they need to curb my sense of mischief. They need to know when I am thinking of doing something that might not quite work. It must be admitted, though, that there are moments of tension, and from time to time we'll have a bit of a blow-up. I actually think that's healthy. A live studio environment is highly pressurised and at times tempers can fray. It doesn't happen often, but when you have strong personalities (and by definition a talk radio presenter isn't shy in coming forward!) there will be times when things are said. If I skewered a politician in an interview, it's often because my producer had spotted a weakness in the politician and suggested a line of questioning to me in my ear that I might not have thought of. And if I didn't get an answer from the politician, they would press me to ask the question again. And again. And again, to the point where I sometimes became embarrassed to do it. But it almost always ends up with us getting a news line, and that's where a good producer excels – spotting an opportunity for a news line that we can then pump out to our media colleagues.

What people don't understand about LBC is that we never have a script. It's all off the cuff. And that is where the role of the studio producer becomes far more important than it might be on other radio stations. The producer has to know when to speak and when not to. He/she needs to know how much info to pass to the presenter and how and when best to do it. It's a real skill, often underestimated by people who've never been in a radio gallery.

I've lost count of the times people say to me: 'God, I wish I had a job as easy as yours. I mean, you just sit there and talk, which is what you love doing anyway.' Oh, if only they knew. Yes of course, if you're a talk radio host you like talking and hearing the sound of your own voice, but there is so much more to it than that. You don't just have to know how to talk, you have to know how to listen too, and be able to hold an intelligent conversation, often about a subject you are by no means an expert on. Or sometimes know nothing about at all, or have no real interest in.

Presenting a talk radio show is a bit like being a swan. To the listener you need to appear completely calm and in control of everything. But under the water your feet are paddling ten to the dozen. Because for the whole of the three hours you're on air you're effectively the personification of the word 'multi-tasking'. At any point in the show you're talking, listening to the producer talking in your ear, listening to an interviewee or caller, checking the time, reading texts and tweets, thinking ahead to the next subject and how to tease it, and much more besides.

It's a real act of concentration, and it's constant. I've never known anything as intense as this.

You're aware that anything you say, with just one word out of place, could spell the end of your radio career. You're also aware that something an interviewee or caller might say might also take you off the air or lead to an Ofcom complaint. In some senses you know that for three hours you're walking a tightrope. Some people walk it with ease, others fall off and a few should never have been allowed on it in the first place.

I came into radio presenting comparatively late in life and, as I've said, have no formal training. But even seasoned broadcasters who've been doing it for years will tell you of the mental strain presenting a three-hour talk radio/news show can bring. It certainly gets the adrenaline flowing, especially on days when there is a huge breaking news story. That's when you're really found out as a news broadcaster. You can either do it, or you can't. There's no halfway house. I well remember the day when the Malaysian Airliner was shot down over Ukraine shortly before we went on air. Instinctively I knew we'd go into breaking news mode, which means we concentrate on that one story almost to the exclusion of everything else. It really is broadcasting by the seat of your pants, especially when there isn't much that you know, little has been confirmed and you're aware that wild speculation is not only often highly inappropriate, but can be very dangerous as well, not to say with a high probability of making you look very foolish if your speculation is way off beam.

Sometimes you read comments on internet forums where people complain that a presenter didn't seem very knowledgeable about a particular subject and why hadn't they prepared better. An understandable complaint on occasions maybe, but on a breaking news programme you have to rely on your general knowledge a lot. That's why it pays to have a few grey hairs – a bit of life experience. The challenge is to make compelling radio on a very light news day.

Nowadays, of course, in our new multimedia, multicamera studio we often either livestream a programme, or programme segment on our website, or record it to put out on social media. This means that as well as conducting a radio show, you're also effectively conducting a TV show. No stripy shirts. No T-shirts. No rude signs to your producer. No facial signs if you think a caller is barking mad. No pressure!

So all this is a roundabout way of saying that when 10 p.m. comes around and the show comes to an end, I am dog tired. Good for nothing. I might as well have run a 10k. I go home, have something to eat. Then intend to watch some TV, but I rarely get past 20 minutes without falling asleep. An hour later, I wake up and slink off to bed. And then the next day I get up and do it again.

Chapter 5

Fake News, Bias and Spin

'Before mass leaders seize the power to fit reality to their lies, their propaganda is marked by its extreme contempt for facts as such, for in their opinion fact depends entirely on the power of man who can fabricate it.'

Hannah Arendt

Over the years there has been an increasing suspicion that there is a cosy conspiracy between the establishment and the media. Some people genuinely believe that politicians and the media have hatched a plot between them to promulgate the status quo. Apparently, broadcasters like me 'take our orders' from on high and just spew out whatever propaganda our masters tell us to. Alternatively, we meekly obey the demands of politicians, who tell us which questions they are willing to answer and which ones they are not. Only once in my broadcasting career have I been told what I couldn't ask, and it wasn't by a politician.

On my first day on *Drive* I scored a real coup by landing the Archbishop of Canterbury, Justin Welby, as my first big-name guest. He had 20 minutes to pre-record an interview. I had never met him before and wasn't impressed when, as I walked into the studio to find him sitting there, he informed me – without even a 'Hello, nice to meet you' – that he wouldn't answer any questions on welfare reform. This was rather irritating for me given that he had been all over the previous day's papers making some rather controversial remarks on the subject. I was in a quandary. If I complied with his request, I'd be compromising my principles as an interviewer. Yet if I did ask him about it, I'd risk him terminating the interview and jeopardise the whole of Global Radio's relationship with him and Lambeth Palace. I am ashamed to say I chose the former course of action. It's the only time in my career as an interviewer when such terms have been insisted on. Did I do the right thing? I still can't answer that question, but the Archbishop certainly went down in my estimation.

I've always believed in the cock-up theory of politics rather than conspiracies. Here's an example that got the Twitter conspiracy theories going during the 2019 general election. Nick Ferrari hosted an hour-long phone-in with Boris Johnson. Nowadays all these interviews are not only filmed, but streamed live. We have a whole host of cameras in the studio, and if we are going to stream something we are increasingly professional with the video production. It's just as much a TV studio as a radio studio.

At one point in the interview, Boris Johnson was seen doing a throat-slitting gesture. He was, at that moment, having some difficulty answering a question about social care.

This was leapt upon by people who assumed it must be Boris Johnson signalling to Nick Ferrari to end this line of questioning and to move on to another subject. It was seen as proof that Boris was much more comfortable in a studio with Nick Ferrari, who would do his bidding in a way Andrew Neil was never likely to.

In a studio environment, all presenters use signals to the producers, who are behind the screen in the gallery. Nick uses a throat-slitting sign to tell his producer to 'shut up' and stop talking in his ear. I use the same gesture if I don't want to speak to a particular caller.

If I want the producer to be quiet – and it does happen, even though I welcome advice in my ear – I tend to do a Larry Grayson 'shut that door' kind of signal in a sort of dismissive hand gesture. With the cameras on, you have to be wary of doing something that might be seen as inappropriate.

All Boris Johnson was doing was mimicking what Nick Ferrari had done to his producer. He clearly found it very amusing. Some time later in the hour, Boris noticed on the TV screen in the studio that Sky were showing a video of him 'throat-slitting'. He then drew Nick's attention to it, Nick explained what he had been doing, and Boris explained he had mimicked Nick. End of story, you'd have thought. As Nick Ferrari explained himself:

> To clarify the PM's gesture this morning on LBC, this is sign language between me and my producer to signify he needs to stay quiet in my ear. It's been in common use for over ten years. End of. NF

But still the conspiracy theories abounded and people who aren't fans of either Boris or Nick delighted in spreading them. Shameful, really. But that's what happens now on social media, and the poor voter is expected to sort the wheat from the chaff.

Take an incident I was involved in during the Labour Party Conference in 2013 in Brighton. If you believe the folklore (or as I would put it, lies) perpetrated by social media, I beat up a frail old pensioner.

It was the day of Ed Miliband's leader's speech. I had to get up early to drive my author, Damian McBride, from a breakfast TV interview, planned to take place outside The Grand Hotel (this detail is important) to the Heart studios in Hove, where he would be talking to Nick Ferrari on LBC. I set my alarm for 7 a.m. but it didn't go off. I eventually woke up at 7.20, which was a bit of an issue given that I was supposed to meet Damian at 7.30. There was no time for a shower, so I threw on some clothes, jumped into my car and headed to the Hotel. There was no sign of Damian. I phoned Biteback's PR director, Suzanne Sangster, and she informed me that GMTV had insisted on doing the interview on the seafront. I was annoyed for two reasons. First, because it was in full view of any passing protester who didn't like the fact that his book *Power Trip* had already overshadowed the conference, but second because it meant I had to navigate Brighton's one-way system and it would be difficult to stop on the seafront main road. Anyway, it turned out there was a layby directly opposite where the interview was taking place with Damian on the seafront and Lorraine Kelly and Eamonn Holmes in the GMTV London studio. At the time, I drove a car with a TV in the dashboard, so I switched it on to see what Damian had to say. But all I could see was a placard protesting against nuclear power. I looked away from the screen and through my car window I could see the GMTV sound engineer trying to keep the protester and his placard out of the picture and failing miserably.

I got out of my car and ambled over to the scene vaguely aware there were other TV cameras there too, but not really intending to do anything. As I stood behind the camera, the protester made another attempt to lunge into shot with his placard and the sound engineer tried to keep him at bay. I remember thinking that anyone watching this at home wouldn't be paying a blind bit of attention to what Damian was saying, they'd be talking about the protester. On the spur of the moment I decided to give the GMTV sound engineer a hand. I walked forward and pulled at the straps of the protester's rucksack to steer him away from the camera shot. It was a gentle tug, not a violent one. He immediately wheeled round and, I guess out of instinct, threw a punch at me, which fortunately missed. We grappled for a few seconds before we both fell over. At no point did I throw a punch or kick, or do anything violent. My only aim was to prevent him getting into the camera shot again. I was also aware that the protester's Jack Russell was yapping through the whole incident and I remember the dog biting its owner, rather than me.

When the interview was over, I went back to the car. Damian got in the passenger seat, aware that something had happened but not quite sure what. All I remember is saying to him: 'I don't think it will become anything bigger.' How wrong I was.

After Damian had done his LBC interview I went back to the hotel for a shower and breakfast with my producer

Matt Harris and our (then) political editor, Tom Cheal. I told them what had happened and they found it all very hilarious. Tom then looked at his phone and someone had posted a video of the whole incident. It still didn't occur to me that this was going to blow up into a major incident.

Around 2.30 p.m. I was told that a senior political journalist had encouraged the protester to report me to the police for assault. By this time, I had learned that the protester was Stuart Holmes, a man I had seen regularly at conferences for years, along with his dog – also somewhat bizarrely named Stuart.

At this point Matt and I decided that I should go to see Stuart, who was standing outside the conference centre. Matt paved the way and at about 3 p.m. I went down, apologised, shook his hand and offered to pay for a new placard. He accepted, and that, I thought, was the end of it. But it wasn't, although I didn't know it at that point.

I went off to do my show, which started at 4 p.m. In the meantime, several people who hadn't even witnessed the incident, but had seen it on social media, reported me to Sussex Police, and I was told that the same political journalist mentioned above persuaded Mr Holmes that he should ignore my apology and report me himself. I've never got to the bottom of whether he did or not.

During the show, Matt kept disappearing from our broadcasting cubicle, and as it progressed, a sixth sense told me something was happening. Matt had my back all day and was brilliant in trying to cope with a situation in which the police were wanting to 'have a word' while I was live on air! I well remember the commercial break when he walked over and said, 'I've sorted it; the police were here, and now they're not.' And at that moment the red light went on. 'You're listening to LBC,' I said, 'live at the Labour Party Conference …' It's moments like those that I'll look back on when I'm in my dotage and dribbling.

I eventually learned that the police had turned up in the media hall asking to speak to me, but Sue Inglish, the head of political programmes at the BBC, knew I was on air and told them I wasn't there, so my show wouldn't be interrupted. They did eventually return, and Matt spoke to them and agreed that I would go down to the police station as soon as I came off air.

While all this was going on, Alastair Campbell came into the booth to do an interview. 'What the hell's going on?' he asked. I told him, and characteristically he offered to help if I needed any advice on how to handle the media fallout.

At 6.30 p.m. Joe Pike, LBC's reporter, now political correspondent on Sky News, came in and during the news break he told me that when the show ended at 7 p.m. I was to follow him and he would lead me down to a waiting police car outside the conference centre. I wasn't to talk to anyone, just to look at the back of his head and walk. I'd never seen him so commanding!

So at 7 p.m. that's just what I did. Waiting for me was a phalanx of lobby reporters, each with a notebook waiting to jot down anything I might say. Various TV crews were there, with reporters shouting inane questions. It's the closest I'm likely to get to a perp walk, I hope. All I remember is the *Guardian*'s Nick Watt and the *Sun*'s Dave Wooding looking at the floor in a rather embarrassed way. Matt followed on behind. He told me afterwards that as I got in the unmarked police car, Gobby (real name Paul Lambert) from the BBC News Channel – the one who would always shout out to ministers 'Are you going to resign, minister?'

– asked him if it was a police car. Matt said he didn't think so; it would be one of mine. 'He's got a lot of cars, you know,' he said, attempting to throw Gobby off the scent.

I was interviewed at the police station and the officer said she imagined I'd be free to go. She then left the room. I looked at my phone and saw that Caroline Lucas had been charged with obstruction over an anti-fracking protest not far from Brighton. It was at that point I suspected this wasn't going to end well. That feeling was reinforced when another police officer appeared. I can't remember her rank, but it was clear she was going to reluctantly do something she knew wasn't really merited, feeling that she had no alternative, given the circumstances. She offered me a caution or the opportunity to go to court. I was fairly confident I'd be able to get a not guilty verdict in a court, but I couldn't have this hanging over me, so I accepted a voluntary caution instead. I was to return to the police station in two days' time. But it wasn't over.

I was one of the leading stories on the BBC and ITV ten o'clock news programmes. Apparently, the video had been running on Sky and the BBC News Channels all day. When I rang my sisters, they were furious with me. 'What would Mum have thought?' they quite reasonably asked. She would have been horrified and deeply ashamed.

And so it was that, two days later, John drove me to Brighton. During the journey I suddenly wondered if there would be any press at the police station. I had no intention of doing another perp walk, so I phoned the police station and asked if I could go in a different entrance. We evaded them, both on the way in and on the way out. I also thought I should write some sort of statement, so I started tapping it out on my BlackBerry while John drove down the M23. I

read it back and it was far too long. I needed a second opinion. So I rang someone I'd always want on my team in a
battle: Alastair Campbell. 'Send it to me and give me ten
minutes,' he said. I also sent it to my sister Tracey, who
invariably has a good eye for these things. Alastair rang
back and said it was far too defensive and long-winded.
Tracey also made some amendments, and she was rather
tickled when Alastair endorsed them. I've always taken the
view that if you're going to apologise for something, you
need to do it without equivocation. Half-hearted apologies
never work.

This incident took place seven years ago. Yet whenever I
hit the headlines for good or ill some people delight in
bringing it to a wider attention by sharing the YouTube
video. The trouble is that they have edited it so it only shows
the bit where we end up on the floor. Because of my media
profile they think they can take me out by using fake news
techniques. I'm used to it now, but the interesting thing is
that invariably the Twitter accounts that share the video
have egg avatars and fewer than twenty followers. Make of
that what you will.

But what message does this fakery send out to young
voters. It's them I feel sorry for. How are they supposed to
work out what's right and what's wrong when presented
with two very different versions of events. Of course, they
consume their media wholly differently to people of my
generation.

Then there are the times when potential guests refuse to
come on the programme for no good reason. In the 2019
election campaign I regularly explained that both the major
parties were refusing to provide guests for interview,

despite having promised to do so. Audiences have a right to know that they play these stupid games. But then they have the cheek to complain you've called them out on air.

Dorothy Byrne, the then head of news and current affairs at Channel 4, raised this issue in her 2019 MacTaggart lecture. She went further than any other news executive has ever done in calling out politicians and government for their attitude to fulfilling their responsibility to appear on current affairs programmes throughout the media. It's always been part of the democratic bargain that as well as subjecting themselves to the scrutiny of their fellow MPs in the House of Commons, prime ministers and ministers will go on television and radio to be held accountable for their actions and to explain their policies. Byrne made the point that Margaret Thatcher would regularly appear on TV for 45-minute or hour-long interviews with the likes of Brian Walden and Sir Robin Day. Nowadays, not so much. If you're not Andrew Marr, you get six minutes, or eight if you're lucky. Byrne commented:

> Politicians have a big job to do if they want us to trust them and the two most important things they can do to win back trust are to tell the truth and come on TV to be held accountable. My message is even more relevant now that the level of trust in politicians is even lower.

No broadcaster has a divine right to demand an interview with a politician. In the 1980s there were only four TV channels. Now there are a plethora of outlets. In radio, in the 1980s there were no national talk-radio stations – or even 5 Live. It was just Radio 4. Now there's LBC, talkRADIO, 5 Live and several others. Politicians often think they get more bang for their buck by doing a succession of local radio interviews rather than appear on Radio 4, where they will inevitably get a grilling, and sometimes a not altogether polite one.

Social media gives politicians the opportunity to talk directly to voters with no filter. Boris Johnson has taken full advantage of this. He pops up on Facebook with a two-minute direct-to-camera video for a folksy chit-chat. In his first six months as prime minister, outside of *The Andrew Marr Show*, he didn't do a single TV interview that lasted longer than a few minutes.

As a result of Dorothy Byrne's MacTaggart lecture, in which she called Johnson a 'liar', the Conservatives decided not to put up ministers to be interviewed on Channel 4 News. When Kay Burley empty-chaired the Conservative Party co-chairman James Cleverly, they boycotted her show too. After Cleverly was monstered by Emily Maitlis on *Newsnight*, they did the same to that show. Radio 4's flagship *Today* programme was the next to get the cold shoulder. Many of these boycotts will no doubt prove to be temporary, but they illustrate the fact that the multiplicity of media platforms has eroded the power of the large TV networks and their programmes in the same way that the influence of national newspapers has been eroded by the rise of the internet.

I once received an email from a 22-year-old:

> I don't buy this line that 'young people are not interested in politics'. We are, although it has to be presented in a manner in which young people who have grown up with the internet feel is relevant to them. A young person is more likely to access something on YouTube than watch

the TV. We don't watch the 6 o'clock News on BBC1; we have the RSS feeds of numerous websites/blogs in our RSS readers. If the Tory party 'get' this concept and harness it, they will be well on their way to mobilising a significant number of young people to vote for them.

To me, that young man encapsulates the problems facing the mainstream media. Advertisers are flooding to the web from newspapers. Young people either do not read daily newspapers, or expect to pick them up for free. Broadcast news bulletins are becoming less popular as people get their news quotient from the internet. Just as satellite TV threatened the hegemony of terrestrial TV channels, social media platforms are doing the same today.

I do quite a bit of public speaking in schools and universities, and when I ask teenagers to put up their hands if they regularly buy a national newspaper it's rare for more than a couple of hands to go up. When I ask how many of them regularly watch the *BBC News at Ten* it's the same. They'll certainly watch news clips on their smart phones, but does that give them a rounded view? They're far more likely to exist within their own echo chambers than older generations.

Do they see the same biases as my generation? The truth is that there is unconscious bias everywhere in the media. As a producer, just by choosing to cover one story or another shows unconscious bias. As a presenter or interviewer there are times when one's personal views inevitably emerge from behind the carefully calculated veneer of impartiality.

I do not believe that individual interviewers show conscious party-political bias, but we need to be very careful how we define out terms. It is clear to anyone who watches them that Channel 4 News has a world outlook that could be described as 'liberal left'. The BBC is often accused of the same bias. Sky News clearly had a pro-Remain outlook during the whole Brexit debate, but none of these broadcasters could be accused of a party-political bias in my view. That assessment is certainly not shared on the Left, who believe the BBC to be in the hands of the Conservative Party and find any excuse to quote their political editor Laura Kuenssberg to prove it. They jumped on a *faux pas* or misspeak by BBC political correspondent Alex Forsyth on election night when she said that Boris Johnson got 'the majority he so deserves'. It was quite clear to anyone who wasn't looking for evidence of bias that she meant 'the majority he so desired'. It was three o'clock in the morning and she was no doubt dog tired, but no one on Twitter gives any room for the benefit of the doubt.

For 20 years, the BBC has been told, even by many of its stars, that it is too biased towards the London liberal elites. Andrew Marr was the first to break cover when he admitted that although the BBC might not have a party-political bias, it certainly had a 'liberal' one.

Peter Sissons, in his memoir *When One Door Closes*, railed against the BBC for its addiction to employing producers who had a single worldview – one that didn't include any understanding of free markets, borders or anything that might have even a slight conservative tinge to it. Lately, John Humphrys has joined the fray.

The problem reached its zenith after Brexit. Like most London middle-class liberals, the BBC couldn't understand why 17.4 million had voted to leave the EU. But then it has never seemed to make any attempt to do so. After the referendum, it panicked, apparently believing that the Leave vote was a consequence of its failure to dispel politicians' 'lies' or 'populism'.

Thus, for the last three years, it has gladly wheeled out its 'Reality Check' fact-checkers to pick holes in the case for Brexit, deploying them only occasionally to question the case for Remain. Its ostensibly impartial presenters, meanwhile, feel the need to stand in judgement over the argument, determining what is 'true' as if viewers were incapable of making up their own minds.

The sycophantic coverage given to 'People's Vote' campaigners (even the use of that absurd moniker to describe people who want to reverse the original people's vote) when compared to the 'look down your nose and sniff' tone the BBC adopts when questioning Brexiteers has been readily apparent to anyone who isn't aligned to the Remain cause.

The dominant mentality in the BBC is not necessarily pro-Labour, but its assumptions are those of middle-class liberals. Look at its coverage of poverty. Judging by its output, anyone would think that Britain is a country solely of billionaires and the very poor: the interests of the majority in the middle are rarely taken into account.

On food banks, the BBC makes out these are a peculiarly British phenomenon, forced on people by a wicked Tory government. There are food banks in virtually every country in Europe, but you won't see that pointed out by BBC producers whose middle-class guilt complex permeates much of their output.

Suggest that it's capitalism that has lifted poor people all over the world out of poverty and it's a quick, 'Sorry Mr

Dale, we don't think that particular documentary idea is right for our audience.' Why? Because they commission programmes for 'people like us'. Perish the thought that the kind of person in Bassetlaw who voted Tory for the first time should be catered for.

One thing you can't accuse the BBC of, though, is spreading fake news. That is almost wholly the preserve of the internet and political parties of all colours. In many ways, so-called fake news is nothing new. Political parties have always exaggerated the truth, or indeed told outright lies about their achievements or political opponents.

The Liberal Democrats are famous for their dodgy bar charts that exaggerate their levels of support. The Conservatives famously faked a video of Labour's Sir Keir Starmer apparently not being able to answer a question on Brexit and created a fake Fact Check Twitter page during a general election leaders debate. Labour faced an investigation for its claim in a faked photoshopped red bus that the Conservatives would be sending Donald Trump £500 million a week of NHS money. They're all at it. However wrong all this fakery is, we can hold the political parties to account for it.

What is more difficult is to identify fake news on social media and in the comments on some new websites like BuzzFeed. At the end of 2019 the BBC exposed a network of Russian-origin social media accounts that was spreading false stories through BuzzFeed and other open-access websites like Reddit. Jeremy Corbyn seized on a document published on Reddit about US–UK trade talks, which he said proved that the Conservatives intended to sell off the NHS to the US. It emerged that it had been placed on Reddit by someone based in Russia.

The trouble with fake news is that by the time it is exposed as such, thousands, maybe millions of people have seen the story and believed it. There's no going back from that. It is surely the responsibility of the news publishing websites to monitor what is put on their sites, whether it is on the main site or in comment sections. Some media organisations have gone so far as to ban all comments because they are impossible to police. The *Daily Telegraph* website did this because it couldn't cope with monitoring the sheer volume of comments it received – many of them abusive, vile and sweary. The *Daily Mail* has persevered, but a quick look through the comments on any particular post and one wonders why they bother to host them. The same with YouTube. Scroll through any YouTube comment feed and you lose any remaining faith in the humanity of your fellow world citizens.

All this was being encouraged by the President of the United States, Donald J. Trump. His own habit of spreading fake news gives licence to both his supporters and his enemies. UK left-of-centre websites like Squawk Box and The Canary have taken the attitude: well, if it's good enough for him, it would be remiss of us not to fight back. In a way you have to understand that point of view. In politics you have to fight fire with fire. It's all very well for the likes of Michelle Obama and Jeremy Corbyn to parrot the virtue-signalling soundbite 'When they go low, we go high', but we all know that politicians get down and dirty, because they realise that negative campaigning works.

There is an upside to all this, though. Young people in general do seem to be more engaged in politics at the moment, either because they are galvanised and inspired by a particular politician (often, but not always, on the Left) or because they feel strongly about an issue. Climate change has galvanised many young people in the way that the fight against nuclear weapons did on the Left in the 1980s.

Perhaps Boris Johnson summed up the whole dilemma facing the establishment media in a *Telegraph* column in 2011:

> A broadcast has been turned into a dialogue. When we write our pieces, thousands of eyes are scanning them for errors of fact and taste – and now our critics cannot only harrumph and curse us. They can tell the world – in seconds – where they think we have gone wrong. We are not just writing columns, we are writing wiki-columns, and if we sometimes get beaten up, we also have the satisfaction of gaining the odd grunt of agreement.
>
> Politicians are being held to account by journalists; journalists are being held to account by their readers – and it cannot be long, the internet being what it is, before the wind of popular scrutiny blows through all the bourgeois professions. What are we going to do about the lawyers?

In the end all parts of the news media have got to decide what they're there for. Is it to inform and educate, or is to entertain? If it's all about the exclusive, all about the 'gotcha' moment, things will look very bleak indeed. I'm more optimistic than that, though. The amount of so-called 'long read' articles now being published, not just on media websites but also in newspapers and magazines, is encouraging. Investigative journalism seems not to have withered away with the death of some newspapers. I'm less optimistic about the broadcast media, though. Seeking viral hits through *Daily Mail*-style headlines is a phenomenon that has infected many parts of the online news media. Surely news journalism has to be about more than that.

PART TWO

POLITICS

Chapter 6

The Language of Politics and the Media

'I always cheer up immensely if they attack one personally. It means they haven't got a single argument left.'

Margaret Thatcher

Human beings rule the planet because of our innate intelligence. We have the ability to articulate our thoughts by the powers of speech and writing. It is therefore only natural that our oral and written utterances will cause either pleasure or displeasure.

Margaret Thatcher received her fair share of personal vituperation in the 1980s, and the language used against her was appalling, yet it wasn't anywhere near on the scale that politicians experience every day on social media nowadays.

Even politicians themselves have fallen into the trap of abusing each other as a matter of course. No politician would have repeatedly called someone from the opposite party a 'liar' until fairly recently. Yet in the 2019 general election campaign Labour frontbenchers were briefed to call Boris Johnson a liar as many times as possible in every interview they did, as well as to invoke the spectre of privatising the NHS. I was on *Any Questions?* during the campaign and was most 'impressed' by Labour Housing Spokesman John Healey managing to do both things within thirty seconds of his first answer. Healey is one of the nicest and most urbane MPs in the Commons, yet he knew he had a job to do. I congratulated him afterwards and he winked at me.

Prime Minister's Question Time has always been a bearpit, but over the years the insults and the language used have got progressively worse. It's the one bit of the parliamentary week people take notice of. I've never bought the line that the general public don't like the argy-bargy of PMQs. After all, it's largely why they tune in. The adversarial set-up of the House of Commons, where MPs stand two sword-lengths apart, certainly leads to a more robust atmosphere, but let's not pretend it hasn't forever been thus. Look back to the parliamentary debates of the 1700s and 1800s and far worse things were said across the aisle.

Generally, as individuals, we rely on self-regulation to inform us as to whether the use of certain language is appropriate, but in both Parliament and the broadcast media things are different.

In Parliament, the following words are considered 'unparliamentary'. Utter them and the Speaker is likely to jump on you like a ton of bricks: bastard, blackguard, coward, dodgy, drunk, git, guttersnipe, hooligan, hypocrite, idiot, ignoramus, liar, rat, sod, squirt, stoolpigeon, tart, traitor, wart.

Similarly, you can't accuse a fellow MP of being 'bought'.

In my world, radio, I know there are words that I simply cannot use on my show; if I did, we would get fined. Ofcom, the broadcasting regulator, has various lists of words that are banned. It takes only one complaint for them to launch an investigation. In 2016 Ofcom commissioned a study into public attitudes to language and words on radio and TV. They found:

Viewers and listeners have become less tolerant of racist or discriminatory words.

The 9pm watershed remains vital for protecting audiences from offensive material.

People say they are more likely to tolerate swearing if it reflects the 'real world'.

Somewhat bizarrely, the study found that swearing was considered more problematic on radio than TV. People regard radio as a more intimate medium and one that children might be listening to without the ability of a parent to regulate it. It's actually quite rare for people to swear on live radio. It's even rarer for a politician to do so. If they do, it can have very serious consequences for the radio station concerned. On most commercial stations there is a dump button that can be pressed by either the presenter or the producer if they hear something they think is unacceptable. Producers tend to be very zealous in pressing the button for the lightest of swear-words, whereas presenters are much more lenient.

* * *

'I've never been so offended in all my life.' How many times have we heard that increasingly irritating phrase in recent times? Being offended has become almost a national sport in this country. The slightest off-colour remark can provoke howls of outrage from people who ought to know better. There's no law to protect people from being offended, and nor should there be if we value free speech.

I doubt there's a gay man or woman in existence who hasn't been offended by a homophobic remark that they have been the target of, or they've heard. But most of us get over it. We shake our heads in sadness that there are still bigots out there. We may sometimes try to educate people out of their ways, but in the end we put it down to experience and move on. It is the same for a member of an ethnic minority, or a disabled person.

There are some people who revel in shocking others. Some years ago, journalist Suzanne Moore angered many transsexuals by writing this:

> We are angry with ourselves for not being happier, not being loved properly and not having the ideal body shape – that of a Brazilian transsexual. We are angry that men do not do enough. We are angry at work where we are underpaid and overlooked. This anger can be neatly channelled and outsourced to make someone a fat profit. Are your hormones okay? Do you need a nice bath? Some sex tips and an internet date? What if, contrary to *Sex and the City*, new shoes do not fill the hole in your soul? What if you aspire to another model of womanhood than the mute but beautifully groomed Kate Middleton? What if your anguish is not illogical but actually bloody spot on?

Did you spot her offence there? If it hadn't been pointed out to me, I'm not sure I would have done. For clarity, it was the bit about the Brazilian transsexual. I am not wholly familiar with what Brazilian transsexuals look like – I must watch more porn – but I am assuming she means they have a perfect hourglass body figure. Her words, though, sent the transgender community into orbit. They were offended. Some of them were so offended that they deluged Suzanne Moore with threatening tweets. So threatening were these tweets that they drove her off Twitter.

You probably haven't ever met Suzanne Moore, but she is a woman not easily intimidated. This vicious hate mob, however, achieved their goal and silenced her purely because they were offended over what most reasonable people would have regarded as a fairly innocuous comment. How they imagine it was an incitement to hate transsexuals, I cannot imagine.

Why is it so difficult to understand the fact that Moore is a polemical columnist? Offending this and that group is what she is often there to do. We all get offended by different things. Some offences are worse than others, but no one has yet been able to abolish the right to be offended in this country. *Yet.* Even Owen Jones has come under attack on Twitter for some sort of injudicious remark, and he was actually defending the transsexual community! What he tried to point out, as I understand it, was that there is a group of hard-Left transsexual activists who act like trolls and give the rest of the community a bad name.

Transsexuals had an absolute right to defend themselves and argue against Suzanne Moore. What they had no right to do is bully her off Twitter. Protecting our freedom of speech is one of the most important things we should all do. It must be cherished, even when a columnist writes something that is bound to cause massive offence to some people.

I get offended by things people write about me most days of the week. I sometimes hit back, but often I ignore it. I don't expect others to intervene and try to get the culprits banned or to drive them from Twitter or anywhere else.

I can't imagine what transsexual people go through. I don't know any transsexual people to even be able to ask them. But I know enough to understand that it's not just the sticks and stones that must be very painful. People fear what they do not know. Transsexual people put up with far worse, I suspect, than gay people ever have, and therefore we must have empathy and understanding. If people write what might be considered ignorant and offensive columns, they should be argued with, not viciously attacked and driven off the internet. The perpetrators of these attacks are no better, and I would argue are worse, than the very people they find so offensive and accuse of using forms of hate speech.

In the end we have to make a differentiation between freedom of speech and hate speech. On my LBC radio show I often get a torrent of texts and tweets from people who don't approve of my lifestyle. I'd love to think there will come a day when this sort of thing doesn't happen, but I doubt whether I will live to see it. Perhaps I have become immune to it, but none of it offends or upsets me. It just makes me a bit sad. All I can do in my job is do it to the best of my ability. I always say to people who describe me as a 'gay radio presenter' that I'm not. I am a radio presenter who happens to be gay. I don't resile from my sexuality. It is a part of who I am, but it doesn't define me or what I do.

Only once have I thought a caller to my show went beyond the norm of what was within the bounds of free speech. She was a Muslim who actively supported ISIS killing gay people by throwing them off buildings. What on earth do you say to someone like that? She was 22. I told her that her parents should be ashamed of themselves for bringing her up with that set of beliefs. Several of my callers told me I should have reported her to the police. I suppose what she said was allowable within the bounds of free speech, but clearly many of my listeners were offended. It's very rare that anyone makes homophobic remarks on air, but on Twitter and in texts it's quite common.

I could spend most of my life being offended if I wanted to, but in the end, life is too short. The very uttering of the phrase 'I find that offensive' effectively means that you want to silence the person who has supposedly offended you. Jews, Muslims, gays and feminists may not have much in common but they are often on the same page in demanding retribution in the form of bans, penalties and censorship of those who supposedly hurt their feelings.

I say, grow up. People have died so that we can retain some semblance of freedom of speech. Each time politicians pass laws that impinge on freedom of speech a small part of democracy dies.

A few years ago I published a short polemical book by Claire Fox, one of the stars of *The Moral Maze*, called *I Find That Offensive*. Anyone who thinks laws banning offensive remarks are a good idea should read it. Fox takes on those who seem to regard taking offence as a professional pastime. She concludes that we should make a virtue out of the right to offend.

We've even got to the point where some students have become obsessed by the idea of 'safe spaces', where no one can say anything that another might take exception to. In some universities LGBT students are even demanding LGBT-only accommodation. What a great way to build more barriers and for gay people to become more isolated. Let's go the whole hog and have student accommodation blocks only for Muslims. Or only for Asians. Where will this lead us? To social apartheid. That's where.

Most people do not set out to be deliberately offensive in what they say or do. Most people want to be liked. It's a natural part of being a human being. Boris Johnson knows he has caused offence with things he has written down the years, but he appears at a loss to understand why some people don't like him. When I chaired ten of the Conservative leadership hustings, he received some very tough questioning from Tory members. In Nottingham, I remember a young British Asian man ask him: 'Mr Johnson, do you not understand the offence you cause to ethnic minorities when you say Muslim women look like letter-boxes? Mr Johnson, you're a racist, aren't you?' Boris Johnson immediately looked at me as if he wanted me to step in, and it was obvious he was astonished and hurt by the accusation. In this respect, he's very unlike Donald Trump, who revels in causing division. Trump can hardly get through a paragraph without causing controversy. He's the ultimate Marmite politician. He inspires hatred in his opponents but devotion from his fans. He is the antithesis of the title of this book in so many ways, and yet he has spent his presidency trying to make friends with President Xi Jinping, Vladimir Putin and Kim Jong-un. At home, however, he wouldn't know the meaning of the word 'bi-partisan' if it slapped him in the face. He revels in insulting his opponents and assumes they have the very worst motives. He whips up his supporters into frenzies in his rallies, and incites them to take out their frustrations and hatred on the Democrats or what he insists on calling the 'liberal media'. Reporters are booed and hissed at and have come to fear for their personal safety, when all they are doing is their job. Trump has created the most ugly atmosphere in US politics since the civil rights riots of the 1960s. And he seems proud of it.

And it's resulted in TV talk show host Ellen DeGeneres having to explain to her viewers and her more tribal fellow lesbians that former Republican President George W. Bush is a friend of hers and she's not going to apologise to anyone for being pictured with him at an American football game in Dallas.

She got a lot of abuse on Twitter, but she highlighted one tweet on her TV show: 'Ellen and George Bush together makes me have faith in America again.' She told her viewers:

> Here's the thing. I'm friends with George Bush. In fact I'm friends with a lot of people who don't share the same beliefs I have. We're all different and I think we've forgotten that's OK … Just because I don't agree with someone on everything doesn't mean I'm not going to be friends with them. When I say 'be kind to one another' I don't mean people who think the same way as you do, I mean be kind to everyone.

I should have asked her to write a foreword for this book.

Chapter 7

The Political Virus

'He knows nothing; and he thinks he
knows everything. That points clearly to
a political career.'

George Bernard Shaw

I contracted the political virus at a very young age, and it's a virus I've never been able to rid myself of. I knew from my late teens that I wanted to be an MP, and even though I often think I have finally got it out of my system, from time to time the virus re-emerges and I ponder whether I should dip my toes into the political waters again. At the age of 58 I know for a fact that I'd be a damn sight better politician than I would have been when I actually stood for Parliament at the age of 42 in 2005.

Politics attracts all sorts of characters. It's far less homogeneous than people think. Forget the backgrounds of MPs, just look at the different types of politicians there are in the modern polity. You can loosely divide them into thinkers and persuaders. The former come up with the policies, the latter sell them. How do they do that? By using language and force of argument to explain the policies to voters. John Redwood, Jon Cruddas and Gordon Brown are all thinkers – people who can think the unthinkable and translate it into new, innovative policy. However, they were not at the front of the class when powers of persuasion were handed out.

Conversely, Tony Blair, Cecil Parkinson, Ruth Davidson and Nick Clegg all proved to be very effective political salespeople. They could latch on to an idea that someone else had come up with and go out and sell it to the electorate using the power of words. Margaret Thatcher appointed Cecil Parkinson to her war cabinet during the Falklands War because she knew he could go out on the airwaves and explain the government position. He wasn't there for his knowledge of military strategy.

It is rare to find politicians who are both original thinkers and political salespeople. Think of all the post-war British prime ministers and I'd venture to suggest that only Winston Churchill qualifies for both categories. In the United States, of all the post-war presidents is it really possible to describe any of them as 'thinkers'?

Most politicians search for other people's ideas, steal them as their own and then articulate why they will make the country a better place. Margaret Thatcher is often thought of as a political ideologue, but she wasn't known as a political 'magpie' for nothing. She latched on to a series of right-wing think-tanks – the Institute for Economic Affairs and the Adam Smith Institute being the two most notorious – and encouraged them to become her brain. Together with Sir Keith Joseph, in 1974 she founded her own think-tank, the Centre for Policy Studies, which rapidly became the provider of more Thatcherite policy ideas than any of its competitors.

Party politics is changing. Ordinarily you expect voters to align with one of the main parties or the other. Given the astonishing events of the last few years surrounding Brexit, party affiliations are now weaker than they have been for many years. Instead of identifying as Conservative or Labour, voters now have a stronger affiliation with 'Leave' or 'Remain'.

Politicians are following the lead of the electorate in this regard and have become far more rebellious over the last decade. Gone are the days when a 'three-line whip' meant 'obey or else'. MPs in the two main parties now regard such an order as optional. Twenty years ago, the electorate viewed MPs as lobby fodder – politicians who troop through the voting lobbies and vote according to their party instructions. Nowadays, the truth is somewhat different. This is truly the age of the maverick. Even government ministers have abstained on a three-line whip in key Brexit votes, and suffered no sanction whatsoever. Ordinarily, they would have been summarily sacked for such a breach of precedent.

Politics has changed a lot over the last decade. It has become more brutal, less kind and increasingly confrontational. Everything is black or white. There are few shades of grey. Nuance is dead. A politician is rarely accused of just being wrong. They're liars.

It wasn't always like this.

My earliest political memory stems from the early 1970s. Prime Minister Edward Heath had called a snap election in February 1974, following a huge amount of industrial strife that had led to a three-day working week and regular power cuts. I can remember spending hours playing cards with my family by candlelight.

One morning I remember walking into my parents' bedroom and telling them why they should vote Labour. Bear in mind I was only 11 years old. I told them that the only thing the Tories had done was take us into the Common Market, which had led to my father having to sell all his livestock. My mother rolled over and told me to go back to bed.

They both ended up voting Liberal, unlike my grand-mother (who lived with us), who was a staunch Conservative. She did more than anyone to spark my inter-est in politics in my early teens. She was a rather regal figure and was known to some as the Queen Mother. She was born in 1894 and was a bit of a feminist. Had she been a teenager today she would have undoubtedly gone to university and had a glittering career. In her younger days she worked for the Post Office and then, in 1922, she went to work at Wembley Stadium for a short time. She subse-quently married my grandfather, a much older man, who hailed from Ayrshire in Scotland and came down to East Anglia in the early 1920s. She lived with us throughout my childhood and was a massive influence on me, largely inspiring my interest in politics. I think of her today and remember her telling me that Michael Foot (a Labour cabi-net minister at the time, who led the party between 1980 and 1983) was a communist and that I shouldn't trust Labour as they always spend more money than the country can afford.

On 11 February 1975, as a 12-year-old boy, I remember rushing upstairs to tell my grandmother, who was ill in bed, that Margaret Thatcher had been elected leader of the

Conservative Party. She started weeping. She was 80 and knew what it meant for a woman to have achieved this high office.

A few years later, having completed my 'O' Levels, I joined a group of my schoolfriends who were doing a project on local politics. We went to interview the Liberal mayor of Saffron Walden. She talked my kind of language, and even though I was only 15 years old I signed up to join the Liberal Party. It didn't last long, as only a few months later, I succumbed to the rhetorical charms of Margaret Thatcher. All I can remember is listening to a speech she made, presumably at the 1978 Tory Party Conference, and thinking to myself: 'Well, I agree with every word of that.'

In that speech, she articulated what I and much of the rest of the country were thinking. A year earlier I had been on a school exchange trip to Germany, and was almost embarrassed to admit I was British. All they could talk about was our strike record and how we were regarded as the sick man of Europe. Margaret Thatcher fastened on to that and articulated what she felt was a better way. That's what all successful politicians do. Tony Blair did it in 1997 and David Cameron did it, to an extent, a decade later.

Most people who end up in full-time politics start out on their road to Parliament by being inspired by someone already involved in politics. It could be a serving MP, a political activist or a local politician, or in more recent years it could be a cause rather than a personality. The running theme is that whoever has provided the inspiration has almost certainly done it through the power of their oratory, writing or leadership abilities. Crucially, these are all positives. Rarely can anyone be rallied to a cause through over-negativity. In the few weeks following Boris Johnson's ascension to the office of prime minister he exuded a sense of optimism and positivity that hadn't been seen in British politics for years. The public warmed to it, even if they doubted there was much substance behind it. It may not have lasted long, but it was tangible.

Let's do another test. Think back again to all the post-war political leaders in both the UK and the US and invariably you find that those who promulgate a message of hope and optimism defeat those who come across as negative and downbeat. Thatcher v Kinnock, Blair v Major, Reagan v Carter, Clinton v Bush, Kennedy v Nixon, Johnson v Corbyn. I could go on.

Ronald Reagan, in particular, was a great example of how upbeat positivity can go a long way in politics. A man with a permanently sunny disposition was often underestimated by his opponents, just as was the case with George W. Bush and Boris Johnson. Reagan was in tune with his country, as symbolised by his 'Morning in America' campaign commercials and the soaring heights of speech-making provided by the incomparable Peggy Noonan. Just like Margaret Thatcher, he was the right leader, in the right place, at the right time.

I lost my political virginity in April 1982 when I was a first-year student at the very left-wing University of East Anglia. I was asleep in my room one morning when there was a knock at the door. 'Oh, you're still alive then,' an anonymous voice said. Still half asleep, I didn't really think anything of it and dozed off again. A few minutes later, the same thing happened. 'Glad to see you're still with us,' said my next-door neighbour. Strange, I thought. Later on, in the communal kitchen someone asked if I had seen the papers yet. I said I hadn't. 'You ought to,' came the reply.

I remember as if it were yesterday: turning to page two of the *Daily Mail* and seeing my name. Killed in action in the Falklands. But it wasn't me, obviously. It was Welsh Guardsman Ian Dale, aged 19 from Pontypridd. It was like being hit in the solar plexus. Tears streamed down my face, as they were to do many times over the next few weeks. Nothing else could have brought home to me the terrible waste of war like this did. I was the same age. It could have been me.

Not long afterwards, I attended a debate at the university between the President of the Students Union and leading light in the University Labour Club, Mark Seddon (who now works at the UN), and someone whose name I now forget but who was also on the hard Left. I was horrified that such a debate could take place between the soft Left and hard Left with no other viewpoint being put forward. So up I stood and defended the sending of the task force and our right to retake British sovereign territory from a fascist regime. That was my first real experience of the cut and thrust of political debate. And I enjoyed it. It was the catalyst for getting involved in politics.

At that time there was no Conservative organisation at UEA, so at the beginning of my second year my friend Dave Larg and I decided to rectify that. We put up a stand at the Freshers' Fair and by the end of the day had attracted several hundred members. It turned out that the Conservative Society was bigger than its Labour equivalent. The Labour leaders were delighted. They were fed up with fighting the Trots. Now they had a different kind of enemy to turn their fire on.

For many of us political virgins it was a baptism of fire. We decided to take part in student union debates, which were intimidating to say the least. One minute I'd be defending the Thatcher government over education cuts, the next taking the Left to task for supporting the IRA. There were, however, a few moments of agreement, where I'd listen to an argument and agree with it. Caroline Flint, later to become a Labour MP but then head of the Women's Society, put down a motion calling for the government to abolish VAT on women's sanitary products. I remember standing up to respond to the motion and telling the assembled throng that, having listened to the arguments, I was fully supportive and would happily add my name to the motion's supporters. The audience erupted with applause and cheering.

The experience taught me that tribal affiliations should not trump common sense, and that there is nothing wrong with agreeing with your opponents when they have said something that is clearly sensible and logical. To me this is a strength, but to other members of the tribe it can seem like a weakness. You can argue it both ways. I have a tendency to see the strength of my opponents' argument and I believe it helps me to better marshal my case against them. If I don't even attempt to see their point of view, how can I possibly deploy the best argument? However, if it really is all about tribes in modern-day discourse, we should be very concerned that what we have come to regard as normal democratic debate and disagreement will gradually disappear and be replaced by one big, permanent online shouting match.

I'm not sure I am typical in my growing non-tribality, though. Some would say this is a primary reason for my having never made it in politics, because I lack the single-mindedness and party loyalty to climb what Disraeli called 'the greasy pole'. Maybe.

In July 2002 I turned 40. I knew that if I wanted to pursue a political career, time was running out. So I made the decision to apply to go on the Conservative Party's list of officially approved candidates. I didn't apply for any seats until the spring of 2003. The first seat I applied for was Chipping Barnet. I shall never forget the moment when, having made my second-round speech, and thinking it had gone quite well, the chairman said: 'And now Mr Dale would you speak for four minutes on the conflicts between Labour's macroeconomic strategy and their micro fiscal policy.' I think I managed three and a half minutes.

You are asked some very odd questions. In Beverley I was asked, 'If you were reincarnated, who or what would you come back as?' Quick as a flash I answered, 'My Jack Russell, Gio.' I got through to the next round.

By the time North Norfolk came around, I was well practised in selection interview techniques. This was the seat I wanted. I was that stupid. North Norfolk had been a Conservative seat since the 1960s, but in 2001 the Lib Dem Norman Lamb upset the Tory applecart and wrested it from the Conservative grasp, with a slimline majority of 483 – a number that would be seared on my mind. I knew the area well. My mother spent much of her teenage years there and I knew what a conservative, with a small C, area it was. It was number two on the list of Tory target seats. If we didn't win there, the game was up. I bumped into the Lib Dem national campaigns manager, Chris Rennard, who I had got to know well. He took me aside and warned me not to go for it. 'Norman will get a majority of 10,000,' he said. Oh, how I laughed. I genuinely thought I knew better. I was taught a painful lesson.

In the first round of the selection for North Norfolk I was up against 19 other candidates, including some well-known names. Apparently, I stormed it and got more votes than any of the others. In the second round I encountered a problem. I had agreed to speak at a fringe meeting at the party conference on gay equality. The meeting was advertised in the conference handbook that some members of the North Norfolk Conservative Association had received, and one or two were clearly perturbed by. The chairman was in a blind panic, but I told him to get someone to ask a question about it in the next round. A lady duly did and asked if this was an issue I felt strongly about. I had prepared a statement, which I read out to them. It was a bit of a tear-jerker. Bill Clinton would have been proud of me. It did the trick. Many of the audience were in tears. At the end, my voice was breaking too.

In the final I beat two strong candidates, one of whom was Harriet Baldwin, who went on to be a Treasury minister. I got 66 per cent of the votes on the first ballot. It was one of the proudest moments of my life.

I was the first candidate to have ever been selected by the Conservative Party having told the selection committee about my sexuality. Theresa May, the then party chairman, was making good progress in encouraging the selection of female and minority candidates. I was one of those minority candidates. When I was selected for North Norfolk, Theresa May rang me up only five minutes after I had left the selection meeting. She knew of the issues I had encountered during the selection over my sexuality and she could not have been more thrilled for me. I really appreciated the call, as it was one she did not have to make.

I invited a stream of political luminaries to come and support my campaign – David Davis, Ann Widdecombe, Theresa May, Boris Johnson, Iain Duncan Smith, the then unknown David Cameron,

We may nowadays think we live in an era when public distrust of politicians is at an all-time low, but things were scarcely better in 2003, in the aftermath of Tony Blair's decision to take the country to war in Iraq.

I gave a great deal of thought to how I could personally address this cynicism about politicians and show people that in me they would elect someone who was different. I wanted to prove I had a high personal moral compass, was a person of obvious integrity and complete openness. I therefore drew up what I rather pompously called a 'Pledge of Integrity', which I made to the people of North Norfolk, in which I promised not to have any outside business interests, to publish all my expense claims, not to employ family members and much more besides.

I was the first candidate to do anything like this. And a fat lot of good it did me. Some Conservative MPs were none too pleased, as they thought they'd have to follow suit. And what a terrible thing that would have been! Party headquarters didn't seem too impressed either, yet at the 2010 election, I noticed with a wry smile that many Tory candidates did something similar. I knew I was setting myself up to be judged, but it was an issue I felt very strongly about.

In my years as a political activist I must have spent thousands of hours knocking on doors asking people how they intend to vote, or if they have any burning issues they'd like to get off their chests. The responses varied, but fell into these categories:

> Not interested.
> You're all the same.
> You're only in it for yourselves.
> Why can't you all just get along?
> I don't vote (usually said with a sense of pride).
> I leave that sort of thing to my husband.
> We always vote the same way.
> I'll never vote for [insert name] while they lead your party.

Don't kid yourselves, during an election, political canvassers aren't interested in persuading you. They have one job on your doorstep, and that's to find out how each person in your house intends to vote. They go back to their headquarters and feed the result into their computers. You'll only hear from them again during the campaign if you've said you're undecided – especially if you have been careless enough to tell them which issue you most care about.

I love knocking on complete strangers' doors. I enjoy it because you never know who's going to answer or what they're going to say. It gives you a great insight into the Great British Public, but it can also thoroughly depress you and make you mull over whether people should have an IQ test before they're allowed to vote. Take this exchange I witnessed in the Norwich North by-election in 2009:

TORY MP: Have you decided who you will be voting for?
MALE VOTER: I normally vote UKIP, but I was thinking of voting Conservative.

TORY MP: That's what I like to hear.

MALE VOTER: Yes, but I am worried about Mr Cameron cosying up to homosexuals. I might as well admit it, you see I am a bit homopathic …

The MP just about managed to retain a straight (if that's the appropriate word) face. On the same day, I encountered a woman in Thorpe St Andrew. Here's how the conversation went:

ME: Hello, I'm calling on behalf of Chloe Smith, your Conservative candidate in the by-election.

WOMAN: Oh yes …

ME: I just wondered who you might be supporting in the election.

WOMAN: Oh my husband makes those decisions for me.

ME: Er, right. So you are not exactly a modern woman then!

WOMAN: No, I like to be a bit old-fashioned. He tells me who to vote for.

The great thing about going canvassing in a team is that, at the end of each session, someone will have a story like that.

I once had a hilarious end to a canvassing session in the North Norfolk town of North Walsham when I called on a lady who had a large Lib Dem poster in her garden despite being a Conservative member. Apparently the Lib Dems just put it up without asking and she said she didn't like to cause any trouble. She also asked us while we were there if we would mind changing the battery in her clock. I said I'd be delighted to. She then told me to fetch the 'durex' battery from the sideboard!

If I am honest, polling day in 2005 was a disaster. We had set up 15 or so committee rooms across the constituency and had teams of people 'knocking up' voters who hadn't yet made it to polling stations. Time and again I kept being asked the same question: 'Are you sure these knocking-up slips are right? We seem to be knocking up Lib Dem voters.' Surely the agent hadn't printed off the wrong codes? I kept asking myself.

I had known for some time that winning was highly unlikely. I remember a day in February 2005 canvassing in the coastal village of Overstrand. Every single house we went to seemed to deliver the same message: 'Well, we're really Conservatives but we're going to vote for that nice Mr Lamb.' I remember going back to my house in Swanton Abbott that night and saying to my partner, John, 'That's it, I know now I can't win.' If people like that weren't going to vote for me, the game was up. But I knew that I couldn't tell that to my supporters, who had sweated blood in helping my campaign. The problem was that Norman Lamb's views and mine were almost indistinguishable on local issues. He was even vaguely Eurosceptic (for a Lib Dem). He had fought three elections and made it his business to be a good constituency MP.

My strategy had been to play him at his own game, and demonstrate that I too would be a good constituency representative – but one who could get things done by dint of being an MP for one of the two major parties. By the time the election campaign started I had undertaken a huge amount of constituency casework, and had got a very good reputation for taking up local campaigns and getting things done. I probably enjoyed better local publicity in local press and radio than any other candidate in the country. We produced good literature and built up an excellent delivery network, but the fact remained: Norman was the MP and I was a mere candidate.

Two other things worked against me. The fact that I was quite often on TV, I originally thought would be a good thing – name recognition and so forth. But all it did was give people the impression I was in London all the time and not local. I could witter on about how I lived in the constituency – and I did – while Norman Lamb lived 20 miles away in Norwich, but a fat lot of good it did me.

So I expected to lose. On top of this, it didn't help that nationally the party wasn't making any sort of breakthrough. Although Michael Howard had done his best, people were still in thrall to Tony Blair. Howard hadn't been able to attract back those soft Conservative voters who had turned North Norfolk Lib Dem back in 2001. Nor, it seemed, had I; Lamb won the seat with a majority of 10,606.

I didn't lose because North Norfolk rejected a gay candidate. I lost because the Lib Dems ran a relentless campaign to persuade Labour supporters to vote tactically. I lost because the national campaign, though highly professional and slick, did not ignite the fires of optimism among an electorate sick of personal insults and negativity. And I lost because the Lib Dem MP had a huge personal vote, far beyond anything I've encountered anywhere else. At the 2010 election, Norman Lamb's majority increased to more than 11,000 – which at least proved it wasn't all my doing five years earlier!

I had hundreds of emails, letters, texts and comments on my blog expressing sympathy. It demonstrated that human beings are fundamentally kind and generous. Even my political opponents got in touch to say I had been a very hard-working and worthy opponent. It meant a lot – more perhaps than they realised. As I'll come on to explain later in the book, I regarded them as fundamentally good people, and it was nice to know they clearly felt the same about me. Given today's toxic atmosphere in politics, I suspect this is a much rarer experience for candidates nowadays.

By the time of the 2015 election I was 52, and I am old enough and wise enough to know that politics in this country has become a young person's game. Few constituencies select people in their fifties, so I didn't see the point in spending five years in the vain hope that I might possibly get selected. It was time to get out. So I did. I was also slightly falling out of love with politics, and having put my partner and family through a lot over the previous seven or eight years, it didn't seem fair to repeat the process. My mother cheered when I told her I wouldn't be doing it again. What an indictment of our politics.

I thought I would come to regret the decision, but ten years on I haven't. Not for a moment. And I mean that. Politics is indeed a drug, and you can never wean yourself off it completely, but my radio career gives me what politics used to give me, and a lot more besides. I'm often asked if I will stand again and I always reply in the same way. Never. I would have loved to have been an MP, for I believe in many ways I would have been good at it and been an excellent constituency MP. But I now know (and probably always did) that the parliamentary side of it might well have become incredibly frustrating for me. I suspect I would have been a whips' nightmare and would have stood no chance of being a minister … not that being a minister ever really mattered.

In truth, most voters don't think about politics very much. They're not like me, or possibly even you. I consume it every day of every year. I have views on most things. I read the newspapers. I listen to political programmes on the radio and watch political programmes on TV. I debate politics with my friends and colleagues. I live and breathe it.

You can divide the electorate into two: those who believe that all politicians are in it for themselves and are lying, thieving scumbags; and those who – in line with the title of this book – believe everything would be fine if only politicians could get along with each other and work together.

This is nothing new. People have always had a deep distrust of the motivations of politicians as a species. They did in 1768, 1832, 1923, and they still do today. Some would argue that in a democracy this distrust is actually rather healthy. Ask people, though, what they think of their local Member of Parliament and they may well give a more positive answer and cite things he or she has done for them or their neighbour. So it's not all bleak.

The demands made on politicians and the skills needed to be one have changed considerably. In decades gone by, a politician might visit the constituency no more than once a year. Nowadays, MPs are expected to be quasi-social workers. I remember an MP I worked for getting a letter asking if he would go round and fix a constituent's washing line. Given it was a highly marginal constituency, he was sorely tempted. Today, the ability to deliver a coherent speech is less important than that of doing a media interview or using social media to political advantage. Potential candidates are assessed on their 'doorstep' manner. Are they able to empathise with voters? This is what political leadership has become. It's less about what you believe, more about how you can communicate a party line.

Politicians have far more contact with their constituents than ever before. The idea that they are 'out of touch' is somewhat far-fetched. They hold weekly or fortnightly surgeries in which they meet all forms of human life. Some of their constituents just want to get something off their chest. Others have seemingly intractable problems. All MPs will have stories of people who, without their help, would have struggled to achieve what they wanted to. There's nothing like a House of Commons letterhead to smooth a way through bureaucracy.

Ann Widdecombe says her greatest achievement in her 23 years as an MP was to get a constituent out of jail in Morocco, by which I mean she got him freed. She didn't spring him. Given that politicians are not allowed to inter-fere in judicial decisions in this country, to do so in a foreign one was quite something to behold. The constituent was a lorry driver who had been convicted of a drugs offence. It soon became clear that no one, not even the Moroccan authorities, thought he was guilty. His wife was at her wits' ends. Widdecombe decided to go to Rabat (at her own cost – in those days the cost of the trip was not claimable on expenses) and plead for mercy. On the day she arrived, the entire Moroccan government fell. But she persisted, and a few weeks later she was able to phone the lorry driver's wife and say: 'Derek's out. He'll be home tomorrow.' The woman's reaction told Widdecombe why it was she had entered politics in the first place. Every MP will have such a tale. They were able to make a difference to someone's life in a way that would never make newspaper headlines. But it meant the world to those who were affected. Macro politics means that politicians can bestride the national stage and pontificate on the big issues of the day, but micro politics is more important for the individuals affected.

Chapter 8

Why Language Matters

'I have written 11 books but each time I think, "Uh oh, they're going to find out now. I've run a game on everybody, and they're going to find me out."'

Maya Angelou

Language played a very important part in my upbringing. Like any good parent, my mother would read stories to me from a very early age. I could read before I started school at the age of five. I devoured Enid Blyton books. *The Magic Faraway Tree* was my favourite. It was the Harry Potter of its day. I picked it up recently and read a couple of chapters. It was like transporting myself back to 1968. The same imagined scenes came back into my mind. To be frank, it made me quite emotional.

Although quite shy, I was quite a chatty child in class. I always had a cheeky one-liner ready. Even at primary school we'd debate things.

Language is one of the most fundamental aspects of human evolvement, and so it has been with me. I didn't have a private education and I don't use language in the flowery way that some of my contemporaries do. I'm fluent, and can hold my own in most debates, but I lack the linguistic flair of a Boris Johnson or Michael Gove. I don't write as well as most of my journalistic contemporaries. At least, I think I don't. Even to this day I have a tremendous sense of imposter syndrome when it comes to my writing.

Very few people go through their careers fully confident in their own abilities. I suppose I have always felt I have something to prove, not just to myself but to others too. I still feel that way, even though I have rid myself of the massive inferiority complex I used to have when I was around people who had been to public school or Oxbridge. They always seem to have an inner confidence that the rest of us struggle to find. It's really only in the last five years that I've not felt inferior around them, and that's been quite liberating.

People have different styles of speaking, different styles of writing and different ways of expressing themselves. We all engage in public discourse in a different way. In today's society and media environment you have to be forthright, concise and the opposite of a shrinking violet. I'm a naturally shy person, which few will believe, and I have to force myself to go into a room of people I don't know. I'm used to making a speech in front of a crowd, because I learned how to do it at school, but I still dread doing so. Yet once I've opened my mouth and the words start flowing I usually enjoy it. I've learned the art of working a crowd. However, you do have to know your audience. Misjudge them and it could go very wrong. For this reason I tend not to do a lot of speeches in schools. I get a lot of invitations, but turn most of them down.

Why? Because I am never sure I strike the right tone. As a 58-year-old, is it ever really possible to relate to a group of 11- to 18-year-olds? I like to bounce off an audience, but find it incredibly difficult to do so with this age-group.

In 2019, however, I spoke to Oaks Park High School in Ilford. They had assembled a group of around 150 pupils in the main hall, ranging in age from 11 to 18. My remit was to talk about my career in politics and the media. As usual, I started nervously, trying to pitch it right. It was billed as a lecture, but I did it all off the cuff. Slowly but surely, the kids came alive, and by the end I could tell they were actually quite interested in what I was saying – unless I got the wrong end of the stick!

Then I asked for questions. This is usually the embarrassing point, where no one puts their hand up. This time was different. At least half a dozen hands shot up immediately. First question: 'How much do you earn?' I roared with laughter. I then explained that I had been on *Good Morning Britain*, having got up at 5.20 a.m., and asked them how much they thought I got as a fee from that. The answers ranged from £500 to £1,000. When they heard the truth there was an audible gasp from some of them. They clearly expected political punditry to be much more rewarding!

Anyway, I answered questions for a good half an hour and enjoyed it hugely. They asked some really good questions too. The whole experience was truly uplifting.

The headteacher wrote to me afterwards and said the kids had felt 'inspired' and that she thought it would be a 'pivotal moment' in some of their lives, 'perhaps the defining moment in determining the career path they follow'. Assuming she wasn't just being polite, that letter has given me the confidence to speak to this kind of audience more often.

I may have 'imposter syndrome' about my writing ability, but it disappears when I have a microphone in front of my mouth, especially when talking about deeply personal subjects.

Finding the right words is something we all struggle with, and that's nowhere more evident than when people ring in to a radio show. If you think about it, it's a weird thing to do. I'm always astonished that anyone does so, to be frank. Most people like keeping themselves to themselves, so when anyone rings in to my show I take it as a huge compliment. It's why I usually try to make a fuss of a 'first-time caller'. The fact that they've bothered to pick up the phone means that something I've said has triggered them to do so, and this is especially the case when I talk about emotional subjects like abortion, rape, addiction or mental health.

On one of my first shows on LBC back in 2010, I covered a story about the Advertising Standards Authority ruling in favour of Channel 4's decision to screen adverts for the Marie Stopes pregnancy/abortion advisory clinics. First of all, I talked to Tory MP Nadine Dorries, who took the view that these adverts should not appear on TV, and then to Simon Blake from the Brook advisory service. He supported their right to be shown. And then it was on to the calls. What I hadn't bargained on was the three women who phoned in, each with a different but equally heart-breaking story about how they had come to decide to have an abortion, and how it had affected their lives. Talking to any woman in private about their traumas would be awkward enough, but doing it on national radio was a real learning experience. I tried to let them talk with little interruption, partly because any significant intervention from me would have been invidious, but also because they clearly wanted to tell LBC listeners how their own experience had impacted on their lives. One of the callers bitterly regretted her decision to have an abortion and described how she thinks about it every day, 20 years later. Carol from Harrow was the last caller and her story almost reduced me to tears. Indeed, she was clearly finding it difficult to hold it together herself. I hated having to cut her off as we had to go to the 8 o'clock news. We phoned her back to check she was OK and she asked my producer to tell me that she had no regrets about the abortion she had. It was the right thing to do at the time, but she now has two very healthy children and she wanted me to know she was very happy. Another lump-in-throat moment.

I remember after that show discussing what had happened with the then Managing Editor of LBC, Jonathan Richards. I expressed my astonishment that people would talk about such personal issues on live radio, and wondered if I had handled the issue properly. He told me people would always want to talk to me, because I let them speak, I didn't constantly interrupt and I had a quiet, reassuring manner. I've never forgotten that. I know now that I enjoy this sort of 'baring your soul' phone-in far more than my usual political fare. In the end it's all about listening and empathising with the caller and using the appropriate language, and not being afraid to admit when you don't know what to say.

'Let's got to Anne in Enfield. Anne, what would you like to tell me?' It turned out to be quite a call. We were conducting a phone-in on rape and its long-term psychological effects. Anne proceeded to tell me something she had never told a living soul, even her husband. Many years earlier, she had been raped at a family wedding, by a family member. As she was speaking, I could tell how difficult she was finding it to continue. I stepped in to reassure her that by telling her story she was helping others who had suffered the same experience and felt that they were the only ones. She explained that, although it had happened many years ago, she still thinks of it every day. 'This giant cloud hangs over me,' I remember her saying. I found it fascinating that she was calling in to talk to me about it, yet hadn't told anyone else. Ever. The call ended and I wished her well.

The next night she phoned in again. She asked to be put through to me, but my producer Laura explained we were talking about a different subject. In a break, Laura told me Anne had wanted to speak to me again. 'Put her on just before the end of the hour,' I said. Somehow I sensed it was important to her. When she came on the line, her first words were, 'Iain, I've told my husband what happened.' I gulped slightly and asked her how it had gone, almost praying it had been OK. 'Iain, I feel I can see blue sky again!' she exclaimed. We both teared up at that point.

Not long afterwards I conducted a phone-in on male rape, by which I mean male-on-male rape. In all honesty, I wasn't sure any man would phone me and talk about it, for obvious reasons. I shouldn't have worried. Within minutes the phone lines were buzzing. It was an hour in which I should have been honest and made an admission myself. I could have revealed that I too was once the victim of a sexual assault, which could have turned into something far worse. It's not something I have spoken about in public before, but perhaps I should have done.

It wasn't that I was ashamed of what had happened, I suppose I just wimped out. Until, in early 2019, I was on *CNN Talk* with Bonnie Greer discussing the sexual assault allegations made against US Supreme Court nominee Brett Kavanaugh by Christine Blasey Ford. Bonnie had written in the *New European* newspaper about a date rape she suffered 40 years earlier. She was asked about her experience by the programme's host, Max Foster, and, as part of her response, she emphasised that sexual assault is something that happens to men as well as women, and that it was important men talked about it. So I did.

I think it is often very difficult for victims of sexual crimes to come forward. This is especially true when people believe there is no prospect of a conviction. They also blame themselves. There's a feeling of shame involved. Embarrassment. 'What will people think?'

Back in the late 1980s and early 1990s, I lived in Walthamstow. One night I met a guy and went back to his flat. His room was disgusting. Clothes all over the place and a mattress on the floor. Still, I wasn't there to judge his tidiness habits.

It soon became evident to me that he was blind drunk. Almost paralytic. I rapidly decided I wanted out of there, but couldn't decide how to do escape without it all being a bit embarrassing. He kept trying to kiss me. I kept pulling away. He made it clear he intended to fuck me and wasn't going to take no for an answer. I made it very clear that this wasn't going to happen. Repeatedly.

He would stop trying for a minute or two, but then start again. Luckily, I was just as strong as him and could fend him off. Someone else might not have been able to do so.

Then he leaned over the side of the mattress and was sick. Over my car keys.

My hope was that the drink would kick in even further and he would go to sleep. And that's what eventually happened. While he was on top of me.

I left it for about twenty minutes and then carefully manoeuvred myself away from him. I rapidly got dressed, cleaned the vomit off my car keys and went to the door. Problem. The door was locked and I couldn't see a key. Eventually I found it, ran out of the building as fast as I could and made a 'Starsky and Hutch' getaway in my car. Five minutes later I was back in my own flat. I immediately threw up.

Reflecting on this nearly thirty years on, I question how I could have been so stupid as to put myself in that situation. Why didn't I realise how drunk he was?

It's not something I think about very often and it only came back to me because of what Bonnie Greer said. But I suspect I am very much the exception and that most men would feel somehow emasculated by going through something like that.

I just kicked myself for putting myself in such a situation. In reality, though, it was the other guy who I should have been blaming, not myself. I doubt whether he even remembers it.

Language is a funny thing. It's completely illogical that we find the word 'bonk' acceptable to use in polite company, yet the word 'fuck' isn't. Why do some people from Manchester object to being called 'Mancs' when Australians are quite happy to be called 'Aussies'? No logic at all, is there? But that's why the English language is such a wonderful, vibrant, living entity.

We tend to sneer at the rhetorical use of language in this country, whereas Americans are completely unembarrassed at the way they use language. They allow rhetoric to soar into areas that would be no-go areas for most British politicians, whose use of language tends to be functional and pedestrian to say the least. In recent years in this country, only Tony Blair has attempted to use language and rhetoric to reinforce a political message. Barack Obama was the Ronald Reagan of his generation, at least in terms of his ability to make a speech that lives on in the memory. Who is today's Obama?

The thread that binds the two is the ability to act, and the possession of the golden halo of celebrity. Reagan and Obama are, of course, politicians, but most people – and I am not just talking about devoted, diehard fans – see them as on a different plane to ordinary mortal politicians. And that is in part because of their ability to act, to ham up, to convince.

Let's not go too far, though. Both Obama and Reagan were capable of making perfectly ordinary speeches too. Not every speech was a masterpiece, but when the occasion called for it, they could rise to it. Think of Reagan after the *Challenger* Space Shuttle blew up.

The crew of the space shuttle *Challenger* honoured us by the manner in which they lived their lives. We will never forget them, nor the last time we saw them, this morning, as they prepared for the journey and waved goodbye and 'slipped the surly bonds of earth' to 'touch the face of God'.

You could just about imagine Tony Blair saying that, but any other British politician? I doubt it.

Of course, they weren't Reagan's words. They were Peggy Noonan's, probably the finest speechwriter of her generation – and if you haven't read her book *What I Saw at the Revolution*, you should.

Obama's speeches were also not entirely his own, but one incredibly important aspect of Obama's success and Reagan's is that their respective speechwriting teams managed to get inside their heads. They knew what their subjects were thinking or would think – and that, I believe, is a large part of what makes a successful speech.

Successful politicians know their own minds, and successful speechwriters know them too. A framework still needs to be set for the speech, and that's up to the politician, but then it's time for the speechwriters to get to work. As relationships develop and confidence grows, a system evolves. A degree of mutual confidence is established.

But what when it all goes wrong? I was chief of staff to David Davis during the Conservative leadership contest in 2005. I was never a speechwriter, but I saw at close hand how not to run a speechwriting team. There were too many people involved, who often disagreed with each other about policy issues. That mattered because, in retrospect, it is clear they were not given a clear enough steer concerning what David wanted to say, and they didn't know his views well enough. Was that their fault or his? Perhaps it was mine for not gripping the process.

I don't have the luxury of a speechwriter. But over a number of years I have established what works for me. I've done a number of parliamentary selections, where I had half an hour to impress the selectorate – a five- or ten-minute speech followed by questions. I normally never attempted to script these speeches, on the basis that if you can't speak for five minutes without notes you ought not to be in the game. I normally decided on a couple of things I wanted my listeners to understand, think of one funny line, and just go in and do it. It worked well normally, but in my last contest, against five others for East Surrey, it all fell apart.

I broke the habit of a lifetime and took advice from a candidate – now a cabinet minister – who had just won a selection. 'They're looking for a cabinet minister,' she said. 'They want weight and gravitas. Write a speech and memorise it.' And that's where the alarm bell should have rung. I'm not very good at memorising anything, let alone five minutes' worth of weighty prose. Anyway, to cut a long story short, it didn't go well. Most of the words came out, but not necessarily in the right order. My delivery was therefore stilted as I tried to get back on track. It wasn't a disaster, but I was only operating at about 50 per cent capacity.

Publicly, I put it down to an off-day at the office, but in reality it was because I broke a winning formula.

The problem politicians face nowadays is that, unless they are a grade-1 premier-league celeb politician, they can make the greatest speech ever, but no one is listening. The media pack are only interested in the party leaders. If you are a frontbencher you really have to go that extra mile to get noticed, and if you are a backbencher, well forget speechmaking. Go on *Celebrity Fit Club*.

Being a speechwriter for a politician is one of the most thankless jobs in Britain. It's because we are all searching for an audience, and the audience is searching for inspiration. The age of celebrity is here, but no one in politics has yet determined what that means for political oratory.

We're constantly told that people's attention span is only a couple of minutes nowadays – which is why we repeatedly hear from radio and TV interviewers that very irritating phrase: 'I'm sorry, that's all we've got time for.' In the House of Commons there is now a rule that backbench speeches must last no longer than ten minutes – sometimes five. In the recent impeachment of Donald Trump, members of the House of Representatives were allowed to make speeches of a maximum of 90 seconds. Ideal to upload on Facebook afterwards, but precious little else.

Most political speeches can only ever hope to garner a maximum of 20 seconds on the evening news, so the need for inspiring rhetoric throughout a speech goes out of the window. Our habits in media consumption are dictating the kinds of speeches we get from our politicians. Around 120 years ago, tens of thousands of people would be happy to stand for hours and listen to Gladstone. And it would be a speech of uniform rhetorical quality from start to finish. Nowadays, if a politician gets an audience of one hundred for a 20-minute speech they think they are onto a winner.

But we are rapidly approaching the day when political speeches may be a thing of the past. Candidate selections now concentrate on the ability to interview rather than the ability to speak. As MPs come to terms with the internet as a means of communicating, the role of the speech in political communication will diminish even further. Politicians, in the end, will seek out their audience. And the internet provides a willing audience. MPs used to turn up their noses at bloggers who get 500 readers a day. But when you ask them how many times they have addressed an audience of 500, they look at you blankly, until suddenly, a light goes on.

So, most politicians will have fewer and fewer opportunities to make speeches. Maybe in the council chamber, or the chamber of the House of Commons, or to their constituency AGMs.

For speechwriters this is a dire situation, as the opportunities for paid work diminish by the year. Or at least, that's the way I see it. I regret this change, because I think inspirational speechmaking is an incredible way of engaging people in politics. As mentioned earlier, the reason I joined the Conservative Party in 1978 was because of a speech I had heard Margaret Thatcher make. I can imagine an 18-year-old Iain Dale in Wichita, Kansas, feeling much the same a couple of years ago listening to Barack Obama.

But the current-day Iain Dale of Melton Mowbray in England? What's going to inspire him?

Chapter 9

Changing Your Mind and the Art of the Apology

'What we've also lost today, especially with this president [Trump], is the humility to know when you've made a mistake and to apologise. It doesn't make you a lesser individual, in fact it makes you a greater one. You can still have attitude without animosity.'

Governor Chris Christie

Having an open mind is at the very core of being able to debate properly. We all like to think we are right and that people who disagree with us are wrong. That may often be so, but not always. If we are not prepared to accept that other people hold genuine beliefs and have every right to do so, how can we possibly maintain we have the optimum public discourse in our society?

Instead, the modern-day tendency is to shout down people we don't agree with, accuse them of having malign intentions. Everyone has a right to hold a view on anything, and if we believe they are wrong we should be able to say so without shouting or being shouted at or insulted.

We need to recognise that it is a human trait to change your mind. If you've never changed your mind on anything you can rightly be accused of being an ideologue. The trouble is that if you go against the modern-day conventional wisdom on some issues, you're treated as a heretic.

In political terms, I have always defined myself as being on the centre-right. I've been fairly consistent in holding relatively Thatcherite views on economic issues, but on social issues I have become increasingly liberal. Indeed, I could easily argue that I am not actually a Conservative at all – I'm a classic Gladstonian liberal in that I believe in *laissez-faire* economics and free markets, but I also believe that the state, so far as is possible, should keep out of our private lives and not concern itself with what any of us do in the bedroom.

Hosting a radio show, where I hear from the general public every day, has made me change my mind on certain government policies. For instance, I could always make a theoretical argument for the so-called Bedroom Tax, but when you hear from a succession of people telling you what the practical effects of it have been on their lives, you'd be mad if you didn't re-evaluate your position. On universal credit, whatever the theoretical benefits are – and there are many, as all political parties agree – when you hear from three middle-aged men in a row, each of whom breaks down in tears live on the radio, you don't have to be Einstein to work out that something is going seriously wrong in the implementation of the revised benefits system.

It's examples like these that have shifted my social compass. Some of the harder, right-of-centre edges have been chipped away. I think I have always been a fairly empathetic person, but you have to have a heart of stone if hearing people's heart-rending stories doesn't affect you and your outlook on social issues.

From changing your mind, let's move on to admitting you're wrong. It's always difficult to admit an error in public. The automatic assumption is that it will diminish your reputation and make you appear foolish. That may be so on some occasions, but at other times you can turn a negative into a positive.

Politicians hate to admit they are wrong, even when there is overwhelming evidence. It's obvious why. They purport to have the answers to everything; mistakes and errors burst their illusion of omnipotence. Personally, I have invariably found that admitting an error and apologising for it is a positive thing, especially when the mistake has occurred on social media. Let me relate an example from a few years ago.

In December 2010 I wrote an article in the *Mail on Sunday*, ostensibly on Julian Assange, but I also used it to criticise the *Guardian*, Alastair Campbell and John Prescott for their pursual of Andy Coulson, David Cameron's then Director of Communications, over his alleged involvement in phone hacking.

It was my view that Coulson had done a good job for Cameron and, so far as I was aware, behaved appropriately. He certainly did in my limited dealings with him. I believed Coulson when he said he knew nothing about the phone hacking. A police inquiry had cleared him, so why wouldn't I believe him? As we all now know, he eventually went to jail.

Where I went wrong, and I apologised for it, was to impugn the worst motives not just to the *Guardian* but also to the various political figures who pursued this issue with such tenacity. I still believe that one of their initial motivations was political; they dearly wanted to get Coulson if they could. But as they dug and dug, what they found led them to a much bigger scalp – that of the whole *News of the World* newspaper itself.

Here's another example of where I tweeted something in good faith but then discovered what I had been told was wrong. You then face a choice: correct the record and apologise, or ride it out. In my experience, the former is invariably the way to go.

In January 2018 I read a story in *The Times* about the Scottish government ordering a change in its flag-flying policy, meaning that the only occasion the Union Flag could be flown on Scottish Parliament buildings was on Remembrance Sunday. Previously there were 14 other occasions when it could be flown. Instead, it would now be replaced by the Saltire.

I tweeted in response:

So @NicolaSturgeon has ordered the union flag to be removed from government buildings. Perhaps the UK government should remove the funding which enables her to spend £1500 more per head of population than is spent in England.

Nicola Sturgeon then tweeted me to say that it was not her decision and nothing had changed since 2010.

I investigated further, and it became clear that the decision on the flags was taken in 2010 when Alex Salmond was First Minister, but the civil service policy guidance had not been updated in the ensuing seven years.

I believed that it was wrong for this decision (a) to have been taken and (b) not to have been made public until now. Obviously, as First Minister, Nicola Sturgeon has to take responsibility for what happens in her government's name, even if the actual decision was not hers. But as soon as I realised I had made an error I got in touch with her directly and apologised for tweeting that it was her decision.

In those circumstances, I deleted the original tweet, which is something I would not normally do.

The online abuse I received over the two days of this stooshie was something to behold. You might suggest that, since I tweeted something that was incorrect, I deserved it. All I will say is that it is possible to disagree and call someone out in ways that don't involve the kind of language and violent abuse that has been freely used by the so-called 'Cybernats'. It's a sad indictment of our public discourse when people who disagree politically can't have a reasonable exchange. If Nicola Sturgeon could have the grace to accept my apology – and she did, publicly – then I'd have hoped that her more vocal supporters could bring themselves to do so as well. It proved to be a vain hope. The more extreme Cybernats are a disgrace to the political party they purport to support. They give Scottish nationalism a bad name and the SNP should do more to bring them into line.

We live in a society where 'sorry' seems to be the easiest word. Apologies are demanded from public figures for the most minor transgression, preferably with tears. And if the apology is not forthcoming, or the apology is considered insincere, the weight of the media descends. Politicians in recent years have thrown apologies around like confetti, thereby demeaning their value. Sometimes they have the desired effect; on other occasions they can rebound. I am still not sure whether Nick Clegg's *mea culpa* over student fees did him any favours or not.

When David Cameron visited Amritsar in 2013, on the final leg of his visit to India, everyone was agog to find out whether he would apologise on behalf of Britain for the massacre of 400 Sikhs in 1919. As it turned out, he called it a 'deeply shameful event in British history' but didn't use the 'S' word. Strangely, the wrath of the Gods of Apology did not rain down on him. One local official, in charge of the memorial site, said: 'He came here, he paid a tribute. It was more than an apology.' We talked about this on my LBC radio show later that evening and were deluged with calls from Sikhs and Indians, none of whom criticised Cameron's reluctance to actually say sorry. Most of them said they felt it was ridiculous for a politician to apologise for something he himself had no control over and wasn't even alive at the time it happened. Wise people. Apologies should be contemporaneous. They must relate to recent events, be genuine, and be full of genuine remorse and contrition. Only then can they really mean something.

Apologies have to be heartfelt. If there's no emotion involved, people doubt its sincerity. One of David Cameron's first acts as prime minister was to formally apologise for the actions of the British army in Northern Ireland on Bloody Sunday in 1972. The words were heartfelt and even diehard Irish nationalists praised him, both for what he said and for the way he said it. Contrast that with the non-apology apology issued by Jeremy Corbyn for the way he and his party failed to deal with the issue of anti-Semitism. His words were robotic, devoid of emotion and did nothing to reassure the Jewish community. Indeed, during the ensuing general election campaign, he couldn't even bring himself to repeat the apology in a TV interview, despite being given four chances to do so by the interviewer, Andrew Neil.

We may be British, but we all have emotions. Traditionally, we Brits don't like emoting in public, especially if we have a Y chromosome. However, I've always believed that emoting is part of who we are and should also be part of our public discourse.

I describe elsewhere the broadcast in which I had to cover the awful breaking news of the terrorist murder of Lee Rigby in Woolwich back in March 2013. The next day we were continuing to discuss it when my producer Laura flashed on my screen a statement from the Ministry of Defence. Normally, I'd skim it first, but on this occasion I didn't. We weren't far away from the top of the hour and I wanted to get it out into the public domain before the news bulletin. So I started reading it out loud. And then I got to this bit:

> A loving father to his son Jack, aged 2 years, he will be sorely missed by all who knew him. The regiment's thoughts and prayers are with his family during this extremely difficult time. 'Once a Fusilier, always a Fusilier.'

As I started to say the words 'A loving father …' my voice began to crack. I couldn't continue. Breathe, I thought to myself, breathe. Pull yourself together. I was probably only silent for three or four seconds, but in radio that can seem like half a minute. I continued and got to the end, but still in a slightly emotional state. I was inwardly kicking myself.

My job was to get the news out there, not to emote over it.

At the end of the hour, I apologised for being unprofessional, and left it at that. And then the texts and tweets started flooding in – and I mean flooded. In torrents. 'Why did you apologise? You only did what we were all doing,' was the general consensus. All these years on, I realise that me breaking down like that pulled me closer to my audience. Showing basic human empathy showed them I was no robot, and I was reacting in the same way that they were. It somehow cemented a trust. And that's why, used properly, the language of emotion is a hugely positive thing.

It is possible to argue that politics is all about emotion. Each political tribe has its own emotional pull. The arguments used by us all to argue for the policies we believe in involve emotion. If they do not, it's as if we don't care. Politics will always be about passion, and impassioned debate, and that's why I have to remain optimistic about our political future. Social media doesn't reflect the real passion of ordinary people. It enables a shouting atmosphere to prevail, which can certainly be described as passionate but is often more shouty and aggressive than it should be. When you talk to real voters on the doorstep, or even down the line on a radio show, you discover people who feel equally passionate about their own particular issues, and are keen to make their voices heard if given the chance. It is for politicians to reflect those views and enable those voices to be heard.

PART THREE

ISSUES

Chapter 10

Brexit: The Angry People of Leave and Remain

'I voted Remain, not just for political reasons
but because my mum's moved to Spain and
I want her to stay there.'

Leo Kearse

Back in 1983 I was a member of the European Movement. In the 1983 general election campaign I remember taking part in a debate in Norwich arguing that Britain's future lay as full members of what was then called the European Economic Community. My Labour opponent in that debate articulated the then Labour Party policy of leaving the EEC. Thirty-five years later I passionately argue the case for leaving the European Union, while most Labour politicians argue the opposite.

I've never been someone whose automatic default is to argue we should leave the EU. Even when the referendum was announced I wasn't entirely sure which way I would vote. I decided to vote Leave when David Cameron failed to secure any meaningful concessions from the EU at the summit in February 2016. It became clear to me then that this was an organisation that was incapable of reform and we would be better off out of it. I didn't announce how I had voted until after the polls had closed at 10 p.m. on 23 June 2016.

The issue of Britain leaving the European Union has been the most toxic and divisive issue of our age and my lifetime. Even the battles over nuclear disarmament in the 1980s seem insignificant compared to the divisions over Brexit. The nation is divided. Families are divided. People have lost friends over their views on the rights and wrongs of the issue. Politicians on both sides of the argument have displayed a lamentable failure to understand the opinions of those who oppose them. So convinced are they of their rectitude, so certain they couldn't possibly be wrong, that they have no interest in trying to understand the opposite point of view.

Many of those on the losing side in the 2016 referendum appeared to have lost the art of accepting 'loser's consent', which lies at the cornerstone of our democracy. By definition, elections and referendums create unequal outcomes. There are winners and losers. If the losers do not accept their loss and, instead, find all manner of reasons to re-fight old battles, the very essence of democracy is at risk. However, loser's consent has to be matched by magnanimity on behalf of the victors, especially when the margin of victory is narrow. Too many of those on the winning side seem to have lost sight of the fact that the result was a narrow 52–48. It's true that Leave scored 1.4 million more votes than Remain, and in theory the winner takes all, but there was little desire on the part of the winning side to heal the wounds of the losers.

Five years on from the June 2016 referendum, the country is as split as it was then. Perhaps even more so. The language used by both sides, instead of softening, has become intolerably shrill. Leavers are stupid, thick, xenophobic racists who had no clue what they were voting for, and Remainers are unpatriotic anti-British traitors who would quite happily sell their own country down the river to Brussels.

Every bad bit of economic news is trumpeted by Remainers as proof that Brexit is having a terrible effect on the economy. Every bit of good economic news is used by Leavers to argue that Project Fear, as conducted by George Osborne and David Cameron during the EU referendum, was a load of hogwash and everything is rosy in the post-Brexit garden.

As ever, the truth lies somewhere in between. There is ample evidence that some sectors of the economy have indeed been affected by Brexit uncertainty, but equally the economy has proven incredibly resilient and performed very well compared to equivalent EU economies.

Take this example. In February 2019 Honda announced the closure – in 2021 – of their plant in Swindon. Naturally, it is a disaster for the town. More than three thousand people will lose their jobs and no doubt that figure will increase in the wider area through the supply chain.

The reaction on social media was immediate. Further proof that Brexit would be a disaster, trilled the #FBPE (Follow Back Pro EU) brigade. People who knew nothing about the automotive sector or Honda as a company claimed as fact that the closure was either entirely or mostly due to Brexit. It wasn't. It was due to global changes in the car industry and the need to launch electric vehicles.

This became part of a trend. Anything negative that happens to our economy is down to Brexit and anything good that happens is despite Brexit or because we haven't left yet. You can't have it both ways.

I'm not some sort of starry-eyed economic illiterate who thinks that the land will be flowing with milk and honey in the immediate aftermath of Brexit, or indeed ever. I've said repeatedly that I believe there will be short-term difficulties, but that in the long term there are many prizes to be had. I do not believe, though, that we're going to hell in a handcart, and I remain suspicious of anyone who seeks to blame Brexit for every economic woe we experience.

Business doesn't like uncertainty, and the continual extensions to Brexit deadlines not only raised many people's ire, they also angered businesses in many sectors of the economy. It is a terrible indictment of politicians both here and in Brussels that even as late as December 2020 we still didn't know exactly what our trading arrangements would be by the end of the year.

Throughout the debate each side has found innovative ways of insulting the other.

In May 2018 someone on the Remain side of the Brexit debate coined the word 'gammon' as an insult to Brexiteers. Apparently, we're all red-faced, white middle-aged men. Some have claimed that the word is being used in a racist way. I wouldn't quite go that far, but it is certainly unpleasant and patronising. I plead guilty to being white and middle-aged, although I don't normally have a red face ...

On the other side, loose lips from Prime Minister Boris Johnson caused widespread outrage when he was unwise enough to use the word 'collaboration' in a Facebook Live session soon after he became prime minister. He was rightly complaining that the actions and words of some Conservative MPs – and he clearly had Philip Hammond, the former chancellor in mind – were persuading the EU to stick to its guns while they waited to see what havoc Parliament could wreak when it returned in early September. Johnson's sentiment was right, but you can't go throwing around words that have World War II connotations and effectively accuse some of your parliamentary colleagues of being quislings or traitors to their country. It debases the debate. Was it deliberate, or did it just slip out? I don't know, but if it was a deliberate attempt to feed into the 'people v. parliament' narrative, well, there were better ways of doing it.

The *Telegraph*'s economics commentator Liam Halligan, who has written a book called *Clean Brexit*, which I published at Biteback, was booed and spat at when appearing at the Bath Literary Festival for having the temerity to suggest in print that Brexit is not only a good idea but will benefit Britain in the long run. Also, during 2017 and 2018, whenever he was on *Any Questions?* he would get hissed at as he was introduced by the host Jonathan Dimbleby, and when he first spoke. He says: 'It happened to me on three occasions. Once, when I was on with Gina Miller, someone screamed out while I was in the middle of my first answer. "We don't want to hear from him. We want to hear from Gina." Live on air. It was totally outrageous … Brexiteers don't behave like that. But apparently it is OK for Remainers.'

But the attacks didn't just come from one side. Newspapers like the *Daily Mail* and the *Daily Telegraph* used virulent, attention-seeking headlines to damn the opponents of Brexit. In April 2017, following Theresa May's decision to call a snap election, the *Daily Mail*'s front page screamed: 'CRUSH THE SABATEURS'. This was aimed squarely at Remainers, or Remoaners as the *Mail* liked to call them. The *Telegraph* put prison-like mugshots of 20 Tory rebels on its front page before one of the meaningful votes. One newspaper published their email addresses, knowing full well the abuse the rebel MPs would get. On the issue of Brexit, newspaper editors appeared to lose any semblance of responsibility for their actions. They just played to their own newspaper echo chamber.

Digital publishers must also take responsibility for what appears on their platforms. Take YouTube, for example. Just look at the comments that YouTube viewers have made under any Brexit-related video. LBC streams many of its programmes live on YouTube, including, at the time, *The Nigel Farage Show*. This was the experience of one of my female listeners, Sam, who phoned in one day to speak to Nigel. They had a perfectly good, calm debate. 'He was respectful, courteous and a real gentleman,' says Sam. 'I was also proud of myself for having had the courage to pick up the phone live to the nation. So, all fine and dandy until I watched back the moment on the LBC YouTube livestream video chats and read the comments alongside the video while I was on air.' She was shocked.

They ranged from unkind and derogatory to hostile, then to just plain abusive, i.e. 'shoot her' and 'throw off the cliff'. For someone who does not use social media a lot and who is just an ordinary member of the public, and is not used to getting abuse, it was shocking for me to experience such a flippant and cavalier manner of hatred aimed towards me. Most of those commenting seemed to have the opinion that I was a weak 'remainer-remoaner' even though, like them, I voted to leave in the referendum. A kind of mob mentality unified them while they listened to me, and in their split-second assertions they subsequently thought it was okay to make offensive generalisations about my worth as an individual and a woman. I also believe most of them didn't realise I was Asian, which I know would have fuelled the fires of hate even further …

The issue here is the responsibility of YouTube, Facebook or Twitter for publishing these vile comments. It is of course within LBC's power to switch off comments on our videos, but given that our strapline is 'Leading Britain's Conversation' it would be a bit odd to prevent people having a conversation or debate. It's the anonymity of the commenters that's the main problem. Virtually all of them have anonymous monikers and therefore think they can say anything without fear of being caught. But for Sam, this wasn't the end of it.

Sadly, my eleven-year-old daughter saw these comments and was absolutely distraught. She is not on social media yet and never faced online abuse before. The intolerance in our society, especially on social media is out of control and needs to be tackled. My daughter was shocked at the amount of hate coming my way from just having a conversation. What she couldn't articulate is that at primary school this type of disrespect and intolerance has already begun. With the wide use and integration of smart phones and tablets, lots of her classmates have already experienced the dark side of social media and unsurprisingly bullying incidents have already had their

head teacher sending out letters to parents. My daughter
is being taught by adults (teachers) about being kind and
respectful to each other, which contradicts the reality of
the world she actually lives in where she sees adults
openly inciting each other with hateful language,
undermining the very principles of the value and trust
she is learning at school.

What a sorry state of affairs. But it's not just in social media
that we have a real problem, it's also the case in the world
of broadcasting. When people watch television, and they
have a certain view on an issue, they hear what they want
to hear. In January 2019 I appeared on *The Andrew Marr
Show*, for the paper review, with the left-wing economics
commentator Grace Blakeley.

This is what Twitter made of it …

I am a sell-out and now support Remain.
I am a hard-Brexit hypocrite who wants no deal.
I minimised the effect of no deal.
I predicted riots in the street if Brexit doesn't happen on
    29 March.

That's quite a record given I am supposed to have said all
that within the space of about three minutes of air time.
This was in the aftermath of Theresa May's deal on Brexit,
which was about to be voted on in the House of Commons.

The divide seemingly has the effect of harming our ability
to listen to one another's views, as the red mist falls faster
than thought processes engage – and not just on Twitter.

There is an assumption among many Remainers that
those of us who voted Leave are anti-European zealots who

wish to pull the drawbridge up. We must all be xenophobic racists who hate foreigners. There is a total failure to understand that for most of us it is the case that we love Europe – we're just not so keen on the EU as an institution.

The urge to conflate the cultural with the political is something that can be seen on both sides of the debate. I voted to leave the EU. But my decision was by no means made due to any sense of not feeling like I have any kind of European identity, nor was it down to being closed to the cultural impact that Europe has had on me – and on the country more generally.

The EU referendum was in itself inevitably divisive. Binary choices always are. You have two choices, with no shades of grey. Leave or Remain. That's it. And since the referendum, things have got even worse. Long-term friendships have splintered. Families have fallen out. Immediately after the vote my two sisters both told me I had ruined their daughters' lives. And they meant it. I was astounded. There were stories of relationships foundering over the fact that two people had voted in different ways. A YouGov opinion poll showed that 40 per cent of Remain voters would be 'upset' if their child married a Leave supporter. The figure the other way around was 11 per cent. Thirty-four per cent of Labour voters would be upset if their child married a Conservative. Only 11 per cent of Conservative parents would be upset if their child married a Labour voter. So much for the liberal tolerance of Remainers or Labour supporters! Surely love transcends politics, or at least it ought to. Supporting a particular political party or cause does not of itself make you a bad person. To be upset that your son-in-law is a Leave-voting Conservative makes *you* the zealot, not him.

Thirty-five years ago, I graduated from the University of East Anglia with a degree in German, and ended up thoroughly fluent, having spent two years living, working and teaching in Germany. I fully intended to become a German teacher, being rather in love with the country, but life often has different plans.

I still speak the language – though with a slight coating of rust – and visit as often as work and life allows. Beyond culture, I also have genetic links to the continent. My grandmother's maiden name was 'French', so I strongly suspect I have French blood in me somewhere. In short then, while I'm no fan of the political entity that is the EU, I feel that – although I identify primarily as English, and secondarily as British – being European is also part of my identity; and what a mercifully multi-faceted range of options and configurations that word covers.

After all, Europe is still there across the water – and in our DNA – even though we've left. Brits will still want to live and work across Europe, just as French, German and Italian citizens will want to do the same in this country. Our trading arrangements may change slightly, but our main markets will continue to be those across the English Channel. We will still buy German cars, French cheese and Italian wine. They will still avail themselves of our financial services, and will remain our main tourist market and export market for all sorts of goods and services.

Chapter 11

Why Racism Matters (and Immigration Is Good)

'Why don't they go back and help fix the
totally broken and crime infested places from
which they came.'

*President Trump on several US-born Democratic
Congresswomen, 15 July 2019*

Racism is a cancer that afflicts virtually every society in the world. It's something I've never quite been able to comprehend, and I think I know why.

I grew up in an idyllic little village in north-west Essex called Ashdon. I attended the local Church of England primary school, along with around a hundred 5- to 11-year-olds. Among us were kids from the local children's home, the All Saints' Home for Boys. Founded in 1885 by the Rector of Ashdon, Reverend Henry Barclay Swete, it housed 24 boys. Many of them were black and came from broken homes in London. They all attended Ashdon County Primary School and became my friends. A five-year-old is incapable of racism, unless it is taught. One of my best friends was Paula, a black girl who had been adopted by the parents of my best friend Roger. The thought of Paula or the Home boys being treated differently because of the colour of their skin never entered my head – or the heads of the other children, or indeed their teachers.

When I walk down the street, or sit on a train, I do not see people's skin colour. I just don't. If I hear people talking a different language, I don't feel threatened, I listen and try to work out which language they are speaking. Sometimes I even ask them. Nigel Farage, on the other hand, feels very differently. Back in 2014 he told a UKIP conference:

> I got the train the other night, it was rush hour, from Charing Cross, it was the stopper going out. We stopped at London Bridge, New Cross, Hither Green. It wasn't until after we got past Grove Park that I could actually hear English being audibly spoken in the carriage. Does that make me feel slightly awkward? Yes. I wonder what's really going on. And I'm sure that's a view that will be reflected by three-quarters of the population, perhaps even more.

Why on earth would hearing other people speaking different languages make him feel uncomfortable? I know Nigel Farage is not a racist, but comments like that give people reason to believe that he might be. Loose use of language in this area allows people to think the worst of you. Boris Johnson has often provided his political opponents with the opportunity to do so.

In a 2002 column he wrote about a foreign trip by the then Prime Minister, Tony Blair.

What a relief it must be for Blair to get out of England. It is said that the Queen has come to love the Commonwealth, partly because it supplies her with regular cheering crowds of flag-waving piccaninnies.

Just for good measure he followed it up with this:

They say he is shortly off to the Congo. No doubt the AK47s will fall silent, and the pangas will stop their hacking of human flesh, and the tribal warriors will all break out in watermelon smiles to see the big white chief touch down in his big white British taxpayer-funded bird.

Responding to the criticism that these examples proved his racism during the 2019 Conservative leadership contest, he said:

If you look at each and every one of those columns and articles, you'll find the quotations have been wrenched out of context, in many cases made to mean the opposite of what was intended.

He also claimed he was being satirical. People will form their own judgements, but the trouble is, they often do so without knowing the full story. The lesson not just for politicians, but for all of us, is to be very careful to use language that is not open to prejudicial interpretation.

As I mentioned in the Introduction, in one famous column for the *Daily Telegraph*, Johnson likened the appearance of burka-wearing Muslim women to letter-boxes and bank robbers. A clear example of Islamophobia you might think, and that's certainly what his detractors would like to have you believe. Yet read the whole column rather than quote two words and you see that he was arguing for Muslim women to be allowed to dress how they like. He was writing about the introduction of a ban on the burka in Denmark.

He said he felt 'fully entitled' to expect women to remove face coverings when talking to him at his MP surgery – and schools and universities should be able to take the same approach if a student 'turns up ... looking like a bank robber'.

> If you tell me that the burka is oppressive, then I am with you ... If you say that it is weird and bullying to expect women to cover their faces, then I totally agree – and I would add that I can find no scriptural authority for the practice in the Koran. I would go further and say that it is absolutely ridiculous that people should choose to go around looking like letter boxes.

He maintained that businesses and government agencies should be able to 'enforce a dress code' that allowed them to see customers' faces. But he said: 'Such restrictions are not quite the same as telling a free-born adult woman what she may or may not wear, in a public place, when she is simply minding her own business.'

Johnson claimed that a total ban on face-covering veils would give a boost to radicals who claim there is a 'clash of civilisations' between Islam and the West, and suggested that it could also lead to 'a general crackdown on any public symbols of religious affiliation'.

I don't consider that to be remotely Islamophobic or racist, but you can see why his political opponents pick out words and phrases and use them without context to further their narrative that he is intent on using dangerous and inflammatory language.

Various European countries have announced a ban on the wearing of the burka or niqab. Only UKIP, back in 2010, has proposed that a ban should be introduced in the UK. We ban too many things in this country, and to ban someone from self-expression is not British. Everyone has the right to dress in their own way. Why not ban punks from wearing safety pins, or goths from wearing eye liner? Go the whole hog and ban nuns from wearing habits! Don't get me wrong, I wish Muslim women didn't wear the burka. I wish they didn't feel the need to set themselves apart from the rest of society. In effect, they are 'othering' themselves, but it's all down to individual decision – or should be.

We should encourage integration into mainstream society, but it is clear that an outright ban on wearing the burka would not, by itself, achieve this. Indeed, it could achieve the direct opposite. That is not to say that as a society we should treat burka-wearing Muslim women differently from anyone else – airport security is an obvious example.

Feminists argue that the burka is a repressive form of dress and that Muslim women are forced to wear it by their menfolk. That may be true in some cases, but I doubt it is any more common than white men forcing their women to slap on the make-up before they go out – which is also a form of repression. The fact is that a growing number of Muslim women – even those born and raised here – are wearing the burka, and they are doing it out of choice, not because they are forced to.

Nowhere in the Koran does it say a woman should wear the burka.

Western women who go to Saudi Arabia are required to respect the dress code of the country and clothe themselves accordingly. Our liberal values don't require the same in return. The day a woman can wear a bikini on a beach in Saudi Arabia will be the day I will totally accept the burka. But ban it? No.

Diane Abbott once started a Twitter storm when she objected to the way in which the term the 'black community' was used as a generalisation. In a Twitter exchange with a friend, she said: 'I understand the cultural point you are making. But you are playing into a "divide and rule" agenda.' Then she added: 'White people love playing "divide and rule". We should not play their game #tacticasoldascolonialism.'

I make no apology for admitting I was among the first to point out that if a white Tory MP had said the same about black people, there would have been hell to pay. All she had to do was issue a quick apology and say that she should have used the word 'some'. But she didn't do that until she was forced to by her less than pleased leader, Ed Miliband.

Abbott came under fire for another tweet in which she reckoned that it is difficult to get a black cab to stop for you if you're black. The papers were in full cry, as were London cabbies. In this case, I had a little more sympathy for Diane Abbott. A few months earlier we were discussing racism on my LBC show and a cabby came on and admitted he wouldn't stop for a black youth. I was rather shocked by this, but then another cabby came on and said the same thing. They had both had bad experiences – one I think had had his passenger run off without paying and the other had had a fare who had puked up. I pointed out that I was fairly sure they would have had the same issue with white youths too. Neither had an answer. Rather bizarrely, a black lady then came on the phone and said that if she were a cabby she wouldn't pick them up either.

It may look like racism to Diane Abbott, and in some cases it may well be. But it could be that the cabby is daydreaming and thinking of what he will do when he knocks off.

Islamophobia is a thing. Some people try to pretend it isn't, on the basis that you can't have a phobia about a religion. They're playing semantics. Ask any Muslim whether Islamophobia is a 'thing' and you'll get your answer. I am not starry-eyed about Islam. I am hugely concerned about the rise of radical Islam in this country and jihadist sympathies, but let's not run away with the idea that normal Muslims in this country have anything other than the same motivations, aspirations and priorities as the rest of us.

The trouble is that with every jihadist terror attack comes the suspicion among non-Muslims that, somehow, other Muslims, deep down, have some sort of sympathy with it. That may be true of the odd brainwashed idiot, but apart from that they could not be more wrong. Ordinary, decent Muslims are as horrified as the rest of us. And they ring my radio show to tell me. I've had Muslim callers in tears explaining that the terrorists do not speak for anyone but themselves. They feel the need to apologise. I explain in return that it is not for them to apologise. I wouldn't feel the need to apologise for Anders Breivik, so why should they?

Islamophobia in this country has become more troubling ever since the 9/11 and 7/7 terror attacks. There are people in our country who genuinely believe that most terrorist incidents around the world are inspired by Islam and perpetrated by Muslims. Somehow this narrative has been allowed to develop and it is the media that can largely be blamed for not explaining the reality: that the vast majority of victims of Islamist-inspired terror attacks are Muslims themselves.

Muslims are understandably at pains to point out that Islamist terrorism incidents in this country are nothing to do with the religion of Islam, which they maintain is entirely peaceful. There are two problems with that. First, the perpetrators of these attacks are very quick to claim that they are doing what they do in the name of Allah. Second, while Islam in many ways does indeed promote peace, the Koran contains some pretty violent passages; but then again, so does the Bible.

David Cameron, who was prime minister at the time of the terrorist murder of Fusilier Lee Rigby, said in statements in Downing Street and Parliament that nothing in the Koran could justify his murder, but in his memoirs he wrote: 'I look back now and think my words were not entirely consistent … There clearly *is* something in Islam; otherwise these extremists across the Islamist spectrum wouldn't quote its scriptures and honour its God.' He goes on to talk about a war within Islam between the moderates and extremists, emphasising that it is the job of all of us to help the moderates prevail. To deny that terrorism has anything to do with Islam doesn't help, he says. And he's not only right, but brave to say so in such stark terms.

Successive governments have never really got to grips with the evils of radical Islamism jihadism. They've devoted millions of pounds to improving intelligence and on programmes like Prevent. Yet religious sensitivities have prevented them from attacking the problem at source – and that is with certain of the radical Wahhabi preachers who infest some of our leading mosques. Token efforts have been made to deny some of these preachers visas, but too seldom are they banned from entering the country.

I'm not a great fan of the 'something must be done' knee-jerk response to a terror attack or tragedy. It invariably leads to the wrong thing being done, and the consequences can be felt for years afterwards. What is needed is calm, cool reflection on what has happened. So what I am about to say isn't actually in response to what happened in any particular terror attack – it's something I have been talking about for a long time on my LBC show.

I have grown very concerned by the number of Muslims I talk to, not just on my show but in everyday conversation too, who believe that Saudi and Qatari money is funding Wahhabi mosques throughout the country, and it is these that are in part to blame for the rise in support for extremist ideas among some British Muslims.

Along with the spread of extremist websites that promote Daesh and their warped ideology, these mosques are now places that many moderate Muslims won't go, having recognised the danger they pose to young minds. This isn't me asserting something; this is what I hear time and time again from Muslims themselves. Some (not all) Imams in these British mosques are starting to turn Sunni against Shia, and the long-term consequences of that can only be imagined. The thing is, this is nothing new, yet no one in Britain has confronted the danger despite the warnings.

I've heard from dozens of ordinary Muslims over the last year or two who feel that something needs to be done.

They've withdrawn their children from classes at the mosques and they no longer attend themselves after witnessing some of the extreme messages being promoted. They will talk to me anonymously on my programme, but have an understandable fear of speaking out 'on the record'. The government needs to listen to these people and then act on what they hear.

In 2010 *Panorama* showed how young people are targeted for indoctrination by a network of Saudi-inspired weekend schools. They discovered 40 such schools that were indoctrinating more than five thousand British teenagers with what were described as the 'warped values' of Wahhabism.

I totally understand that Britain wants good relations with Saudi Arabia and Qatar, but for how much longer can we ignore what both these oil-rich states have been doing, yet pretending otherwise. It's not enough to ban the odd extremist Wahhabi cleric from entering the country. The government must go much further.

Their bluff needs to be called, and the way to do that is to cut off the funding of these mosques. The government should legislate to ban any foreign funding of British mosques. Indeed, if it makes it more politically acceptable, I'd say it could be broadened to include a ban on funding for any religious institutions. American fundamentalist Christian organisations tried in vain to influence the recent Irish gay marriage referendum by pouring money into the No campaign. I'd be quite happy for a law such as this to apply to any religious organisation whether Muslim, Christian, Sikh or Mormon.

We would not be blazing a trail here, either. In 2015 Austria banned mosques from receiving any monies from abroad, and Denmark is going down a similar route.

For far too long we have been too sensitive about dealing with Islamist extremism. Government should resist the siren voices that say they must just continue with the 'hearts and minds' Prevent programme. It hasn't achieved what it set out to. It's time to adopt a more hard-line approach to fight extremists.

And to those who say that all this is no doubt promoted by someone who hates Islam and hates Muslims, all I can say is that what they need to do is listen to my LBC show and they will see that they are very far from the truth. I am regularly criticised for my defence of Muslims and my belief that they are unfairly traduced by the media in all sorts of ways. I believe what I have said here is what most Muslims would agree with, whether they feel they can say it openly or not.

Over the past few years I've talked to several government ministers, all of whom think this is the right way forward, but none of them have had the guts to do anything about it.

Since I started presenting on LBC more than a decade ago, I have lost count of the times I have hosted phone-ins on Israel, and much more latterly the issue of anti-Semitism and anti-Jewish hatred. Producers hate doing phone-ins on anything to do with Israel because they believe the subject attracts the zealots from both sides. They're right, but if you set down the ground rules and make clear you intend to have a sensible discussion and you won't tolerate extremist views, people will generally respect that.

One of my proudest moments on LBC came in 2016 when I persuaded the Israeli Ambassador, Mark Regev, and the Palestinian Representative in London, Manuel Hassassian, to debate with each other live in the studio. Something like that had never happened before and to say

I was nervous about what might happen was quite an understatement.

Hassassian had been a regular guest on my show and I always enjoyed interviewing him. I had first interviewed Regev back in 2006 when he was the main spokesman for the Israeli Foreign Affairs Ministry and had followed his career ever since. Australian born, he is an extremely eloquent and articulate front-man. If only all Israeli politicians and representatives could be like him, Israel might have a far better reputation than it currently enjoys.

The hour sped by as the two of them sparred and debated with each other. We rather cheekily dubbed it the LBC Peace Process. In some ways it was living proof that the question posed by the title of this book can be answered: we can.

As the hour came to an end, I thanked them both, then the unthinkable happened. Regev reached over and offered his hand to Hassassian. It was quite a moment, given I had been told by Hassassian's press officer that on no account would he shake Regev's hand on camera. But he did. And everything seemed right with the world.

I'll always remember that hour. Neither of them 'won' the debate, but both seemed to prove that we could be optimistic about the future of Israel and Palestine. And both spoke with respect for each other and the other's standpoint. In a debate on the Middle East, this is unusual, but we can all learn from their example.

Anti-Semitism has, of course, always existed, yet until 2015 it didn't really rate as an issue that I'd have thought merited a phone-in, as it was generally consigned to the margins of far-Right or far-Left groupings. In 2015 it became mainstream. For some reason, as soon as Jeremy

Corbyn was elected leader of the Labour Party, it became a 'thing'.

Membership of the Labour Party mushroomed and people who had been consigned to the fringes of the Socialist Workers Party or the Workers Revolutionary Party started to join Labour in their thousands. Many of these people were and are Israel haters. They deny the right of Israel to exist. They see Jews as people who control large parts of world finance and the media. They willingly devour any anti-Jewish trope that's ever been created. Mainstream Jewish Labour MPs were targeted by them. Their lives were made a living hell. Eventually Jeremy Corbyn was forced to commission an inquiry into anti-Semitism in the Labour Party under the auspices of the ex-head of civil rights group, Liberty, Shami Chakrabarti. Her anodyne report, which essentially said 'move along, nothing to see', provoked much ridicule, yet she was rewarded with a peerage.

Jeremy Corbyn himself stood accused of being an anti-Semite and eventually the Equalities and Human Rights Commission launched an inquiry into whether the Labour Party is institutionally anti-Semitic. Quite something for a party with a proud record of fighting racism.

Several MPs quit. They'd had enough of the online abuse dished out to them. The sheer level and frequency of the abuse would have been enough to drive any sane individual into a slough of depression. Yet the party leadership did little to quell it. In a meeting with Jewish leaders, Jeremy Corbyn barely uttered a word. Even when the Chief Rabbi came out and urged British Jews not to vote Labour, Corbyn barely uttered a word in response. His formulaic response to the problem sent a message to British Jews that he didn't care and didn't take their concerns seriously. He just retreated into his usual pedestrian words on the subject, unable to differentiate anti-Semitism from racism, falling back on his favourite word, 'scourge'.

One Jewish friend of mine called a family meeting to discuss what they should do if Jeremy Corbyn won the election. All ten of them decided they would no longer stay in Britain. They were not alone.

What links all the different subjects in this chapter is the fact that words matter. If political leaders use the wrong words, they send out the wrong message. If they use weak words when strong words are called for, evil people feel they have licence to continue in their efforts to sow division, disharmony and discord.

On race issues everyone may appear to be walking a tightrope. Use one word out of place and an online storm may be provoked, or a political career may be prematurely ended. We don't all have to become so woke that we can't see the wood for the trees, but we do perhaps sometimes need to think more about the hurt that can be caused by an insensitive use of language – especially on matters of race and religion.

The trouble is, people fear what they don't know. It's usually an irrational fear, and it's not one that is easily dispelled. When we refer to immigrants, or asylum seekers, or refugees, we lump millions of people together. A big group of people can be a scary group of people.

Not long ago I was speaking to a friend who rather breathlessly told me that a Muslim family was moving in next door to him. Why is that an issue, I asked him? 'Well, you know …!' he said plaintively. 'No, I said, I don't know.' A few weeks later I ran into him and asked him how it was going with his new neighbours, who he clearly thought were going to bomb him or something else equally ludicrous. 'Oh mate,' he said, 'they're great! We're in and out of each other's houses all the time.' Again, the known triumphs over the unknown. As Republican governor Chris Christie's mother once told him: 'It's hard to hate someone up close.'

It's a bit like the theory that while, historically, we British appear to hate the French, we like and love individual French people. Stereotypes invariably lead to us having a negative opinion about an amorphous group of people.

The language of race and immigration fascinates me. People of my parents' generation would routinely describe members of ethnic minorities as 'coloured'. My mother would do so without a second thought. She wasn't being racist. That's just the word that everyone used. Trouble is, she would use it when it had become a word that wasn't used in polite society.

I've had to pull up callers on LBC who used the word without thinking. It's all very well telling people that the phrase we use now is 'people of colour', but they look at you quizzically and you can almost hear their brains whirring and thinking, 'Well what's the difference between using the word "coloured" and the phrase "people of colour"?' My answer is to encourage them to have that conversation with a person of colour and let them explain.

When we use the terms 'immigrant', 'asylum-seeker' or refugee we are indulging in an insidious form of 'othering'. We group people together in a way that is subliminally pejorative. We may not intend it to be, but that's often the effect. What we often fail to understand, though, is that if we were in their situation, we'd act much as they have done. Whether they're fleeing from a war-zone or persecution, or whether they're economic migrants seeking a better life for themselves and their families, they're doing exactly the same as we would do in similar circumstances. Would we not want to flee a war-zone? Would we not want to avoid persecution? Would we not want to do the best for our families?

Ah, but people say, why do they have to come to Britain? Why don't they settle in the first country they arrive in? Why do refugees and migrants congregate at Calais to cross the Channel? It's very simple actually, and if we bothered to listen to them, we'd know the answer. I've done a couple of phone-ins where I have encouraged people who have come to this country illegally to call me and explain their motivations for coming to the UK. In virtually every case, the ability to speak the language is a prime motivating factor, and the fact that we have a reputation as a tolerant and welcoming country. Not a single one was motivated by our generous benefits system. They all eventually regularised their employment status and most of them had become pillars of society. One had started a business that now employs 40 people. I'm not naïve enough to believe that there aren't people who come here to fleece the system and who, while they are here, indulge in bad behaviour, but to labour under the illusion that the majority of legal or illegal migrants are motivated in this way is utterly delusional.

Unfortunately, part of the reason why immigration gained traction as a big political issue was precisely because some politicians reckoned that anyone who was concerned by increasing immigration was an obvious racist. But large-scale immigration that is allowed without the consent of the people, and without providing the necessary infrastructure in public services to cope with it, will inevitably lead to tensions.

I make no secret of the fact that I am as wet as a lettuce on immigration. It played no part in my decision to vote to leave the EU. Freedom of movement is not something that causes me any concern whatsoever, but I am in a minority on that. What I deprecate is the hypocrisy of politicians who have argued that immigration should be cut to tens of thousands rather than hundreds of thousands. The very same politicians who made that promise in the 2010 Conservative manifesto made little or no effort to restrict immigration from outside the EU, which they were in a position to do. They didn't do it because people from other countries were needed to fill both skilled and unskilled jobs, which couldn't be filled by British people because they either didn't have the requisite skills or refused to do menial jobs.

I do not believe in open borders. Given that we're a relatively small nation in terms of land mass, it would be mad to suggest that anyone who wants to come here should be allowed to. There's nothing right wing or racist in believing that we should police our borders properly. But to suggest that we are 'full up' is plainly wrong. Only 7 per cent of our land mass is built on. Fly from London to Edinburgh and it's quite obvious that there is room to build more houses without hugely impinging on our green and pleasant land. This is only possible, however, if the rest of the required infrastructure like more schools, hospitals and roads accompany the new houses. So far, they have not, leading to complaints that because of high immigration people can't get appointments with their doctor, or they can't get their kids into the local school, or the waits at A&E are rising because of the number of non-British people using casualty departments. Simplistic stuff maybe, but you can't blame people for making the connection. To them it's as clear as night follows day.

Few politicians, even on the Left, appear willing to explain the benefits of immigration. They fail to tell us that large parts of our economy would not function without migrant labour. Have you ever heard any politician explain that most of us are part immigrant? Very few of us are 100 per cent pure British. When I signed up for the Ancestry DNA scheme, I found out I am 11 per cent Middle Eastern and also part French. Most of us have foreign blood in us somewhere, and perhaps sometimes those with anti-foreigner sentiments should think on that a little more deeply. Ironically, it is occasionally immigrants themselves who are set on pulling up the drawbridge behind them. I well remember various calls to my LBC show from people with Indian accents telling me the country is full up!

I delight in spending time explaining to my listeners why they are wrong if they think immigration is overall a bad thing. Every so often I host an hour where I ask immigrants to phone in telling me how they contribute to our society. No doubt it infuriates anyone with a racist bone in their body. Good. But if it provides a lightbulb moment for a few people, my mission is accomplished. Just in case you, yourself, are someone who doubts the benefits of immigration, let me briefly explain why you're wrong, because, let's face it, very few politicians will ever do it for you.

1. Nearly half the new doctors and nurses employed in the National Health Service have qualified abroad and we *still* have shortages of medical staff.
2. Immigrants use fewer NHS services than British people.

3. Immigrants pay more in taxes than they take as benefits.
4. We have an ageing population. Without working-age immigrants we won't be able to afford their pensions or provide their social care needs.
5. Immigrants are twice more likely to start a new business than native Brits.
6. Immigrants contribute massively to the diversity of our culture, food, music and language.
7. Immigration boosts productivity and incentivises native workers to up-skill and employers to invest.

Perhaps this is breaking through. According to the YouGov-Cambridge Globalism survey in 2014, nearly half of all British people believe that immigrants have either a positive or neutral impact on the country. In Germany the figure was 19 per cent.

Twenty-eight per cent of Britons believe that the benefits of immigration outweigh the costs, 20 per cent believe they are neutral and 16 per cent are not sure. However, 27 per cent believe the costs of immigration outweigh the benefits, although on the bright side this is the second lowest of any European country after Poland. In Italy the figure is 50 per cent, in apparently tolerant Sweden 49 per cent, in France 42 per cent and in Germany 40 per cent.

Interestingly, these figures change markedly when taking into account the reason for immigration. If an immigrant already has a job lined up prior to coming to the country, 80 per cent of Britons believe qualified professionals have a positive impact, compared to only 56 per cent in France. The figure for unskilled labourers arriving with a job is 41 per cent, the highest of any EU country except Spain.

These attitudes to immigration and race, and the conversation surrounding both issues, are very much influenced by what people read on social media, especially Twitter.

Sunder Katwala, the British Indian director of the think-tank British Future, says that he experiences more racism on Twitter in four weeks than he has in his forty-odd years on this earth. Without Twitter, his life would be totally harmonious. But he's addicted to the medium, despite all the nastiness, and doesn't wish to leave it. He's tried to get Twitter to take racism more seriously and to take action against people who transgress its rules. In August 2019 he wrote in the *Guardian*:

> What sorts of racism does Twitter let users get away with? You probably won't get away with calling somebody 'nigger', but I was told by Twitter that 'You are not British, parjeet – you people are shitting in the street' was acceptable. I emailed back to ask what more the user had to say to break the 'hateful conduct' rules. A response just said it had been checked and upheld. I wondered how often a human being was reading my messages – and how often an algorithm.
>
> Twitter says it abhors racism on the platform, but its current rules permit racism and racist speech, only banning users who promote violence or make threats or harassment on racial grounds. It did tighten its anti-hatred policies this month and dehumanising tweets against faith groups now violate the rules. Twitter gave examples: 'We need to exterminate the rats; the Jews are disgusting' would now be out of order. I was astonished that it wasn't already. Yet say exactly the same thing about black people and it's still OK. That is, tweets

dehumanising racial groups are deemed by Twitter to still be acceptable. Changing their policies on this is an urgent necessity.

It's not only a necessity, it's a matter of corporate social responsibility. I've reported racist trolls to Twitter and on not a single occasion has the complaint been upheld. If this doesn't change then Twitter users themselves will have to rise up and take the only action that will make Twitter take notice – leave the platform en masse, and I'm not far away from deciding to do that.

Chapter 12

Crime and Punishment

'One way to make sure crime doesn't pay would be
to let the government run it.'

Ronald Reagan

As with immigration, the language of the whole debate about crime and punishment prevents real debate and meaningful policy change. If any politician of any colour gives the slightest impression they are less than tough on crime and tough on the causes of the crime, they're accused of being soft on criminals and sympathising with them. As in so many areas of policy, things are never quite that clear-cut.

Just as we tend to judge the NHS by our own experience of it, the same is true in the field of crime and punishment. If we have reason to deal with the police, it's usually because something bad has happened, and we judge the police on the way they respond both in words and actions.

Back when I worked in London's Doughty Street, one Sunday a burglar broke into our offices before being frightened off by the alarm. On the Monday a bike was stolen from outside our offices and on Tuesday five cars were broken into, including my own. Naturally we rang the police, but unsurprisingly they didn't want to know.

This is a prime example of why many people have little confidence in the police. If they're not willing to investigate five car break-ins, just what are they willing to do?

And that's why crime appears to be falling. It's in part because people like me don't bother to report them, because there's no confidence that anything will be done. The crime figures aren't worth the paper they are written on.

One morning in January 2018, my new mobile phone was snatched out of my hand by a man on the back of a moped. I'd only had the wretched thing for six days. It happened so quickly it took a few seconds for my brain to compute what had happened. At first you feel a fool, then you feel angry. It was only when someone told me I'd been lucky I hadn't had acid chucked at my face that I started to realise how serious it could have been.

Back in 2004, only a week after someone stole my mobile phone from the front seat of my car, I was the victim of a road rage attack – by a cyclist! It culminated in me chasing after a man who had attacked my car and smashed the car window with a D-Lock metal bar. With the help of a passer-by, I apprehended the culprit and the police were called. The man was arrested and charged with causing criminal damage. The attack shattered my car window and left several dents in my car. I spent nearly three hours at the police station making a statement. It just wasn't my day – while making the statement I received a parking ticket. The police promised to help get it cancelled!

The police let the man off with a warning, despite the fact he had been violent towards me and had damaged my car. I couldn't believe it. They had the evidence and multiple witnesses, yet refused to do anything more because it was a first-time offence. Forgive me if my confidence in the police was as shattered as my car window that day.

These crimes happened to me some time before the well-publicised cuts in police numbers, and I am not someone who thinks that crime will automatically fall if we have more police. More police walking down our high streets may do wonders for public reassurance, but it does little to prevent or solve crime. I'm ambivalent about more visible policing. In some ways it's a luxury we simply can't afford. With the changing face of crime, and in particular the rise in cyber-crime, we have got to think quite radically about the way we police our nation.

It's the same at the other end of the crime and justice system in our prisons. If our police service is in a state, prisons policy is a complete and utter shambles. The only way prison works at the moment is that people are locked up and not able to commit further crimes. Beyond that, it doesn't work at all.

Just look at this country's rate of repeat offending. Our prison population is at an all-time high. Indeed, it's double what it was in 1993, and yet we're told that non-violent crime rates are at an all-time low. Something doesn't compute there, does it? I am very happy to lock up serious offenders, people who are a danger to society. Indeed, I'd lock most of them up for far longer. However, there are thousands of people in prison who don't need to be there, if only we were able to dream up alternative forms of punishment.

What is the point of putting people in prison if they are no danger to society, if their crimes are not serious? What is the point of imprisoning someone for not paying a TV licence fine, or council tax? And, of course, once people get to prison, they end up on the highway to hell. They're locked up in their cells for most of the day due to a chronic lack of prison officers to look after them. Educational resources are at a minimum. Sixty per cent of released prisoners can't read or write. Is it any wonder then that it's becoming increasingly difficult for recently released prisoners to find a job?

Add to this the drugs. Stories are legion of people who go into prison never having taken a drug in their lives but come out addicted to the hard stuff.

There are constant calls for prison regimes to be tougher and less like a holiday camp. This is short-sighted thinking. If you treat people like animals while they are incarcerated, don't be surprised if their behaviour doesn't change when they are released. I'm not saying prisoners should live in the lap of luxury, but surely losing their freedom is punishment enough for the crime they have committed. Imposing Victorian conditions merely means that a violent rebellion is at some point inevitable.

When he was Justice Secretary, Jack Straw banned prisoners at Whitemoor Prison from learning about how to write a comedy script or do stand-up. They were taking part in an eight-day course as part of an education programme. What harm could possibly have been done by learning about comedy script writing and improvisation? I'd have thought learning how to defuse potentially harmful situations by the use of humour was a good thing. Instead, Jack Straw jerked his knee and responded to tabloid outrage. Not only that, but he ordered an inquiry! He then issued a Prison Service Instruction to all governors, telling them that, when making decisions about arts interventions, they must ensure projects 'meet the public acceptability test' and consider how the activity might 'be perceived if open to media scrutiny'.

Prison is a balance between punishment and rehabilitation. I don't believe in going soft on people in prison – but neither do I believe that activities that make them want to learn and develop should be discouraged.

Goethe once wrote that 'The decline of literature indicates the decline of a nation.'

Back in 2014 when the coalition government announced it was banning friends and family from sending books to prisoners in jail, I scratched my head in disbelief. If you're banged up in a cell for 23 hours a day, surely allowing prisoners free access to books is just the sort of thing a prison governor would want to encourage just to keep them occupied. If you believe the maxim that the devil makes work for idle hands, it is a pretty obvious thing to do.

The government justified the ban on the basis that drugs, and other things, were being sent into prisons, hidden in packages, including those containing books. An understandable response maybe, but in my view totally over the top. Prisons have libraries, so books are available to prisoners, but quite often these have a fairly restricted choice. They are not run by prisons but by local authorities.

Given the claim that things were being smuggled into prison, I didn't think it unfair to suggest that the Prison Service needed to look at its security procedures. And in addition, was it beyond the wit of the Ministry of Justice to come to an arrangement with Amazon or Waterstone's so that family and friends could order books from them to be delivered securely to prisons?

Being tough doesn't just mean locking people up and throwing away the key. A tough politician will take tough choices – and that means locking up fewer people and devoting more resources to preparing prisoners for life on the outside. Only in that way will reoffending rates drop. Prison is indeed about punishment, but it is also about rehabilitation. You don't have to be left wing to believe that. It is the mark of a decent society.

I've only been to prison twice. Thankfully not as an inmate. Once I visited a man in Shepton Mallet prison who was serving 25 years for murder. He wanted to write a book when he came out. For various reasons it never happened. The second occasion was to visit a friend who had been sent to prison for a relatively short sentence. I have a policy when a friend is in trouble or falls on hard times – I stand by them. It's what friends do. What I have found time and time again is that this is when people in trouble really find out who their friends are.

I arrived at Lincoln prison with a certain degree of trepidation. I suppose I was afraid that the conversation might be a bit stilted and that five months in this rather Victorian institution might have really changed my friend. I queued up in the waiting room along with all forms of human life.

My time soon arrived and I was led through three gates to the visiting room. I'm not sure what I was expecting, but I was led to a numbered table where my friend was waiting. It was all fairly informal, with us sitting on a sofa and soft chair. The time flew by and two hours later it was time to leave.

I was glad I went. My friend seemed to really appreciate it. It had been a round trip of three hundred miles or so but I am pleased I took the time to do it. I know if it had been me, it would have meant a lot. And you know, there really was a feeling of 'there but for the grace of God go I'. I don't think I have ever done anything that could have merited going to prison, but then again, in my opinion, nor had my friend.

One of the big challenges facing the prison system is how to deal with prisoners who have been convicted of terror offences. The fact that Usman Khan, the man who killed two people on London Bridge in November 2019, was released on licence, despite being a clear and present danger to society, demonstrates that things need tightening up, as does the release of the Streatham knife attacker Sudesh Amman, who had only served half of his 16-year sentence, yet under the law had to be released. Scandalous. But he's not the only person to be released far earlier than most people would think he should have been.

In October 2018 the Islamist hate preacher Anjem Choudary was released from prison after serving only three years of a five-a-half-year sentence for inciting Muslims to join Daesh.

The then Prisons Minister Rory Stewart gave an interview to the *London Evening Standard* in which he said Choudary 'poses a genuine threat' to public safety and is a 'deeply pernicious destabilising influence'. He said MI5 and the police would need to 'watch him like a hawk' to stop him from inciting further violence.

We know, after all, that various terror perpetrators in this country, including the two killers of Lee Rigby, were disciples of Choudary, as was Khuram Butt, one of the London Bridge attackers.

So one has to ask why on earth was he released? Why didn't he serve his full sentence? As with Usman Khan, it's apparently because the judge who sentenced him gave him a 'determinate' sentence, and by law he had to be released after serving half of it, unless he had misbehaved in prison. Well, given that he had to be transferred to a so-called 'Jihadi Jail' in County Durham because he had been trying to radicalise other prisoners, you'd have thought his was an open-and-shut case for the prison authorities to insist he should serve his full sentence.

You'd have also thought that the Home Secretary or the Justice Secretary could intervene on national security grounds. Again, apparently not.

You do have to wonder what is the point of being Prisons Minister, or even Home Secretary, if they can't intervene on cases like this. Michael Howard sold the pass in some ways when he was Home Secretary and took away his powers to intervene in life sentence cases. Choudary, of course, was not serving a life sentence, so even if Howard hadn't changed the rules, the Home Secretary couldn't have intervened in this case.

Many called for Choudary to be deported. But where to, and under what grounds? He was born in Welling and is a British citizen. You can't just deport British citizens who hold a British passport. And which other country would take him anyway?

We are where we are. You'd have thought the prison authorities might be able to find some reason not to release him, but perhaps they were only too keen to get him off their hands. But what about the probation authorities?

Surely in order to be released you have to accept you've committed a crime, and also to show some remorse and repentance. It's clear that Choudary has done neither.

In the long term I think we need to look at some law changes. The maximum sentence for crimes like the ones he committed need to be increased to life imprisonment. At the time of writing the government has introduced emergency laws to prevent terror offenders being released automatically after having served their sentences. But that's just a stop-gap, sticking-plaster law. It just delays the inevitable release.

We also need to have a debate on whether the offence of treason needs to be reintroduced.

I believe it is treasonous to pledge allegiance to a proscribed terror organisation that seeks to bring about the destruction of the United Kingdom by random acts of terror. If people still pledge allegiance to Daesh when they know the consequences, then I believe they should be tried in a court of law for that offence, as well as any others they have committed. They should then receive an indeterminate sentence that enables them to be kept off the streets of our towns and cities for as long as is deemed necessary by the parole authorities. Yes, the human rights lawyers will scream very loudly, but the balance of legal scales has tipped far too firmly in their direction over the last 20 years.

The problem is, there is no single answer to this problem. Short-term solutions rarely work. It's a bit like the knife-crime issue. It needs a long-term solution, not all of which is about law or policing. A lot of it is about attitudinal change, which is necessarily long term.

You could treble the policing budgets, double the amount of money going into MI5 and the prison system, but if you can't root out the cancer of Islamist Jihadism, it will all be for nothing.

The language of crime and justice is necessarily toxic. Politicians feel pressure to appear tough and it's only when they're out of office that they suddenly discover their liberal side. For me as a talk show host, the easy thing to do is pander to listeners who think hanging or flogging is the answer to everything. I merely try to deploy calm logic to explain that being tough on crime is all very well, but prevention is far better than cure. And given that prisons are about the worst place to 'cure' an offender, it's far better to look at other ways we can punish or rehabilitate those found guilty of crimes. I might as well whistle in the wind sometimes, but at least I can try to make people think again and challenge some of their inbuilt prejudices.

Chapter 13

The Opium of
the People

'I am an Agnostic because I am not afraid to think. I
am not afraid of any god in the universe who would
send me or any other man or woman to hell. If there
were such a being, he would not be a god;
he would be a devil.'

Clarence Darrow

Even when I was a campanologist (no sniggering at the back), ringing the bells at our village church, I didn't believe in God. OK, I was only a teenager, and I was only ringing the bells each Sunday as the lesser of two evils. It was that or being a choirboy.

I had a typical rural upbringing. I went to the local Church of England primary school, my mother did the church flowers once a month, partly out of a genuine sense of community duty but also because as a farmer's wife it was expected of her, and every so often we'd be dragged along to the Sunday morning service to take Holy

Communion. I hated the wafer-thin fake bread and loathed the red wine even more.

I remember sitting there willing the hour away. I quite liked the hymns, but I just couldn't get my head around reciting a whole lot of religious doggerel and worshipping some imaginary supreme being. By that stage I didn't believe in Father Christmas or fairies at the bottom of the garden either. My father rarely came to church, but on one occasion that he ventured there I remember the vicar saying rather sarcastically how nice it was to see him there. He snapped back: 'I don't need to attend church every Sunday to prove my Christian credentials; I do that every day of the week.' Collapse of stout vicar.

There are two sorts of Christians – those whose entire life and philosophy is governed by strict adherence to scripture, and those who try to live their life by what they think Jesus Christ would have done, or would have wanted.

I've never felt I needed moral guidance from a religion of any kind. I know what's right and I know what's wrong. My parents taught me that. However, I have always been fascinated by religions of all kinds, mainly because I can see that millions of people get a lot out of them. I've tried to understand what that is, but have never succeeded. When I was at university I had many friends who were members of the chaplaincy – nowadays renamed the UEA Multifaith Centre. I went along to quite a few of their meetings in a vain attempt to see if I could relate to them. I remember many a late-night chat discussing religion and why I wasn't religious. No one tried to convert me, but I have to say I was open to it. It never happened. Why? Because even though I am not scientifically trained, I do try to deal with facts and logic. I cannot for the life of me understand how people who are clearly intelligent can on the one hand believe in a God, yet on the other decry the existence of the supernatural. Surely the two go hand in hand.

I'd love to believe there is an afterlife and that in some way I could be reunited with my parents, my grandmother, my godmother and my dogs. But there isn't. It's scientifically impossible. Our so-called spirits die with our bodies. We don't go to heaven. We don't go to hell. We are buried or cremated. The end. We only live on in other people's memories, on film or through the words we have written. I'd love to believe it is otherwise.

Religious advocates maintain that they bring peace and love to communities all over the world. All religions maintain that their purpose is peace, yet the truth is often very different. It may be a lazy claim, but without religion, many, if not most, of the world's greatest conflicts in history would not have happened. Political leaders may sometimes use religion as a convenient pretext for their wider aims, when it is just cover for the emptiness of their rhetoric or policy. Similarly, many religious leaders are often nothing of the sort. They use their positions to promulgate political messages that have scant to do with the religion they purport to represent, but religion again provides a useful cover.

These are the very people who sow division and thrive on it. No number of appeals to dial down the rhetoric will have any effect on them whatsoever. Creating division and discord is what they are all about. Without that, they are utterly ineffectual and impotent.

It doesn't matter which religion we are talking about, religious fundamentalism is wrong, but it's on the rise across the globe. In a world in turmoil, more and more people seem to be turning to extremes for the answers, whether it be in politics or religion. My religion, right or wrong, encapsulates a position that too many people are adhering to.

Take what is happening in the United States, where religious fundamentalists have far too much influence both nationally and at state level. When I first went to the United States in 1987, I was proud to support the Republican Party of Ronald Reagan. There were a few differences between the Republicans and the UK Conservative Party, but there was little doubt that they were sister parties.

Since the mid-1990s, the two parties have drifted apart in both philosophy and politics. The Republican Party has in large part been taken over by religious zealots. It is less of a political party nowadays, more of a religious sect. Take this example.

In May 2019, 25 white, middle-aged Republican state senators in Alabama voted en bloc to ban abortion in Alabama. Not restrict it; ban it. Even in cases of rape or incest. They've done it in the full expectation, or even hope, that it will be challenged in the courts. Their expectation is that it will be used to overturn *Roe v. Wade* (the 1973 landmark ruling that enshrined protection of a woman's right to choose to have an abortion) in the Supreme Court. They believe that Trump's three conservative Supreme Court appointments, Neil Gorsuch, Amy Coney Barrett and Brett Kavanaugh, will vote the 'right' way.

We'll see. It's very difficult now for any pro-choice Republican to run for office any longer. Absolutism has won the day. And if you show any signs of not being a fully-fledged God-fearing Christian, then you're well advised to do something else with your life. I don't know how many agnostics or atheists run for Republican office nowadays, but I suspect it's a very low percentage.

God help this country (if you'll pardon the expression), or indeed the Conservative Party, if we ever venture down this road. But there are already signs that religion is playing a far larger part in UK domestic political life than it ever used to.

Some religious adherents seem to think they are above the law. They use 2,000-year-old practices to justify why they should be able to ignore laws that the rest of us regard as perfectly sensible. Take animal rights and male circumcision, for instance.

Balanced broadcasting is all about offending people equally – so in May 2019 I furthered that cause by offending both Muslims and Jews. Twice. On successive days, I hosted phone-ins on whether Iceland is right to ban male circumcision, and then on whether Halal and Kosher animal slaughter should be outlawed in the UK, as the Danes have done.

It's safe to say that peace and harmony didn't break out on either subject. I'm quite clear that I don't believe in inflicting unnecessary pain on babies or animals – a view that doesn't seem to be prevalent among proponents of either religion. Indeed, it was seriously argued that circumcision causes no pain to babies because they can't feel it. It was likened to a paper cut, can you believe?

It was also argued that it's more hygienic not to have a foreskin. The point no one could counter was when I said that if God hadn't wanted us to have a foreskin, he wouldn't have given us one. And if it was so useless, why hasn't it been bred out of us?

People also argued that slitting an animal's throat causes it no pain. They claimed it severed a nerve. Luckily, a vet rang in to explain that they have been misled, and that the animals would be in a great deal of pain. The fact that many Halal/Kosher abattoirs fail hygiene tests didn't seem to worry the proponents of religious slaughter.

I was also informed by my guest from Halal Consultations that the Prophet Mohammed himself had decreed that animals should be slaughtered in this way. I perhaps didn't help interfaith understanding by telling him: 'I don't care what your prophet thinks: we live in the twenty-first century, not the Dark Ages' – but there we go. If we can't, as a society, agree that if we have to kill chickens, sheep and cows so we can eat them, then pain must be minimised as much as possible, how can we describe ourselves as humane?

Another example of religious fundamentalism rearing its ugly head is in the area of same-sex education in schools. It is the law of the land, under the Equalities Act, that primary schools must teach their pupils that not all children live in families with a mummy and a daddy. Some have only one parent, some have a mummy and a mummy, others have a daddy and a daddy. This is not teaching children about sex; it's about relationship education. This distinction seems to elude those who oppose the teaching of relationship education. It came to a head at the Anderton Park primary school in Birmingham where the award-winning deputy head had drawn up a series of lessons designed to address these issues. Demonstrators said the school was using 'children as pawns' by teaching LGBT equality in lessons that are 'over-emphasising a gay ethos'. Whatever that is. These demonstrators comprised parents – predominantly Muslim parents – but also some professional agitators.

I interviewed the local MP, Roger Godsiff, who had come out against the lessons. I accused him of 'pandering to religious beliefs', and suggested that he was just after votes from parents. Mr Godsiff said I was 'entitled to make that assumption'. I was astonished that he was a Labour MP who seemed to be against equality even though he had voted for the Equalities Act, as well as other recent legislation relating to 'relationship education'. He said it was not a 'question of content'. I responded: 'No, it's a question of hypocrisy.' I accused him of voting for the legislation but not supporting its enactment. Mr Godsiff maintained: 'I do believe it should be taught,' but he said he did not believe the material was appropriate for primary-school-aged pupils. I then asked him if he thought teachers were a better judge of what subjects are age-appropriate than an 'MP who is purely after Muslim votes'. Teachers are entitled to have an opinion, but so are parents, Mr Godsiff said.

This Labour MP was not used to having his views questioned in a robust manner, and he came close to ending the interview at one point. To me, he represented all that is wrong with some modern-day politicians. He's not alone in pandering to religious minorities, but that can't excuse his appalling sense of moral values. To be fair, many of his fellow Labour MPs were as appalled as I was.

The Anglican Church, of which the Church of England is the leading player, is split asunder on the issue of homosexuality. Just recently the leaders of the Anglican Church voted to sanction the US Episcopal Church for its liberal stance on homosexuality in general and gay marriage in particular. It was a murky decision. Some felt that the values they held of Christian empathy and inclusion were sacrificed on the altar of what Bishop Stephen Lowe called the 'altar of false unity for Anglican Communion'.

If marriage is such a great institution – and it is – why is it that some of the more recidivist members of various religions find it so wrong that gay people want to access its benefits too. How does my being married to a man threaten or undermine anyone else's marriage or relationship?

Some Christians cling on to the fact that certain passages in the Old Testament apparently clearly condemn the 'evils' of homosexuality. But other passages censure the evils of eating shellfish or of wearing mixed fibres, and claim that the best way to deal with adulterous women is to stone them. However, depending on which translation you read, the New Testament barely mentions homosexuality. Just as importantly, if a 'New' New Testament were to be written today, does anyone seriously think there would be any condemnation of homosexuality at all?

Fundamentalist Christians would do well to actually study the life and beliefs of Jesus Christ himself. I may not believe in God, but I do believe Jesus existed. And from what I know he would be one of the last people to condemn anyone who found true love. Even if he still abided by the belief than 'man shall not lie with man', he would be compassionate and empathetic to those men who did. Or do. He certainly wouldn't want anyone publicly shamed, stoned or thrown off the top of a building.

I'm afraid there is no way of keeping the Anglican Church united. Women bishops started the fragmentation. Gay vicars and gay marriage are likely to lead to a schism. The dogmatic and recidivist views of the African Anglican Churches will never reconcile with the increasingly liberal attitudes displayed by many in the leadership of the Church of England or the US Episcopal Church.

Having written all of the above, I've probably given the impression that I am an out-and-out atheist. The truth is somewhat more nuanced. If anything, I class myself as an agnostic, purely on the basis that I can't prove one way or the other whether God exists or not, and until someone can provide me with evidence, how can I possibly be anything other than on the fence? Some people consider atheism to be a religion in itself, and I can see why. It revolves around the kind of absolutism and certainty of mind that motivates religious zealots all over the world.

The title of this book is one that people of all religions ought to relate to. If they did, perhaps there would be far less religious conflict in the world.

Chapter 14

The Gay Thing

'My first words, as I was being born … I looked up
at my mother and said, "That's the last time I'm
going up one of those."'

Stephen Fry

In gay-world, language seems to matter more than ever.
We're no longer part of an LBG or LGBT community, it's
LGBTQI or even LGBTQIAPK. Yup, me neither. For gay
activists these letters are incredibly important, but to the
average gay person living a normal life they are not life
defining. I am a man who happens to be gay, not someone
who's gay who happens to be a man.

There is a theory that suggests we're all on a spectrum of
gayness. If you draw a line, with 1 being 100 per cent straight
and 100 being 100 per cent gay, we're all somewhere on that
line.

I always knew I was different. I probably didn't know it
meant I was homosexual. I just had this feeling, which I
knew was different. Well, when I say always, I mean I knew

I was different to other boys from the age of seven or eight. I have absolutely no doubt that I was born gay, yet I find it bizarre that some find that difficult to accept. There are still misguided souls who believe that people choose to be gay.

I must have been around 12 or 13, I suppose, when I got out of bed and crept into my parents' bedroom. 'Mum, I think I've wet the bed,' I whispered. She got out of bed, grabbed some new sheets and ripped the old ones off the bed. She looked at me slightly quizzically and said, 'Er, you haven't wet the bed. Hasn't your father talked to you about this?' I was totally mystified. She sat me down and explained that I'd just had a wet dream. I was, of course, mortified.

My father hadn't discussed the birds and the bees with me, nor had my mother.

It was little better at school. We had to wait until we were 14 to get any form of sex education, and to be honest it was a joke. Mr Maidment, head of Geography and Mrs Mathias, head of Needlework, broached the subject in General Studies. Mrs Mathias would rather have been anywhere else than teaching sex education to a group of 100 giggly teenagers, while Mr Maidment rejoiced in telling us how he would 'hump' Mrs M every Saturday night without fail. It was titillation rather than education at Saffron Walden County High in 1976. And God forbid the thought that anyone should mention homosexuality, which had, of course, only been legal for a decade at that point.

Forty years on, not a lot has changed in some families. Mothers and fathers up and down the land recoil from the embarrassment of discussing condoms and cunnilingus. Schools may be rather more enlightened than in the 1970s, but the standard of sex education is incredibly variable. Even in 2020 some parents even withdraw their kids from it, and they're invariably the sheltered kids who most need it because they won't be told it in the home environment.

It's time that there was a complete review of sex education in this country. Children encounter sexual issues at an ever-younger age. I was 14 or 15 before I even knew what the word 'wanking' meant. By contrast, the eight-year-old daughter of a relative of mine learned what a clitoris was in her sex education lessons a couple of years ago. Most 11-year-olds have viewed pornography. It's all a long way from the 'I'll show you mine if you show me yours' of my youth.

There are still teachers out there who are reluctant to talk about homosexuality for fear of contravening Section 28. They don't even know the Blair government got rid of it. And what of the parents, often ones with devout religious views, who refuse to allow their children to take part in what are now known as Relationships and Sex Education (RSE)? Should the state overrule their wishes in the interests of the children?

In the long term, we have to realise this subject can only be taught by professionals, rather than geography and maths teachers whose hearts aren't in it and who aren't experts in the subject. I'd like to see an army of Relationships and Sex teachers recruited and trained, who would travel from school to school within their borough or county. Yes, there would be a cost to that, but if it helps children cope with the emotions and trials of puberty and adulthood, wouldn't it be money well spent?

I remember as a young teenager being turned on by graffiti on the walls of public toilets. I remember at the age of 14 or 15 making an advance on a school friend, which wasn't reciprocated. Looking back, that fear of rejection sent me back into the closet. I went out with girls and had genuine feelings for them. There was even one I would have happily married. But when it came to sex, I went so far and no further. Looking back, I know I broke more than a few hearts. I remember the look of incomprehension and hurt on one girl's face when she realised I didn't want to have full sex with her.

People who believe we all choose to be gay should think back to when I was growing up in the 1970s. Homosexuality wasn't illegal, but it might as well have been. Being raised in a small village in Essex meant conformity to a relatively conservative rural lifestyle. I loved my childhood, but it did mean hiding a part of who I was, even from those closest to me. To have come out would have been unthinkable.

To most people, homosexuality came in the form of John Inman and Larry Grayson. It meant camp cries of 'shut that door' or 'I'm free'. It meant furtive fumbles in public toilets. In short, it was seen as a perversion, which few were willing to even try to understand or empathise with. Why anyone would have chosen to be a homosexual in those days is anyone's guess.

Today it is very different. In some ways, it's cool to be gay, so for some of our more bigoted members of society, you can sort of understand why they really believe it is a lifestyle choice.

Believe me, I am very comfortable in my own skin. Were I now given the choice of being straight, I wouldn't take it. But I suspect most of us, if we really examined ourselves deeply, might have given a different answer at the age of 15.

Because life is undeniably easier if you're straight.

In some jobs being gay is still a big no-no. Gay people continue to suffer from discrimination, especially outside metropolitan areas. Being gay in some religions can lead to excommunication and total exclusion from one's family. From a personal viewpoint, I have absolutely no doubt I would now be a Member of Parliament were it not for the fact that I was/am gay, and eventually didn't mind who knew it.

On my LBC show I had a caller recently who told me she detested the 'gay act' and it was terrible that people should choose this lifestyle. She clearly hadn't got a clue, poor love, who she was talking to. So in my usual loving, caring way I gently pointed out, from one who knows, that being gay wasn't a choice. You were born like it. She still didn't click. 'I knew I was gay at the age of seven,' I then said. There followed an awkward two-second silence, which on the radio sounds like two minutes. Whether I provoked her to examine her own prejudices I have no idea.

And then on Eurovision night it all started again. This time on Twitter. A fellow West Ham fan called Brian – someone who clearly believed it's not possible to be gay and shout 'Come on You Irons' every fortnight – told me that 'nature, history and religion are against you. It is nurture and environment and perverse thinking.' Thanks for that. He continued: 'Our minds are malleable and can be turned.' Speak for yourself, mate. And finally came this little gem: 'We are all born heterosexual and get influenced to be gay in our twisted minds.' When I asked him if, as a straight man, he could be turned, strangely, I didn't get an answer.

You may think it bizarre, but I don't regard people like my LBC caller and Brian as homophobic. I just think they're scared of something they have a fear of. Because they think that we've all chosen to become gay, they think we could persuade their kids to turn gay too. You might think it's laughable, and it is, but it's up to us all to show that being gay is nothing for them to fear.

Why is it that people who know they're gay find it so difficult to acknowledge it to themselves or to others? One of the reasons is because having the 'coming out' conversation with friends and family is a very daunting thought. Even in these enlightened days there are still many gay people who find that particular conversation difficult to have.

I had that conversation at the ripe old age of 40. My parents had known my partner, John, for five or six years and he often joined me for the weekend at their home. But the penny hadn't dropped. He was my friend and they liked him very much. But the fact that he was more than that never seemed to click with them. By way of contrast, my partner came out to his parents at the age of 16 and didn't like the fact that I wasn't prepared to rock the parental boat. He was right, of course. I was being a coward.

But when I decided to try to be a Tory MP, I decided that I had to tell my parents I was gay. Everyone in Westminster knew, and I didn't want my parents reading about it in the *Daily Telegraph* or one of their friends saying something inopportune. I decided to do it when I reached the second round of a parliamentary selection – possibly not the best or most courageous criteria to use to come out.

I remember that drive round the M25 and up the M11 as if it were yesterday. I rehearsed in my mind what I would say, but nothing ever seemed right. Everyone kept saying to me, 'Don't worry, it won't come as a surprise to them. They must know.' I doubted that very much. After all, I knew my parents, and they didn't.

My dad was always good in a crisis. He was a man of few words, but I was fairly confident he would be OK. My mother was the sweetest and most kindly woman in the world, but I sensed it would be more difficult for her. I won't go into the details of the conversation, but it wasn't an easy one. There was incomprehension, bemusement and a degree of horror. I explained that John was much more than a friend, that I loved him very deeply and I hoped they could bring themselves to accept that. My dad gave me a hug, but my mum just had a far-away look on her face. The next morning she told my sister that she wished she had never woken up.

But all was well that ended well. They continued to welcome John into their home and came to treat him as a son-in-law; both also came to our civil partnership ceremony in 2008. However, the subject of my gayness was never spoken of again. My mother died in 2012. I loved her with all my heart, but in my soul I know how much I had hurt her. In the end, though, we can't live our lives for other people no matter how much we love them. We have to be true to ourselves. That's not being selfish, it's being honest.

I find it incredibly frustrating that the old gay stereotypes still remain, and probably always will. We're all either incredibly camp, have lots of facial and stomach hair, and probably sleep with any other male who shows a vague interest. Oh, and we're all incapable of being in a relationship without sleeping with other men, we have an unhealthy interest in Shirley Bassey, we all boogie away in nightclubs with our shirts off with white powder up our noses, and spend our evenings engaging in orgies or feasting our eyes on gay porn.

The truth is that most of us live very ordinary lives and consider ourselves normal, law-abiding members of society. We do the same things other people do. We live in perfectly ordinary houses without a sex dungeon (actually I did know someone who had one of those, but it ruins my thesis …), we drive the same cars, because, believe it or not, we don't all like the open-top Jeeps the bloke in *Queer as Folk* drove. We buy normal people's magazines. For goodness sake, I even have subscriptions to *Stuff*, *FourFourTwo* and *GQ*.

Society likes to box us into little homogeneous groups, and in a media-driven age it suits a lot of agendas to pretend that somehow we are all the same. But we're not. We're individuals who each lead totally different lives with different tastes, habits and proclivities.

In many ways the internet age ought to have liberated us all from the stranglehold of stereotypes, but in some ways the opposite has happened. Mainstream media narratives still dominate. Tories are still rich toffs. UKIP supporters are racist little Englanders. Liberal Democrats are basket-weaving sandal wearers. Labour voters wear flat caps and own whippets. If a black man drives a BMW he has probably stolen it. Anyone wearing a hoodie is likely to mug you. Gay men will shag anything with a penis. You get the picture.

It is clear to me that one of the things that drives the promulgation of stereotypes is often fear of the unknown. Often it is a perfectly understandable fear. Animals fear what they don't know, so why shouldn't humans? Let me give an example. I took a call on my radio programme during a discussion on street crime. An elderly white lady phoned in to tell me how she feared being mugged by the various groups of hooded kids on her estate. One day she was walking home and saw a group of them looking menacing on a street corner. She panicked and dropped a bag of shopping. Immediately one of the hoodies came over and, instead of nicking the shopping, helped her put it back in her bag and even carried it home for her. She said she felt thoroughly ashamed for thinking the worst was about to happen. Another barrier broken down.

We bought a house in Norfolk in 2013. I suspect we're the only gays in the village. I have to say that everyone has been incredibly friendly, but I had to laugh when one of the neighbours blurted out: 'You're both very normal, aren't you?' I didn't know whether to laugh or cry. Normal for Norfolk, as the saying goes.

Virtually every gay couple I know I consider to be 'normal'. OK, one or two may be slightly more exotic than others, but that's the same in the world of 'straightery' too. Perhaps we are too defensive about gay stereotypes and, instead of fighting them, we shouldn't give two hoots about them. Because in the end, we know who we are. We don't need to be told by society.

Whenever I do phone-ins on gay issues on the radio, I am pleasantly surprised by the enlightened view taken by my callers. Most of them, even those on the hard Right, can see the case for gay marriage. Why? Because nowadays they all know someone who is gay. That would not have been the case 20 years ago. People fear the unknown and that's totally understandable. Nowadays they may have a gay son, daughter, nephew, niece, postman, doctor. They see gay people represented in the media. Gay has become normal in everyday life.

Back in the late 1980s, Section 28 allowed many tabloid and broadsheet newspapers to launch vicious attacks on gay people, the like of which I'd like to think we wouldn't see today. Indeed, it is fair to say that, by and large, even papers like the *Sun* and the *Mail* are far more sympathetic to us than they have ever been before. That's not to say there isn't room for improvement; there is.

However, it would be crass to pretend that on issues like civil partnerships, and celebrities and sportspeople being comfortable to declare their sexuality, times haven't changed. Even on equal marriage the most homophobic parts of the *Daily Mail* have struggled to be as outraged as they once might have been.

The truth is that most newspapers are led by the lifestyles and proclivities of their readers, and the editor of the *Sun* knows full well that most of his or her readers have a much more liberal attitude to gay issues than they did even ten years ago. That's why when Tom Daley came out, their copy oozed understanding and empathy in a way that scarcely five years earlier would have been incredible. Even when they had a front-page 'EXCLUSIVE' on his boyfriend being the ripe old age of 39, the article itself was less prurient than a normal *Sun* reader might have expected. And the next day, its front page not only ran a story with the sympathetic headline 'POP HUNK PAL WHO HELPED DIVE STAR COME OUT', but also ran another about a girl who believes she is a boy. This wasn't a sidebar story; it was the main front-page splash. Twenty years ago, one can only imagine the headline Kelvin MacKenzie might have used, but instead, in December 2013, it was headlined 'I'M A BOY, SAYS TWIN GIRL 6 – MUM FIGHTS BIGOTS'. And inside was a double-page spread giving a totally sympathetic hearing to the mother.

The fact that celebrities declaring themselves gay is still considered news shows that there is still some way to go before full equality is achieved. The day when a boyband member, or a celebrity like Philip Schofield, doesn't consider it necessary to announce to the world he is gay, but merely turns up to an awards ceremony holding hands with his latest beau, will be the day when we can think to ourselves that our work is done.

It's easy to criticise the press, especially the tabloid press, but let's not pretend that their coverage of how gay people are being treated in other parts of the world is anything other than exemplary. Vladimir Putin will have been furious to see page after page ridiculing his anti-gay laws.

So yes, the media can be infuriating and outrageous at times. But let's acknowledge that its coverage of gay people and gay issues has changed for the better in the last few years. Credit where credit is due.

Not every battle is yet won, however. Back in the 1960s and 1970s, most people took the view that the words 'homosexual' and 'paedophile' were more or less interchangeable. If your predilection were of the male-on-male variety, you didn't particularly differentiate between men and boys. That viewpoint is still shamefully held by many, especially if they write on this subject for the *Daily Mail* or belong to some sort of religious fundamentalist group.

I remember a time, not so long ago, when I was involved in a discussion with a senior Tory MP about gay adoption. His line of argument was based around the apparently harmless notion that we must always 'think of the children'. I got rather angry. 'What you're effectively saying is that gay men are more likely to abuse a child than straight men.' He started blustering, but that was exactly what he meant. He also came out with the old canard that gay parents would inevitably turn their children gay, even if they didn't mean to. I don't know any gay parents whose kids have grown up to be gay, although by the law of averages some no doubt do.

It is, of course, nonsense to suggest that gay men have any greater predilection for underage sex than straight men. Or women come to that matter. I'd no more want to have sex with an underage boy than my own grandmother, and she's been dead for 40 years. Of course there are paedophiles among gay men, just as there are among straight men, yet from the way the issue is still covered in some newspapers you'd think the proportion was 90/10. For some reason, newspapers seem titillated (if that's the right word) by priests or politicians who get caught with young boys. They cover these stories with a sexual prurience that you just don't find in stories about a builder abusing his 12-year-old daughter. The truth is that most abuse occurs in the home or between family members, regardless if it is between family members of the same sex or otherwise.

These myths about gay stereotypes can either be reinforced or shattered by the way gay people are portrayed in the media. Think about the gay characters you see in TV and movie dramas and then think about how many of them accurately reflect your life, if you're gay, or the characters of your gay friends. Not many, are there?

On the positive side, there are many more gay characters in soaps and other TV shows, but they do tend to be of a 'type'.

Equality will only be achieved in this country when our sexuality becomes almost an irrelevance. Just as I cringe whenever I hear the phrase 'the gay actor' or the 'gay Labour candidate', I inwardly smile whenever I see an article about a gay person of note that doesn't even mention their sexuality because it's just not relevant to the piece. I well remember my irritation when, many years ago, I was described in the *Observer*, by their left-of-centre political editor, Gaby Hinsliff, as 'Iain Dale, the gay Conservative candidate'. It wasn't that I was ashamed. Far from it. But I was a political candidate who happened to be gay, not the other way around. They didn't do it again.

The battle for equality is unlikely ever to be totally won. All we can do is make progress.

Chapter 15

The Language of Business

'There are no secrets to success. It is the result of
preparation, hard work, and learning from failure.'

Colin Powell

Business pays 27 per cent of all UK tax revenues. In the
2018–19 tax year this amounted to £196 billion, up from
£188 billion the year before. Yet from some of the language
used about businesspeople you could be forgiven for thinking they didn't pay any tax at all – that they were modern-
day misers, desperate to avoid any form of tax – entirely
motivated by profit and exploiting their workers. There
appears to be little comprehension that without these tax
revenues we would have no money to fund the main
components of a modern-day welfare state. I don't pretend
all businesspeople are angels, but the language that is used
about them and their motives, usually by uninformed politicians or media commentators, is both destructive and
damaging. In some ways, it's their own fault. Just because
they understand the world of business and commerce, they

sometimes imagine that everyone else does too. Even worse, they often don't think they need to do any persuading. They believe their case is so obvious. In recent years this has changed and we've seen the rise of the commercial lobbyist.

In essence, there is nothing wrong with political lobbying. Most people don't know their way around Westminster and Whitehall, so they hire a public affairs consultant to help them, just as they would hire a lawyer to advise them on the law or an accountant to advise on finances. But in the end, it's money that talks. Individuals haven't got £20,000 a month to pay lobbyists, so if you're fighting a big corporate, it's always an uphill task.

In the 30 years since I entered this murky world of lobbying it has changed a lot. But the one thing that has remained constant is the fact that lobbyists use language to further their clients' aims. What's changed is that the lobbyists have stepped back from advocating a client's case themselves. Instead, they put the words in the client's mouth, and he or she then parrots it to receptive politicians. Another thing that has changed is that it's no longer legal for a public affairs consultancy to pay a Member of Parliament a monthly retainer. Indeed, nowadays it seems outrageous that the practice was ever allowed. It was commonplace for MPs to make speeches in the chamber of the House of Commons or put down parliamentary questions on a client's behalf. It is perfectly proper for an MP to do both of those things if they believe in a campaign, but it should be the power of belief that motivates them, not the persuasive power of monetary remuneration. This sounds obvious now, but in the 1980s and 1990s it wasn't. It was a form of low-level corruption, which was only eradicated in the years after the 'cash for questions' scandal of 1997.

Like me, many ex-House of Commons researchers fall into working for political consultancies by accident rather than by design. Some will be recruited because of who they worked for and their contacts. For example, if a consultancy has clients in the transport field, they will actively try to recruit Commons researchers who might have worked for a transport minister or shadow minister. Let's face it, that was why I beat 200 competitors to the job with the British Ports Association. They were, or so they thought, buying my contacts at the Department of Transport.

Lobbyists portray themselves as strategic advisers, but most lobbyists get into the sector by pimping out their contacts to their clients. It made me feel slightly grubby, but it was part of what you had to do. And it still is.

Let's not pretend, though, that lobbyists don't do valuable work. They do. They help their clients marshal their arguments to the best possible effect. They use the power of language – both written and oral – to persuade politicians and civil servants that they deserve a hearing and that policy needs to be changed. The challenge for those same politicians and civil servants is to determine which parts of the arguments are valid and which are transparently full of bullshit.

Ultimately, it's all about winning hearts and minds. You don't persuade anyone by just presenting cold facts in a worthy, academic document. If you're running a campaign, you don't simply need to appeal to politicians, you also want to persuade other stakeholders to put pressure on the decision makers too. If you're campaigning against the HS2 rail link, for example, it's not enough to say that the business case doesn't stack up; you need to explain what the effect will be on businesses, farms and individual residents in the area that is affected. You run a media campaign designed to put secondary pressure on the decision makers. There's nothing politicians dislike more than being assailed by a combination of newspapers, radio and TV.

The reason the Stronger In campaign lost the Brexit referendum was in large part because they failed to appeal to people's hearts and minds. They used logic, mechanical language and fear to persuade people to vote Remain. By contrast, the Leave campaign projected a message of hope, optimism and positivity. They appealed to people who had never voted before – three million of them – and demonstrated that this was the best chance they would ever have of giving the political establishment a good kicking. They used a negative and turned it into a positive.

Social media has in some ways democratised lobbying. A concerted campaign on Facebook, Twitter and email costs peanuts and can be launched by an individual, but the trouble is, social media campaigns can often be dominated by people whose hearts are in the right place, but whose actions and use of ad hominem language can subvert a campaign or even destroy it. Just on a human basis, if a Member of Parliament is sympathetic to a campaign, he or she is likely to be turned off it if they receive a stream of aggressive social media messages calling into question their motivations and asking why nothing is happening.

Words matter. Careless talk can cost campaigns. Any lobbyist worth their salt knows that. In today's internet-dominated world, campaign leaders cannot control their supporters in the way that was possible 20 years ago.

Command and control is a concept that is now dead. And this is another reason why public discourse has declined. We are allowing emotions to rule our heads in a way that is destructive to the very causes we believe in. Instead of shouting at the TV, we now have the opportunity to shout at politicians and celebrities directly via social media. This lack of emotional self-discipline undermines the very core of the body politic.

I spent the best part of ten years in the world of political lobbying. Some of my best friends are lobbyists, as the saying goes. Would I ever want to darken its doors again? It's highly unlikely, unless I were masterminding a campaign for a cause I believe in very strongly, rather than being paid to do so.

Back in 2015 London Underground drivers went on strike. I was on the train into London listening to one of my colleague James O'Brien's monologues. His main message was that all employers wanted to exploit their workforces, and London Underground was a good example. It was a ten-minute tirade against business, employers and profit. I could hardly believe what I was hearing, so I thought I'd take him to task on my drivetime show. Here's part of what I said:

> Let's start from the premise that not all employers get up
> in the morning thinking, 'How can I exploit my
> workforce today for maximum advantage?' The difference
> between James O'Brien and me is that, so far as I am
> aware, he's never run a business, never employed anyone,
> never created wealth. I have. I've started or run seven
> businesses over the years and I treat people who work for
> me as colleagues, not peasants who I can exploit. I've

probably employed more than 400 people over the years and I'm confident enough to say that not a single one of them would think they have been treated badly by me or any company I have run.

Tube drivers aren't downtrodden workers scratching around for a living. They aren't migrants who come to this country and are exploited by a gangmaster at two quid an hour. These are people on double the average wage in this country. The only people who are suffering are the travelling public whose taxes and fares pay those salaries and who find themselves massively inconvenienced today.

I'm not opposed to all strikes. I had great sympathy with the firefighters, for example, for their fight to protect the pensions they thought they had signed up for. But that's totally different to this. James reckons that employers nowadays have more control over our lives than at any point since the Second World War. Again, an easy soundbite which some will lap up, but it is of course simplistic rubbish. We have equal pay, the 48-hour week, the minimum wage, minimum holiday entitlement, maternity pay, paternity pay, parental leave. None of these things were available in 1974 let alone 1945.

Yes, there are rogue employers, just as there are rogue employees. Yes, there are greedy employers who pay themselves far too much. But we've got to a state in our society where anyone who runs a business, takes a risk, or makes a profit is seen by some in our society as a symptom of what's wrong with this country rather than something to celebrate. It should be the reverse.

When employers get things wrong, we shouldn't be afraid to say so but we shouldn't get it into our heads that

the first thing they do when they get out of bed in the
morning is to think, 'How can I shaft my workforce
today?'

How often do you hear anyone on the media defending
employers or businesspeople? Very rarely, if ever, I'd venture
to suggest. This is the age of the entrepreneur and we should
be shouting about it. The entrepreneurs themselves should
be shouting it from the rooftops, yet they are too busy
making a success of their businesses.

There's never been a better time to start a business, yet
all we hear from the media is gloom and doom. Business
news bulletins are full of high street chains going out of
business, scandals in the city and falling profits. The
maxim that bad news is news and good news is advertising
is nowhere more true than in the world of business. When
did you hear a story about a company experiencing record
profits being reported in an entirely positive manner? I'd
wager to say, never. Even if a record profits story makes the
news, it's invariably accompanied by sneering about the
salary or bonus package of the managing director. It has to
be said that some of these packages are indeed obscene
and cannot be defended, but they are the exception, not
the rule.

Why is it as a society that our default is to look for the
bad in people, rather than the good? The bad businesspeople rather than the good ones? Is it envy, political ideology
or just plain ignorance that leads us to brand all businesspeople as bad apples?

It has to be said that there are a few more business-re-
lated programmes on TV and radio. *Dragons' Den* and *The
Apprentice* attempt to introduce new generations to the

business world, yet is the impression they give the right one? On *The Apprentice*, businesspeople are portrayed as utterly ruthless, mendacious, self-obsessed people who would sell their own grandmother if it earned them a quick buck. Nice people don't succeed is the subliminal message that Lord Sugar gives out, whether he means to or not.

Dragons' Den has become a tabloid caricature of itself. Gone are most of the original dragons, to be replaced by business ogres who too often appear to delight in humiliating the poor saps who are after their investment money.

Since the demise of Adrian Chiles' *Late Lunch* daily business show on BBC2 there has been nothing to replace it. Given the BBC is a public service broadcaster you might think there might be some duty to cover the business world in a meaningful way. Even the hourly business bulletin on the *Today* programme is something that many think the BBC would dearly love to shelve if it could. Radio 5 Live's business coverage has become pedestrian to say the least. News bulletins across the media hype up a minuscule 0.1 per cent fall in GDP yet often don't bother to report a larger rise.

ITV, Channel 4 and Channel 5 fail to cover business matters to any great degree. Sky News is a beacon of business-friendly broadcasting, with its daily hour-long mid-morning business show presented by Ian King.

Why is there such a dearth of business coverage? One reason is that most people who work in broadcasting are liberal arts graduates who have never spent a day of their working lives in the world of commerce or business. They have been educationally programmed to view business with scepticism and suspicion.

One of the big failings of organisations like the CBI, the Institute of Directors and the Federation of Small Businesses is an inability to find ways of selling UK business success. They think facts speak for themselves. Far too often, radio or TV producers ask them to put up someone to comment on a business story, but they have no one available. Eventually, producers give up, and who can blame them? In addition, I suspect viewers tend to switch off when they hear the words 'Confederation', 'Institute' or 'Association'.

If business leaders don't explain their motivations and record, who will do it for them? For too long they have let their reputations be collectively trashed without feeling the need to set the record straight.

Capitalism has its failings, but unless the case is made for it, and why free markets work, the case will go by default. Too many young people are being seduced by socialist economics without understanding its flaws and dangers. They see a capitalist system that isn't currently offering them the benefits it offered their parents and grandparents. It's hardly surprising that they are turning away from capitalism if they can't see any opportunities to accumulate the kind of capital that is needed to put down a deposit on a house, for example.

Ask someone about the company they work for and they will mostly say something positive. But ask them their opinion of business in general and you may well get a rather more negative answer.

There is a compelling case to be made for business, capitalism, entrepreneurialism and free markets, but at the moment there are few people prepared to stick their heads above the parapet to make it. It's what free-market think-tanks or pressure groups like Aims of Industry used to do in the 1970s and 1980s.

The trouble is that the CBI has only ever represented the corporatist interests of its larger members. In effect, it has become an anti-SME organisation. It cares not a jot for the family business employing a dozen people, and its lobbying is often directly counter to the interests of smaller businesses. Its lobbying in Brussels and on Brexit has been particularly insidious. Because of its financial backing, the CBI is able to lobby government and Brussels in a way smaller business organisations or individual smaller companies could never dream of. Indeed, the European Union tries only to deal with massive trade associations like the CBI and often just ignores the interests of the 'little guy'. This is why many have come to see the EU as the personification of the interests of global capital.

Globalisation has been a force for good in so many ways, but its benefits haven't been explained to sceptical consumers. Instead of cheering the benefits of increasingly free trade, they are fed a diet of stories on how multinational companies are exploiting their workforces, ruining the environment and avoiding taxes. They see global economic and political leaders descending on Davos every January and assume they're meeting to discuss how to further their own interests rather than those of the ordinary person. Davos is the personification of the global elites – elites who preach the benefits of environmental conservation, yet arrive in their individual private jets. They appear on camera in their expensive ski jackets with snow-covered mountains as a backdrop, and the global TV audience looks on and shakes its collective head in disbelief.

The global business community suffers from exactly the same affliction as the domestic businessperson who doesn't like appearing on the media and shouting about their successes.

If I asked you to take a few seconds and write down some benefits of globalisation, could you come up with more than a couple? I'd bet if I asked you to write down some of the failings of globalisation you'd find that a much easier task. Given the intelligence of everyone who is reading this book, ask yourself why that is?

Globalisation encourages lower prices for consumers as well as a greater choice. It enables domestic manufacturers or service providers to sell their wares in bigger export markets. It promotes greater competition and economies of scale.

OK, not exactly sexy, but someone needs to get out there to tell us why globalisation is a good thing, because if not it will further the ever-growing gaping chasm between normal people and those who govern them, both politically and economically.

Even when business lobbies government, it strikes entirely the wrong tone. Former Downing Street adviser Jimmy McLoughlin explained in an article in *The Times*:

> During my three years at Downing Street, business leaders regularly would cite their concerns over the accumulation of costs facing business – the apprenticeship levy, business rates, the national living wage and auto enrolment, to name a few. Often the creative ways that they were benefiting society were left to the final five minutes.

There are business leaders who are willing to put their heads above the parapet – Richard Reed, the creator of Innocent Drinks, is an evangelist for business, and the Managing Director of Iceland, Richard Walker, is a regular on programmes like *Question Time*. There are others, but I doubt you'd be able to list more than ten if I challenged you to.

And that's what needs to change.

Chapter 16

Calling Occupants of Planetary Dogma

'The concept of global warming was created by
and for the Chinese in order to make U.S.
manufacturing non-competitive.'

Donald Trump

As I start to write this chapter, the climate change protest group Extinction Rebellion has brought central London to a standstill. Obediently, a pliant media broadcasts hours and hours of footage from the protests, never once stopping to question the people taking part about the extra emissions they are causing. It came a few days after the same group had used a diesel-fuelled (untaxed and uninsured) fire engine to drive into Whitehall and coat the Treasury building with fake-blood red paint. Having in the summer of 2018 successfully got us all talking about the growing importance of the so-called climate change crisis by mounting a different form of polite protest, Extinction Rebellion seem to have changed tactics.

For the avoidance of doubt, I don't deny the existence of climate change or global warming. Nor do I deny that part of it is due to man-made influences. But I do deny that the debate is over about the actual extent of man's influence. Climate change has happened since time immemorial. That, it is safe to assume, is something surely everyone can agree on.

I consider myself an environmentalist. Being brought up on a farm, I'd like to think it goes with the territory. I learned the art of conservation from my father. He considered himself the temporary guardian of his 220 acres of land. He went out of his way to protect local wildlife and was the careful custodian of a Site of Special Scientific Interest.

My introduction to the world of environmental protection came during a year living on the edge of the Black Forest in southern Germany. I witnessed first-hand the havoc caused by acid rain on the forests of the Schwarzwald. I can lay claim to being the first person ever – in 1986 – to make a speech at a Conservative Party Conference on acid rain and the need to rethink our approach to environmental policy. I think I even got a clap.

But being pro-environment does not and should not mean being anti-growth or anti-business. As ever, there is a balance to be struck. Just as I deprecate ultra-Green activists who would happily ban all sorts of means of travel and take us back to an agrarian economy, I also cannot understand those who think that in 2019 it's still OK to carry on with the polluting policies of the 1960s as if we were in a time warp.

One thing we all ought to agree on is that discussing the environment and debating the way forward is a good thing. If only it were so.

I remember at 18 Doughty Street TV, back in 2007, I phoned Greenpeace to invite them to take part in a panel discussion on climate change. They refused on the basis that the argument was won and there was nothing to debate. Sound familiar? This was 13 years ago! It's attitudes like this that make people very suspicious of the climate change industry, which is supported by people whose fanaticism borders on the religious.

It has indeed become a religion to those people who like to jump on the bandwagon of such causes. If you dare to speak out against their creed, you're attacked as 'mad'. I dislike the messianic side of those like Al Gore who treat climate change as a pseudo-religion that, if you deign to question, you're considered slightly unhinged.

I do question it, but I do it out of curiosity, not out of dogma. I am prepared to listen to the arguments of the climate change sceptics, just as I am to those I respect on the other side of the argument.

Back in 2013 the then Environment and Climate Change Secretary and Lib Dem MP Ed Davey seriously suggested that the media should refrain from giving a platform to climate change sceptics. How very 'liberal' of him. I invited Ed Davey onto my show to discuss his views. First, he was coming into the studio. Then the interview was to be conducted via ISDN. Then on the phone – first at 6.20 p.m., then at 6.30, then at 7.20. Then not at all. A meeting, apparently. It happens. But if any of his staff were listening, they might have been rather worried to discover that, with one exception, every caller expressed some degree of scepticism about climate change. I'd say that proves the argument is far from won and that people like Ed Davey need to up their game.

On the evening I was supposed to be discussing climate change with Ed Davey, I received a text during my show from Justin, a geography teacher. This is what he had to say:

> Until two years ago I used to teach both sides of the climate change debate and invite students to discuss the issue and reach their own conclusions based on the evidence available. I have now been stopped from doing this – apparently it confuses the students. I am now only allowed to teach the 'climate change is real' evidence. So therefore I have moved to teaching students WHAT to think, rather than to THINK for themselves using the evidence available.

How chilling is that?

Roll forward a few years and the BBC made a BBC-wide editorial decision not to invite people like Nigel Lawson onto their news programmes to put the other side of the story. Like Greenpeace in 2007, in their view there was no need to provide balance, because the argument was won. Except that, as long as a significant number of people believe that climate change isn't man-made, the argument isn't won. Not by a long chalk. Just because people say they've won the argument doesn't mean they have.

The very same sort of people who warned the world in the 1980s about the coming nuclear apocalypse are now warning about the end of the planet. In the 1980s we had politicians who were able to expose these zealots for what they were. We now have cabinet ministers who go along with them and give them money. And have the cheek to tell people on radio stations that they shouldn't be providing platforms for climate change sceptics.

The climate change movement is lucky to have a whole host of articulate supporters who lose no opportunity to put the case for drastic action by governments around the world to ameliorate the effects of global warming before, as they say, it is too late.

Their latest and most powerful advocate is the 18-year-old Swedish schoolgirl Greta Thunberg. It was she who started the school strike movement. She soon became the symbol of a youth movement around the world. Her stance proved an inspiration to teenagers across the globe. She had a simple message and almost instantly her name became synonymous with climate change. Indeed, it is not outlandish to claim that she has done more to alert people to the potential dangers of climate change that any other individual since Margaret Thatcher first talked about it in speeches in the late 1980s. You didn't know that, did you? Charles Moore explains in the third volume of his biography of Thatcher that in September 1988 the then prime minister declared that because of rising population, the greater use of fossil fuels, the methane and nitrates produced by agricultural modernisation, and the cutting down of tropical forests, there had been 'a vast increase in carbon dioxide' in the atmosphere. 'It is possible,' she warned, 'that with all these enormous changes (population, agricultural, use of fossil fuels) concentrated into such a short period of time, we have unwittingly begun a massive experiment with the system of this planet itself.'

She concluded that changes in atmospheric chemistry, enabled by greenhouse gases, could lead 'some to fear that we are creating a global heat-trap which could lead to climatic instability … Protecting this balance of nature is therefore one of the great challenges of the late 20th century.'

According to Moore she followed this up in her party conference speech at the beginning of October, reiterating her fear of 'a kind of global heat-trap and its consequences for our climate'. She then convened a group of experts to conduct a one-day-long seminar to discuss an 'assessment of the science, options for mitigating the greenhouse effect' and possible policy responses.

A year later she was out of power.

Just like Margaret Thatcher, Greta Thunberg has an instinctive knowledge of how to lead and then influence a debate. However, it has come at a cost. The bile used against her on social media, particularly Twitter, has to be seen to be believed. It's not just online trolls who are abusing her. Dinesh D'Souza compared her look to a Nazi propaganda poster. The self-styled 'bad boy' of Brexit, Arron Banks, floated the possibility of her boat capsizing in the Atlantic as she headed to the UN General Assembly. A Fox News contributor called her a 'mentally ill Swedish child'. Even Piers Morgan accused her of 'abusing loads of adults' – as if he had never done that himself.

But the abuse is not all one way. Environmentalists seem to think it is quite acceptable to use the phrase 'climate change denier' to describe those who, for whatever reason, seek to argue that global warming is not man-made.

It's a not so subtle way of trying to equate climate change sceptics with Holocaust deniers. That's the only other context in which the word 'denier' is habitually deployed. Even supposedly impartial journalists and broadcasters use the term now as if it's a perfectly acceptable thing to do. It's not. Language matters and it's being abused here. If you want to take the word literally, yes, they are denying that climate change is happening, but it doesn't take Einstein to work out that the phrase is meant to imply something much more sinister.

Rather like Brexit, climate change has seen people retreat into their own echo chambers and refuse to accept there is any other opinion than their own.

Extinction Rebellion supporters have completely bought into the narrative that unless carbon emissions are reduced to zero by 2025 the planet will self-combust by the time people reach their old age. Their opponents – those who don't believe in man-made climate change at all – think that nothing is happening and people should move on because there's nothing to see. And never the twain shall meet.

Except of course, in real life it does. Over the last few decades we've all been taught that conserving is good. Most of us recycle nowadays as a matter of course. We've grown used to shopping without a raft of plastic bags. We don't like unnecessary use of plastics. Sky's Ocean Rescue campaign has alerted us to the dreadful effects of thrown-away plastic on our sea creatures. Some of us have stopped buying products that we feel have unnecessary plastic wrappings. In the end, we as consumers can drive change. Yes, governments can help too, but they need to give us more carrots and fewer sticks. People's behaviour can change, but it's not necessarily higher taxes or extra regulation that makes them do it. Incentives can often work better than force. Markets respond to consumer demand, and that can be a far quicker driver of change than a prohibitive law. Winning over hearts and minds is far more effective than a slap on the back of the legs.

But you don't win over hearts and minds by making apocalyptic threats, with little evidence to back them up. We're told by the adherents of Extinction Rebellion that if we don't act immediately the planet will end and 'billions' will die.

The trouble is we've heard it before. Thirty years ago, on 30 June 1989, the Associated Press reported this:

> A senior U.N. environmental official says entire nations could be wiped off the face of the Earth by rising sea levels if the global warming trend is not reversed by the year 2000. 'Coastal flooding and crop failures would create an exodus of "eco-refugees", threatening political chaos,' said Noel Brown, director of the New York office of the U.N. Environment Program, or UNEP. He said governments have a 10-year window of opportunity to solve the greenhouse effect before it goes beyond human control ... 'The most conservative scientific estimate is that the Earth's temperature will rise 1 to 7 degrees in the next 30 years,' said Brown.

The fact that we've heard it before doesn't necessarily mean that the similar warnings being issued today are necessarily wrong, or even exaggerated, but it does mean we shouldn't just accept the dire threats being issued as gospel truth. It also means that environmentalists who want to persuade us of their case need to explain it using facts and proper scientific research rather than just hyperbole.

Extinction Rebellion's Zion Lights appeared on *The Andrew Neil Show* during the October 2019 protests in London. She claimed that 'billions of children will die in the next 10 to 20 years' because of climate change. She was quoting Roger Hallam, one of the founders of Extinction Rebellion, who said in April 2019 that 'billions of people are going to die in quite short order' and 'our children are going to die in the next 10 to 20 years'. She then admitted that the claims have been disputed, with many scientists saying they are utterly fanciful.

When challenged, she continued: 'We don't have exact numbers, but there will be deaths and mass suffering. Any amount is enough as far as we're concerned.'

Andrew Neil then claimed that there was 'no reference to billions of people dying or children dying in under 20 years' in the IPCC report on climate change.

He pushed Ms Lights further and asked where her scientific evidence for that came from and how exactly people would die. She replied: 'Mass migration around the world, which is already taking place due to prolonged drought in countries, particularly in south Asia. Wild fires in Indonesia and the Amazon rainforest, Siberia and the Arctic.'

Neil was having none of it. He continued: 'You talk about weather disasters and there seem to be a lot of them around at the moment and people die from them. But from what I have seen, 100 years ago, weather-related disasters killed half a million a year. Today it is 20,000 a year. Still 20,000 too many, but a reduction of 95 per cent. It doesn't lead to deaths of billions. You are scaring people with this rhetoric.'

Lights hit back: 'I think there is a danger of scaring people simply because we are not taking it seriously enough and people are feeling desperate to be heard on this. Unfortunately, alarmist language works, which is why we are discussing it right now.'

Neil appeared appalled, replying: 'Does it work? I have seen young girls on television part of your demonstration, the school ones when they take the day off to demonstrate, crying because they think they are going to die in five or six years' time. Crying because they don't think they will ever see adulthood. And yet there is no scientific basis for the claims that your organisation is making.'

So, there we have it. A TV interviewer doing his job and holding people to account for their alarmist language, and Extinction Rebellion admitting that they are using such language to further their aims, but that they are not based on fact, merely to scare.

The debate about the dangers and implications of global warming needs to be conducted in a measured manner. If you're trying to persuade people of a coming apocalypse, then you need more than a few pliable celebrities on your side to make that case. The case has to be believable, and the suggested policies to lessen the effects of climate change need to be portrayed in a realistic manner. The mixture of carrot and stick is vital. There are grounds for optimism that the general public are changing their ways and recognise the need for positive action by their governments. It's only in this way that governments can gain the consent of the people for some of the more dramatic measures that may become necessary if some of the world's more poverty-stricken countries like Bangladesh are to be saved from the dire effects of global warming.

Chapter 17

The Fraudulent Debate about Poverty

'In a country well governed, poverty is something to be ashamed of. In a country badly governed, wealth is something to be ashamed of.'

Confucius

'Poverty is considered quaint in rural areas, because it comes thatched.' So said former Environment Minister John Selwyn Gummer at a conference I attended in the mid-1980s. I've always remembered it because it seemed to betray a certain attitude towards poverty.

Unless you've lived in real poverty, you can't possibly understand what it means. I never have, so I won't pretend that I can put myself in the position of those who exist on a day-to-day basis without a penny in their pockets. The only time that has happened to me was on a cold Friday afternoon in 2004 when I was wandering around Cromer with 16 pence in my pocket. My overdraft was at its limit. My credit cards were maxed out and I didn't know how I was going to get through the weekend. Irony of ironies, I was the Conservative prospective parliamentary candidate for North Norfolk.

The language surrounding poverty has been distorted and hijacked by those in the poverty lobby. It is defined in the *Cambridge English Dictionary* as 'the condition of being extremely poor'. So far, so good. But nowadays we have to differentiate between 'absolute poverty' and 'relative poverty'. If you live in 'absolute poverty' your household income is so low that it makes it impossible to meet the basic needs of survival, including being able to find housing, buy food, procure safe drinking water, education or healthcare. It means that even if the general economy is doing well, it has little effect on you as you live below the poverty line.

'Relative poverty' is when households receive 50 per cent less than average household incomes. They do have some money but not enough to afford anything above the basics. Some people describe it as 'relative deprivation' because people in this category are not living in absolute poverty but they are unable to access the same standard of living as anyone else.

It is also possible to argue that poverty is about exclusion. It means that your financial circumstances could exclude you from the opportunities everyone else in society is able to enjoy – things that most of us take for granted in our everyday lives.

All this sounds perfectly reasonable, but I do wonder if the word poverty hasn't become somewhat debased. Ask someone in sub-Saharan Africa who can't get access to clean water if they think that not having access to Sky Television constitutes poverty. Ask a textile worker in Bangladesh who is paid a dollar a day if they think a British family of six on benefits is living in poverty.

We have a rich language, yet we use the word poverty nowadays to include a lifestyle that is anything below the average.

We are told that there are 14 million people living in poverty in Britain, among whom four million are children. That's what the official statistics for 'relative poverty' inform us. Question those figures on social media and be prepared for a tsunami of abuse.

The existence and proliferation of food banks is cited as proof that one of the richest countries in the world is going to hell in a handcart. It's a point of view, but it is lazy and fundamentally flawed. If this is the case, the same thing is happening in equivalently rich European countries too. Germany has a higher GDP than we do, and German people are on average individually richer, yet it has around the same number of food banks as us – around two thousand – although admittedly its population is slightly higher. The number of people using food banks in Germany rose by 10 per cent in the year 2018–19 to 1.65 million. Among older people the rise was even higher, at 20 per cent. In France, 3.5 million people rely on food banks, at least three times more than the number in the UK.

Britain, Germany and France all pride themselves on having advanced welfare states, yet the services provided apparently aren't good enough to enable millions of people to afford to feed themselves. As a consequence, private charity has stepped in to fill the void. Organisations like the Trussell Trust have done a fantastic job in setting up food banks and ensuring no one goes hungry. This is in the great tradition of charitable giving and they should be praised for it, just as the people who give food supplies deserve huge credit too. Some see this as a complete failure of the state, and attribute the rise in food banks to the government's austerity policies. Up to a point. Food banks didn't really exist in Germany until 1993, and in this country until 2005. This, though, was well before the financial crash of 2007–8 occurred and austerity became 'a thing'. The Trussell Trust, when it set up its first food bank, realised there was a demand, and therefore soon created a national network. If you provide a supply, the hitherto unmet demand will be met. The proliferation of food banks doesn't necessarily mean that the situation has got worse across the country – it just means that the latent demand, which was always there, can now be met.

One of the big issues with our welfare system is the demonisation of those who are on benefits or use food banks. The language used is appalling, and nowhere has this been worse than in our tabloid newspapers. But it now goes wider than that. TV companies delight in feeding our apparent appetites for 'poverty porn'. Channel 4's *Benefits Street* series took us behind the scenes of an impoverished community in Birmingham. It wasn't exactly poking fun at the residents of Benefits Street, but it certainly provided ample opportunity for the show's viewers to have many of their prejudices confirmed. It singularly failed to enable its viewers to either understand or empathise with the people it portrayed. Instead it provoked ridicule, insults and anger in equal measure.

The fact is that although some of the residents of James Turner Street were on benefits, the impression given was that they all were: that they were all screwing the state – and, through the state, the taxpayer – for every last penny they could get, with no sense of responsibility whatsoever. Channel 4 exploited both the individuals and their community in order to supply their viewers with five episodes of welfare state rubbernecking. Edifying it was not.

Similarly, hardly a week goes by without the *Sun*, *Express* or *Mail* carrying a story about a larger than average family fleecing the benefits system, as if this were happening in thousands of families across the nation. Their agenda is simple: make hard-working people angry that feckless breeders are getting freebie handouts at their expense. Here are a few examples:

> Is this Britain's most shameless mum? Cheryl Prudham has 12 children and gets £40k in benefits. The mother-of-12 tells Channel 5 cameras she 'isn't bothered' what the public think of her and the £40,000 she receives from the government, and teases a shocking revelation about her future as a mother.
>   *Daily Mirror*, October 2015

> 'We are ashamed we have to do this': Couple with seven young children open up a GoFundMe after having their benefits slashed – leaving them just £480-a-month to survive on and forcing them to rely on food banks.
>   *Daily Mail*, December 2019

There are 15 families in the whole of the United Kingdom with 13 children or more, and 430 with 10 or more. That's fewer than one per parliamentary constituency. I totally get that these families are objects of curiosity – things that deviate from the norm always are. Not all of them will be claiming benefits. The Radford family in Morecambe have 22 children and don't claim benefits. A common refrain from people is that if you can't afford to have children, don't have them, and there is a certain logic to this viewpoint. However, blanket responses rarely take into account individual circumstances, and everyone has a different life experience to relate.

Nowhere is this more apparent than in the field of rough sleeping and homelessness. These are two of the most vilified groups in our society. We rarely stop to think about how a rough sleeper got into the situation. We rarely stop to engage a rough sleeper in conversation. We console ourselves that the advice from homeless charities is not to give money to street beggars or rough sleepers and we move on and continue with our lives.

This is going to sound an odd thing to say, but I love doing phone-ins on homelessness. Why? Because when I ask people who've experienced rough sleeping or homelessness to phone in, they each have the most fascinating story about how they got into it and how they eventually turned their lives around. I've also had quite a few current rough sleepers phone in. I remember a man in Bournemouth who called from his car in which he was spending the night, and a woman who was sleeping rough because she was too frightened to go home because of her violent husband and there was no room at the local women's refuge.

Politicians have always struggled to deal with rough sleeping. Some have taken the view that it's an insoluble problem. It is indeed impossible to eradicate it because there will always be some people at the margins who won't accept help from the state. Similarly, there will always be those with mental health problems who, whatever is done to help them, will continue to sleep rough.

Rough sleeping hit a peak in 2003, but by 2009 it was at an all-time low, largely down to the initiatives launched by Tony Blair's 'homelessness tsar', Dame Louise Casey. She is the most untypical civil servant I have ever met. She's someone who knows that to make an omelette you have to crack a few eggs and use a bit of industrial language. Never one for a quiet life, she got things done.

And then it all went wrong. The financial crash came. Austerity measures were introduced, the Casey initiatives were axed, and local authorities decided that most things were more important than maintaining facilities for rough sleepers, and by 2018 rough sleeping peaked, although the numbers have declined slightly since then.

It's not just the streets of London and Manchester that have seen a dramatic upsurge in rough sleeping. Wander around those of some of our idyllic market towns and you'll also see people sleeping rough. This is a phenomenon that I do not recall happening in the recessions of the 1980s and 1990s.

One Saturday night in December 2019 I found myself sleeping rough in Trafalgar Square after Dame Helen Mirren had read me a bedtime story. A few months earlier, I had another dame whom I greatly admire as a guest on my LBC radio show – yes, the aforementioned Dame Louise Casey. We were talking about the exponential rise in the numbers of rough sleepers, and she mentioned a forthcoming mass charity 'sleep out'.

Before I knew it, I'd committed to joining the World's Big Sleep Out, a global initiative founded in 2016 to raise awareness and funds, and which this year saw 60,000 people from 50 countries taking part.

I'd always been sceptical of this type of initiative in which a lot of middle-class people signal their virtue by spending a night in the open and then go back to their comfortable lifestyles the next day. However, given Louise Casey's involvement, and her record on the subject, I thought, OK, I'm up for it. Frankly, I've always hated camping, and had not spent a night under the stars for more than 35 years.

I'll admit it was a pretty unpleasant experience. I had developed a bad cold and a hacking cough, to the point that a couple of days before the event I seriously considered pulling out, given that it was only a week away from the night when I'd have to broadcast for 11 hours on the night of the general election. I simply couldn't afford to be ill. Yet I knew if I pulled out, I'd be letting down all the people who had sponsored me. What helped me decide was the thought that a homeless person doesn't have the option of sleeping indoors if they go down with a cold.

I have two main memories of the night. First, the noise. OK, Trafalgar Square was never going to be quiet, but even at 3 a.m. there was a constant hubbub. And second, the rain. It started at midnight and continued through most of the night. We were given orange plastic bags to put over our sleeping bags, but with me being 6 foot 2 inches tall it didn't go up to my head. They then gave me a second one, so I tried to put it across (rather than over!) my head. It kept blowing off. Needless to say, I didn't get a wink of sleep all night.

But it's not my lack of stoicism or the cold winds and heavy rain that drenched us from midnight onwards as we cowered under orange plastic sheets that have put me off repeating the experience. Rather, it's the torrent of foul-mouthed and mean-spirited abuse that my participation unleashed on social media, most of which I'd rather not repeat.

I was forced to block hundreds of people on Twitter because of the level of vitriol directed at me.

My 'mistake' was to publicise my night in Trafalgar Square via my LBC show and my own social media feed.

The point of the exercise was, after all, to raise awareness and money, and through my job I am lucky enough to have a platform that enables me to reach hundreds of thousands.

But because I don't fit the hard Left's notion of a social activist – I am of a small 'c' conservative persuasion and once stood unsuccessfully for the Tory Party – I am regarded as beyond the pale.

Among the milder comments I received are the observations that I'm a 'self-serving egotistical git', a 'parasite' and someone who was having a 'charitable laugh at the austerity homeless'.

I was dismissed by one Twitter antagonist as the 'sneering face of the right who want the homeless to have to beg for charity'.

Well, I wasn't expecting a peerage or a Nobel Peace Prize for my small, personal gesture of solidarity with the thousands of men and women forced to sleep rough on the streets of our cities and market towns.

But I did want to know more about the experience of the anonymous rough sleepers I hurry past on my way to Charing Cross station each night. I am all too aware that each of them will have their own, deeply human story.

That, however, was never going to protect me from contemptuous abuse, and I learned a lot about the hard, Corbynite Left during that night on the pavement – many of them self-identified their allegiance with the hashtag #JC4PM (Jeremy Corbyn for Prime Minister).

This is what I discovered.

Many of these hard Leftists think they are on the side of the angels, but social media amplifies their obsessions and shows them to be intolerant and vile. They share a loathing of Tories (or those who might be assumed to be such); they also seem to despise charities and the human impulse of private charitable giving, believing only in the miraculous powers of the Big State to deliver everything.

The other striking common theme in this river of hatred is the total absence of interest in or empathy with people on the streets.

Jeremy Corbyn likes to visit a homeless shelter on Christmas Day, and good for him for doing so. But why do many on the Left assume in him the purest of motives while they subject people like me to vile abuse for also highlighting a social scourge?

It is strange to be accused of the basest of motives by people I have never met and who know nothing about me.

Is it not possible for anyone on the centre-right to entertain the same human empathy and compassion as people on the Left? Give me a break.

I happen to agree that the rise over the past decade in the numbers of the homeless is a stain on our nation. I also agree that there is no doubt that Tory austerity has exacerbated the problem, though I would say there is blame all around, in national and local government. Money that could have been spent on more housing or homeless shelters has been spent elsewhere – to govern is to choose, as the old maxim goes.

And the longer I work in broadcasting, talking to those

who call into my show and hearing about their problems with housing or universal credit, the more nuanced the world seems to me, and the less tribal my politics become. However depressing it has been to read the abuse I've been subjected to online, I refuse to become as cynical as my critics.

Most of us in this country still believe in the power of the individual doing good things, and in the charitable impulse. We know that it is the individual who should exercise power over the state, not the other way around.

'Have a laugh at the haters,' someone tweeted even before I joined the Sleep Out at Trafalgar Square that Saturday; 'it will keep you warm.'

So it did – and more importantly, it created a backlash among the quiet battalions of the generous, open-minded people who pushed my fundraising above my wildest dreams with donations topping £34,000.

Chapter 18

Do We Really Love the NHS?

'The NHS is the closest thing the English have to a religion.'

Nigel Lawson

The NHS makes me angry. Yes, I know that is a strange thing to write, but it is the debate surrounding the NHS, or lack of it, that really makes me very irritable. Sadly, anyone who tries to critique the NHS, even in a constructive way, is immediately accused of wanting to provoke the whole-sale destruction of the institution. Suggest a modest reform to the way it is run, and it's as if you've suggested the mandatory killing of the first-born. No matter what your protestations are, they are dismissed with a wave of the hand and you're cast into outer darkness.

So when I got an email from a brain surgeon who listens to my show inviting me to deliver a lecture at Queen's Hospital in Romford, my immediate thought was to politely decline. However, as I was typing the email, the thought struck me that I was being too hasty. After all, the institutional failure in one particular hospital led directly to the death of my mother, and later my father, so here was a golden opportunity to publicly say what I really thought about the way it could sometimes fail the very people it is there to look after. It's not as if I hadn't said it on the radio often enough. So I deleted my draft email and started again. 'I'd love to accept,' I said. And thus, in January 2014, I stood up and addressed a hundred or so consultants, doctors, nurses and administrative staff with a lecture entitled: 'The NHS – Things That Need to Be Said'.

Forty-five minutes later, I started to take questions. Much to my surprise, all the people who spoke agreed with most of what I'd said. I was astonished. I half expected to be hounded out of the room for daring to question some of the most treasured covenants of the NHS. Even the union rep came up to me afterwards and said she thought pretty much everything I'd said was bang on.

Each and every one of us uses the NHS. We have shared experiences, both good and bad. We all have opinions about what the NHS does well and what it doesn't do so well.

Any government wanting to get the best out of the NHS starts from the position of knowing that the NHS has huge amounts of public support. A 2018 YouGov poll showed that 87 per cent of Britons are proud of the NHS, placing it above the armed forces (83 per cent), the royal family (64 per cent), the BBC (60 per cent) and the House of Commons (28 per cent). Furthermore, according to the Ipsos MORI Global Trends Survey, of those countries surveyed, Britain is the second most positive country, out of 19, about the quality of their healthcare, with only Belgium rating their healthcare more highly.

In many ways, senior health professionals and those in government and opposition have much in common – even if that thought might fill the latter with a degree of horror. The government is trying to wrestle with the demands of an empowered, knowledgeable twenty-first-century consumer base, while NHS staff are all operating within a structure designed for a mid-twentieth-century command-control system of healthcare provision. There is another commonality of interest: NHS staff all have a fair idea of what needs to be done, but no one in politics is courageous enough to articulate either the problems or the solutions. No one is prepared to think the unthinkable, say the unsayable, much less implement the doable.

The language we use surrounding the NHS is very telling. Politicians on the Left don't call it 'The NHS', they always call it 'Our NHS'. They do it to signal that it was the Labour Party that invented it, and that it is an institution different to all the others. Even Conservative politicians have now taken to using the word 'our', on the basis that they have been in charge of it for 44 of its 72-year-long existence. Labour also ran a campaign under the banner 'I ♥ the NHS'. Is it even possible to love an inanimate institution? Do we love the armed services? The BBC? If we do, it's a very different kind of love.

Politicians treat the NHS as a political football – insisting on initiative after initiative – to prove that there really is 'Action This Day', and yet they consistently fail to plan for the long term. They seem to think that structural reform and targets will yield results – and sometimes, in the short term they do, but who can think of a single health secretary who has been able to plan for the long term – of either party? During the 13 years of the last

Labour government there were six different health secretaries.

The Conservatives under Margaret Thatcher and John Major did a little better and managed only seven in 18 years. The latest Conservative government (in coalition for its first term) has had three different health secretaries so far. So a health secretary serves for an average of a little over two years. Since 2010, the average has increased to more than three – a small improvement depending on whether you think Andrew Lansley, Jeremy Hunt or Matt Hancock have performed well.

Of the 16 holders of this post since 1979, very few had any direct experience of health policy before they took on the job. Typically, they spend six months reading themselves into the position and the last six months of their tenure trying to save themselves from being sacked. This gives each of them roughly a year to make an impact.

Bearing in mind that the NHS is one of the world's largest organisations, this way of running it is utter madness. If IBM or Glaxo changed their chief executive every two years their share prices would plummet and within a short time the company would be considered a basket case.

Unsurprisingly, then, we constantly hear pleas to take the politics out of the NHS. Liam Fox, when he was Shadow Health Secretary, said it. Various Labour ministers said it. Andrew Lansley said it. Jeremy Hunt actually believed it. But surely none of them can be so naïve.

After all, the fact that the Health Service eats up £130 billion – a sixth of all public expenditure – means that the way this money is spent has to be made accountable, and that has to be through the political system. So any politician who calls for politics to be taken out of the NHS is likely to be doing it to get a cheap round of applause on *Question Time* and can safely be ignored. It's not going to happen, and nor should it.

You simply can't take politics out of the NHS. We need to be having a big national debate about the NHS and the future provision of healthcare, but we are being denied that debate because whenever any politician on the Right or Left – but mainly the Right – has the temerity to criticise the NHS, he or she is jumped on and warned about the consequences of having a go at a beloved institution.

If you point out that outcomes in the NHS are in most areas way below other comparable nations you are accused of denigrating people who work so hard in the NHS, or advocating privatisation even when you're not. If the NHS can't stand up to robust critique, it says an awful lot about the arguments of its very vocal defenders.

Defenders of the status quo refuse to engage in the argument about how services are provided. Even though the private sector has always been heavily involved in the provision of healthcare in this country, many on the Left regard it as an evil. In the 2019 general election Labour made clear it would seek to eliminate any private sector involvement whatsoever. The Shadow Chancellor, John McDonnell, brazenly told me he would happily take Britain's 14,000 pharmacies into the public sector. Labour even wanted to stop buying drugs from the very pharmaceutical companies that had spent millions developing them – purely on the basis of political dogma. Instead, they wanted to create a nationalised NHS drug supplier, ignoring the fact that such an organisation would only be able to supply generic drugs.

The 'public good, private bad' mindset that bedevils politicians on the Left is equally matched by the 'private good, public bad' attitudes often prevalent on the Right. Only in this country could this happen. Even in these days of supposed consensus, these attitudes still prevail.

Do any such politicians think people care if people are treated privately or in an NHS hospital if they get the treatment they want, where they want, when they want it? Of course not. Yet people who use private healthcare are made to feel as if they are somehow being elitist, rather than being praised for taking responsibility for their own healthcare and not burdening the NHS with their demands.

Beveridge and Bevan never meant for the NHS to have to meet every single demand ever made of it. Two systems can work happily together as long as each respects the other. For too long in this country Labour politicians have seen private medicine as a class enemy and Tory politicians have viewed the NHS as something for other people to use, not them.

Let's not pretend that private sector involvement in the provision of healthcare is anything new. Most people use private sector dentists. GPs are effectively in the private sector, as are most osteopaths and physiotherapists.

Drugs are provided by private sector suppliers. Chemists and dispensaries have never been in the public sector. It was recently reported with some horror in the *Guardian* that 70 per cent of NHS contracts are with the private sector.

Opponents of the private sector also raise the spectre of the NHS introducing charges, conveniently forgetting that patients already pay prescription charges. From time to time, the issues of charging for hospital food, or for GP visits, are floated, but these are quickly ditched once the howl of public outrage subsides. However, on radio phone-ins such as my own, the idea of charging for NHS services is quite popular in some areas. For example, people ask why the taxpayer should pay for the treatment of people who bring their own misfortune on themselves.

People who binge-drink on a Friday night and end up in A&E. Why shouldn't they be charged? People who regret getting a tattoo and can apparently have it removed courtesy of the NHS. But where do you draw the line? Charge smokers for lung cancer treatment? Charge obese people for diabetes drugs? Another one for the 'too difficult' box, I suspect.

We all make judgements concerning the NHS depending on whether we work for it, we are patients ourselves or we have family or friends who use the NHS. All our judgements are based on our own experience or that of those close to us. Indeed, doctors, surgeons and nurses are not immune to this, with surveys showing that as many as 30 per cent of them would not want their own family members to be treated in the hospitals in which they work.

It's all anecdotal evidence, but that's the only evidence an individual has got. So when learned academic studies are published that are at variance with our own experience we tend to speak out. Clearly, people always tend to highlight the negative rather than the positive, which is why whenever I host a phone-in on my radio show about a particular aspect of the NHS, I am always careful to solicit positive as well as negative callers.

Ann Clwyd, the recently retired Labour MP, became a bit of a *bête noire* for some in the medical profession when she told of the terrible care her husband had received courtesy of a hospital in Cardiff. He died. She made a tearful speech telling of their experience and was later asked by

David Cameron, the then prime minister, to head a review looking into complaints against the NHS.

Her report made very sad reading for all concerned with the standards of nursing care in this country. I regret to say it chimed with me, for my mother went through a terrible experience at Addenbrooke's Hospital in Cambridge, after which she sadly died. It was a horrible experience for her, for my father, for my sisters and myself. Throughout it all, we felt powerless. It turns out that she was put on the Liverpool Care Pathway. We were never told about it. No one seemed to be able to tell us what was happening to her.

She was put on the wrong drugs. She kept telling us, 'They're trying to kill me.' We put it down to the effects of the drugs, but in the end perhaps she was trying to tell us something that we were too deaf to hear. We put our trust in the hospital and they let us down. More importantly, they let her down.

The standard of nursing care was lamentable. Different nurses every day. I reckon she had 150 different nurses in the three weeks she was in that ward. I'd love someone to tell me how there can be any continuity of care in such circumstances.

I queried why, whenever I visited, there was never a nurse that I recognised. 'Oh, it's the 48-hour week that's to blame,' one said. 'And we get put on different wards each day.'

Half of them seemed to be agency nurses, some with a variable grasp of English – never a good thing when dealing with older patients. They kept trying to feed her totally inappropriate food, when a cursory look at her notes would have told them she was unable to digest it.

She was left sometimes for hours in soiled sheets. In the end my two sisters operated a shift system, because we couldn't let her be alone. We ignored the visiting hours, and the nurses allowed us to, as it took work away from them.

And the thing is, it wasn't that there weren't enough nurses. There were. When we eventually realised that my mother was going to die, we decided to take her home. The thought of her dying in that place was too awful for us to contemplate. But even then, they were so incompetent that I was forced to book a private ambulance to take her home, because the NHS ambulance repeatedly didn't turn up.

She spent two weeks at home, and it was here that the NHS came up trumps, with her wonderful GP visiting at least twice a day and providing just the support that she – and we, her carers – needed. I shall never forget what that amazing GP did that week. My mother died at home looking out on the garden she loved, surrounded by her family.

I should have made an official complaint against Addenbrooke's. I should have raised merry hell with the hospital bosses, but, to my shame, I didn't. I just couldn't bear the thought of reliving it all.

I let down not only my mother, but also others in that hospital. While she was lying there, unable to do anything for herself, I kept thinking about other patients who had no family to care for them. We were in a position to do things, but there are many older people whose families can't or won't support them in the way we could.

It was only when I read about Ann Clwyd's experience that I actually did something about it. She had received thousands of letters and emails from people who had gone through the same thing. Blame is easy to ascribe, but it is often misplaced.

I have thought long and hard about how these things are allowed to happen. In truth, there is no single person or group of people who is to blame. And let's face it, blame rarely gets us anywhere. But there are clearly questions to be asked about current standards of care in some of our hospitals.

So when I heard Jeremy Hunt say, almost on his first day in the job as Health Secretary, that he was concerned about the fact that nursing care was becoming increasingly depersonalised, my ears pricked up.

When he suggested, though, that nurses should do a year's on-the-job training before embarking on degrees, he was met with a hailstorm of abuse from the usual vested interests.

'A really stupid idea,' said the Royal College of Nursing. That's the kind of response one might expect from a trade union but not from a Royal College.

It seems to me that aspects of nursing training are not fit for purpose. Jeremy Hunt once said that this 'culture of defensiveness' must cease, and doctors and nurses must 'say sorry' when things go wrong in the NHS. Administrators blanche at that, saying, 'think of the legal consequences', but surely he was right.

Of course, things will go wrong. In any organisation the size of the NHS, and with the risks involved in most medical procedures, there will always be mistakes made on occasion. The challenge for the NHS is to find a way of acknowledging this in a way that doesn't undermine the whole system.

The NHS would collapse without foreign nurses and doctors, but I have always been slightly queasy about overtly recruiting them from countries that, frankly, are so poor that the best form of international aid we could offer them is not to steal their most capable medical staff.

It was the Blair government that promoted the theory that people much prefer to be treated in their own homes, and therefore fewer hospital beds were needed. In addition, new technology and faster treatments meant that, whereas in the 1980s someone might need a five-day hospital stay, nowadays that might be reduced to one or two, or even none if the treatment could be done in a day. It's a policy that has continued since that time under all shades of government. Small hospitals in rural areas in particular have been hit, with many being closed altogether. The very concept of a convalescent hospital has virtually disappeared.

There has been a perfect storm. Although the number of doctors and nurses has increased, and brand-new hospitals have been built (often funded on the never-never, or as a Private Finance Initiative, as we have come to call it), the population has increased exponentially. This seems to have come as a bit of a surprise to NHS executives. On top of that, instead of the population becoming healthier, we've become more obese, prone to be diabetic, and generally more ill, more often. Again, this seems to have taken the NHS by surprise. Demands on mental as well as physical health services have increased hugely in recent years, yet the number of mental health beds has declined sharply. Not only that but non-residential mental healthcare funding hasn't kept pace with demands in any shape or form. As I say, in short, it's a perfect storm.

So why do politicians still refuse to acknowledge the reality that more beds are needed? One explanation is that the advice from NHS England remains that the policy shouldn't change. But isn't it the job of politicians to challenge that advice?

The trend couldn't be clearer. Under all governments in the last 30 years, the total number of hospital beds has been cut – or slashed depending on your viewpoint.

The total number of beds in the NHS has declined by more than half, from around 300,000 in 1987 to around 148,000 now. In 1987 the UK population was 56.8 million. The population now is around 66.2 million. An increase of 17 per cent, yet the number of hospital beds has declined by more than 50 per cent. Medical advances have certainly been made, but surely not to that extent.

If we look at the number of general and acute beds, which is the biggest category, the numbers are startling:

1987–8 – 180,889
1997–8 – 138,047
2010–11 – 108,958
2016–17 – 102,369

The average decline in beds per year during the Blair/Brown government was 2,909. During the coalition and subsequent Conservative years, the figure is 1,098.

The figures for mental health beds are even more stark:

1987–8 – 67,122
1997–8 – 36,601
2010–11 – 23,448
2016–17 – 18,730

The biggest cuts in mental health beds came when Care in the Community was launched. However, it's continued ever since. In the last 30 years, bed numbers have been cut by 72 per cent. This is astonishing.

The average decline in mental health beds per year during the Blair/Brown government was 1,315. During the coalition/Conservative years the figure was 786. These figures demonstrate that hospital bed cuts are part of a long-term strategy that governments of all colours have implemented. And they've done this at the behest of the medical establishment.

This leads us on to the real issue here – and that's social care. NHS professionals and administrators have been very keen to cut bed numbers on the premise that once patients have been discharged it's up to the social care system to take over – especially with geriatric patients. The trouble is that this side of the healthcare equation has been largely ignored, despite politicians constantly telling us that it's a policy dilemma that needs solving.

I know from personal experience how elderly people take up beds in hospitals even though they shouldn't be there. They should be in care homes, but the places just don't exist. Since 2002 an average of 7,000 new care home beds have opened in the UK every year, but by 2026 there will be an additional 14,000 people needing residential care home places per year. How will these beds be financed? There's little doubt that, along with housing provision, social care is one of the two biggest social challenges facing government.

Chris Hopson, the head of NHS Providers, has said that ten to fifteen thousand new hospital beds are needed if we are to avoid the kind of crisis we're seeing at the moment in hospitals up and down the country. That's between 60 and

90 per acute trust. Bear in mind that some acute trusts have more than one hospital.

Each hospital bed costs the NHS around £150,000 per year. The annual cost of increasing bed numbers by 15,000 would be around £2.25 billion.

It's all very well for healthcare professionals and politicians to call for billions of pounds of extra funding, but what would it be spent on? We all remember the huge amounts of extra money that went into the NHS in the early Blair years, but the overwhelming amount of it went on salaries, not into directly improving healthcare.

If we are going to spend a higher percentage of our national income on the NHS then we surely need to decide on our priorities. I would suggest that reversing the decline in hospital beds ought to be fairly near the top of that list.

Politicians will tell you that the NHS is their number one priority. The NHS has achieved the same status as the Queen Mother in the nation's affections.

But I do not see an appetite to change it fundamentally and, as a consequence, I think over time it will become a much hotter political potato than it may be at the moment; as expectations increase, performance will lag behind. The challenge facing all politicians will be how to square this un-squarable circle. The truth is that they will abdicate responsibility to health professionals and then blame them if it all goes wrong.

In future, most government initiatives are likely to be centred around preventative measures rather than structural ones. Preventative healthcare has grown in visibility in recent times. An anti-obesity drive is always guaranteed to provoke big headlines in the mid-market newspapers as well as intense discussion on radio phone-ins.

Such initiatives give the appearance of action, even if they can be incredibly expensive in terms of PR costs. Politicians love them. They are great for photo opportunities, soundbites and gimmickry.

So expect to see a lot more of nannying politicians exhorting us to eat less, drink less and exercise more.

There needs to be a national and rational debate about the scope and extent of the NHS. Should it cover illness, injuries or both? Should people insure against injury – probably a small cost – as opposed to illness. But I pity the first politician to even suggest such a heresy. This is a perfect example of where politicians need to come together and 'get along'. There surely has to be scope for cross-party agreement on the way forward for both the NHS and the social care system.

Can we afford to maintain the 'cradle to grave' scope that Beveridge established, although I doubt that he foresaw the range of treatments currently available and their cost. I doubt also he foresaw a health service where 2,600 people earn more than the prime minister, and 7,800 people earn more than £100,000 a year.

The obvious truth is that until we accept that the NHS can't and never will be able to meet all the demands made on it, we can't actually have a proper and rational debate.

The pity is that no one currently on the NHS scene seems to have much idea of the questions, let alone the answers. Parliaments drift by and the issues remain the same: expensive reorganisations take place with little or no real benefit. And anyone who dares to criticise or critique the NHS gets their head bitten off by people who profess to *love* it.

So the real, overwhelming question is this: if we were in a position to set up a health service now, from scratch, what

Chapter 19

Last Night a DJ Saved My Life

'What mental health needs is more sunlight,
more candor, and more unashamed
conversation.'

Glenn Close

One in four of us will suffer from mental health difficulties at some point this year. I'm lucky. I never have. Even in the darkest moments of my fifty-plus years on this earth, I've never come close to wanting to end it.

A quarter of those who have mental health problems won't visit their GP. The real question is what happens if they do visit their GPs. Anecdotal evidence from my listeners suggests that not enough GPs are equipped to deal with mental health issues. Maybe older GPs didn't have the same kind of mental health training that is available today, but time after time people tell me that their GPs seem out of their depth on these kinds of issues. And perhaps this explains why the prescription of drugs seems to be the automatic default for so many GPs.

Part of the problem is that people suffering from mental health problems, or their families, face a bewildering system that is so complex that even those who are familiar with it find it baffling.

OK, we have mental health trusts, but there are also acute trusts that provide liaison psychiatry services and some A&E services for mental health patients. Ambulance trusts may or may not be commissioned to provide mental health conveyancing services outside of emergencies, whatever they may be.

Clinical Commissioning Groups commission some services, while specialist trusts commission others. And then of course there are GPs who provide primary mental healthcare to some 83 per cent of mental health patients. Finally, you have local authorities who oversee and/or directly employ Approved Mental Health Professionals – or at least those who are not employed by or seconded to the NHS.

We talk about mental health more openly now than we ever have done, but for some it remains very difficult. They still see it as a sign of weakness and fear that could be exploited. But when celebrities and even politicians now feel able to bare their souls about their struggles with depression, it can only give hope to those who still find dialogue difficult. For those who do want to talk, the key thing is for others to listen.

My interest in mental health was first sparked when I became a volunteer on my university's 'Nightline', aimed at providing a local Samaritans-like service for students. I did a day's training as a counsellor and then would spend some very lonely hours sitting by the Nightline phone waiting for it to ring. It never did. I bet it does today, though.

In 2004, when I was a parliamentary candidate in North Norfolk, I led a campaign to save a dementia care unit in North Walsham called Rebecca House. It provided respite care. It had only been open a few years when the local primary care trust decided to close it. It was a lifeline for carers and they were distraught. I was invited to meet some of the relatives. I assumed it would be very informal, but after a tour of Rebecca House I walked into the main social room to find thirty or forty people. I hadn't prepared a speech, but got up and reassured them I would do all in my power to reverse the decision. I rang my opponent, Norman Lamb, and put party politics aside, as I thought the only way this was going to work was for him, as well as me, to lobby the government. In the end we failed to prevent it closing, but it wasn't for the want of trying on either of our parts.

The people I met at Rebecca House made me realise how mental health really was, and still is, the Cinderella service. Think about it: we care about our physical health, but we regard mental health as of secondary importance. But to those with mental health problems, it's far from that. It dominates more or less every waking moment of their lives. People who are outwardly extrovert and have very successful careers and happy home lives can often be prime examples of people with chronic depression. The most common response is to tell them to 'snap out of it'. It's the worst possible thing you can say. Because it's impossible to do. If you could, you would.

But mental health is far from being all about depression. Mental health issues come in all shapes and sizes, as I have discovered presenting my LBC radio show. When I started at LBC I never for a moment imagined I would host phone-ins on depression, dementia, bereavement, coping with trauma, the psychological effects of child abuse. Who on earth, I thought, would phone in to a radio station and talk about such personal matters? Well, I soon found out that many people do, and regard it as a huge release to be able to talk about things in such a forum. My boss at LBC at the time said that I would always get a good reaction on these subjects because I am a good listener and don't interrupt all the time. 'You've got a comforting, non-threatening voice,' he said. 'People will open up to you in a way they might not to others.' And so it has proved to be. Some of my best programmes have involved talking about mental health. We've had some tears, we have had a lot of emotion, but above all, people feel they are helping others by demonstrating that other listeners are not suffering alone.

In a way, that's the secret of talk radio. Let the listeners do the talking and only intervene if they start breaking down or need a bit of guidance. Just listening to people relate how their depression dominated their entire lives, or how people had recovered from it and were now optimistic about the future, was an inspiration. I have never got to the end of an hour discussing mental health and thought it had been a failure. Think about it. If you suffer from mental health issues it takes balls of steel to ring up a radio station and tell the whole country about it.

Perhaps the most difficult thing to talk to anyone about is the moment you tried to take your own life.

My first experience of talking to someone about this subject was Bill on the M25 back in 2012. He phoned in towards the end of the hour and very calmly informed me that he would take his own life later that night. I was blindsided. I hadn't expected that. I told myself to keep calm, but knew that one word out of place could have potentially tragic consequences. I watched the clock tick up to nine o'clock, but I knew there was no way I could terminate the conversation. For the first time ever, I dropped the top-of-the-hour news. I listened and let Bill talk, sometimes for minutes without interruption. He saw no future for himself and felt that taking his own life was the only way out. After twenty or twenty-five minutes I knew I had to bring the conversation to a close. I asked him to stay on the line and talk to my producer, Laura. I could see her speaking to him for at least another twenty minutes.

The next night he phoned in again and asked Laura to put him through to me. We were covering a completely different topic, but I knew all those who had been listening the previous evening would want to hear from him again. This is what I recall him saying: 'Iain, I did try to kill myself last night. I took a lot of pills, but then I thought about what you and Laura had said, and I phoned 999.' He and I both became a little emotional at that point. I've thought about Bill a lot, and often wonder what became of him.

'Iain, you're my number ten,' said the voice on the phone, late one Saturday night in December 2018.

At around a quarter to midnight my phone rang. It was someone who I knew from the world of politics, but not well. We had texted a few times, but met only once. Initially I assumed it was a pocket call, but I knew from Twitter that this person had had a few personal problems of late, so I took it. As soon as I answered I knew something was very wrong. Michael is not his name, but for the purposes of what I am about to tell you, that's what I am going to call him.

'I'm so sorry to have rung you, but I didn't know who else to ring. I'm in a bad way and I have 40 pills in front of me and I want to kill myself.'

Those were his opening words, so far as I recall.

He explained that he was often having suicidal thoughts following a traumatic personal experience a few months ago. He had tried to get treatment on the NHS but was told there was a lengthy waiting list. He had been to see an NHS crisis team and told them of his state of mind. Their advice was to compile a list of ten people he could call if he ever felt suicidal again. The second thing he said to me was that I was number ten on his list and he kept apologising for the fact. Eventually, it transpired that the other nine people hadn't picked up. I talked to him for around 45 minutes with the rather obvious aim of talking him down from what he was intending to do. Though I had very little experience of this, I knew that one wrong word could have some very tragic consequences.

I won't go into all the details of the conversation, but during it Michael told me that when he was referred to NHS mental health services, he was told there would be a two-year wait for treatment. Even when he phoned the Samaritans, he was told there would be a 30-minute wait to talk to anyone.

I can't remember all that I said. I do remember asking him to think about the effect on his friends and family if he did go through with it, and how upset they would be. The most important thing to try to persuade him of, I felt, was that there was something to live for. That he meant something to a lot of people. That it wouldn't always be like this. But, as I've already said, listening to him explain why he felt the way he did was probably more important.

I needed to convince Michael of the consequences of his intended action. I think it registered.

By the end of the conversation it had become more normal and I was relieved when I heard Michael laugh.

It is quite clear that Michael and many others like him are being let down by the NHS. It is simply not acceptable for someone who has suicidal tendencies to be told they will have to wait months, or even years, for proper treatment. The *Spectator* journalist Isabel Hardman explained how she had a similar experience and had to spend her life savings going private. But what about those who don't have any savings to fund such treatments? I often argue that the NHS fails some patients because of structures, rather than a lack of funding. But it is clear that in the field of mental health, funding is indeed the main issue. And it is one that must now be addressed.

Since that initial conversation, I have had at least six other similar calls from Michael. I suspect I've moved up his list from number ten. On one occasion I noticed people talking about him on Twitter. Somehow, I and others managed to find his address and the police went around just in the nick of time. He called me the next day from hospital.

At the time of writing, Michael is in a good place. New job, new home, a fresh start in life, able to put some of his more painful memories behind him.

There is little doubt in my mind that the state of public discourse on social media is partly to blame for the rise in suicides among young people and the recent explosion of self-harming. I do not pretend to understand what motivates a 13-year-old to cut themselves. It's easy to put it down to a cry for help, but surely it goes deeper than that.

Bullying used to be a physical phenomenon, but in the last 10 or 15 years it's become a mental issue. Most bullying is not done face to face, it's done in text conversations or anonymously on the internet. The 11-year-old daughter of a friend of mine was bullied remorselessly on social media by an anonymous troll, but no one could have foreseen the identity of the bully. It was her best friend. The pressures on today's teenagers are hundreds of times greater than they were when I was a teenager in the 1970s. It's not only the pressure to succeed. For middle-class kids, that's always been there. It goes far beyond that. A teenager's self-worth and self-image is too often the driving force in their lives.

We all know the saying about sticks and stones and names. But language does hurt, and not only does it hurt, it can have tragic consequences. The daily grind of looking at your Twitter page or Facebook page and seeing all the terrible things that people say about you can have a deleterious effect on your mental health whatever age you are.

I'm not especially in favour of the language police, but in mental health I will make an exception. Let's stop saying 'commit suicide'. It infers a degree of criminality and shame. We should always use the phrase 'take your own life'. I once upbraided Nick Clegg for using the word 'nutter' in an interview. I reminded him that mental health professionals regard it as the mental health equivalent of 'poof' or 'paki'. He looked shocked. Sadly, I heard him continue to use it in ensuing interviews. It's not that he did it deliberately. It's difficult to wean yourself off using words that you've used your whole life.

It's the same when we talk about death or grief. The old-fashioned among us might like to think that when we discuss dying, we do so with some degree of reserve and respect. And usually that is the case. But switch on your social media feeds and it feels like you've entered a parallel universe. Wishing someone dead is commonplace on Twitter. Former Tory MP Antoinette Sandbach published an email she received the night after her local Conservative Association passed a motion of no confidence in her.

> You ignorant Remain MPs deserve all you will get keep looking over your shoulders your family must be very proud of you by putting their future in jeopardy by trying to stop Brexit make sure you and your Remain twatish [sic] MPs keep looking over your shoulders because BOOM BANG you are all dead.

What happens to someone when they come to believe it is perfectly normal behaviour to email a death threat to an MP just because she has the temerity to disagree on a matter of policy? I could fill the rest of this book with similar such missives.

It really matters how we use language when we discuss political matters, and it especially matters how politicians comport themselves. Labour MP Paula Sherriff made her name for taking Boris Johnson to task in the House of Commons for using hyperbolic language and for invoking the name of her murdered colleague Jo Cox, saying that the best way to honour her would be to 'get Brexit done'.

In a controlled rant at the prime minister she said:

> I genuinely do not seek to stifle robust debate but this evening the prime minister has continually used pejorative language to describe an act of parliament passed by this House … We should not resort to using

offensive, dangerous or inflammatory language for
legislation that we do not like. And we stand here under
the shield of our departed friend with many of us in this
place subject to death threats and abuse every single day.
And let me tell the prime minister they often quote his
words 'surrender act, betrayal, traitor'. And I for one am
sick of it. We must moderate our language and it has to
come from the prime minister first. I would be interested
in hearing his opinion, he should be absolutely ashamed
of himself.

Boris Johnson responded by saying:

I think the threats against MPs and particularly female
MPs are absolutely appalling and we're doing a lot of
work to give MPs the security that they need. But then
there's another question, which is – can you use words
like 'surrender' to describe a certain act or a certain bill?
And, quite frankly, I think that you can, and if you say
that you can't then you're kind of impoverishing the
language and impoverishing political debate because,
after all, the use of that kind of metaphor has been going
on for hundreds of years.

On the same day Jess Phillips tweeted: 'I'm not scared of an
election, I am scared I might be hurt or killed.'

I believe her. But I said at the time that it was unwise of
her to tweet such a thing in case it encouraged someone to
actually try to do it.

A disturbing poll at Cardiff University and the University
of Edinburgh found recently that a majority of voters on
both sides of the Brexit debate said violence against MPs

was a 'price worth paying' in order to get the resolution they wanted. Think about that.

All this culminated in many MPs – particularly female ones – deciding the game wasn't worth the candle. Conservative, turned Change UK, turned Lib Dem MP Heidi Allen quit at the 2019 election, writing to her constituents:

> I am exhausted by the invasion into my privacy and the nastiness and intimidation that has become commonplace. Nobody in any job should have to put up with threats, aggressive emails, being shouted at in the street, sworn at on social media, nor have to install panic alarms at home. Of course, public scrutiny is to be expected, but lines are all too regularly crossed and the effect is utterly dehumanising. In my very first election leaflet I remember writing, 'I will always be a person first and a politician second' – I want to stay that way.

This deeply held view should worry us all if we are to continue to attract not only people of quality, but also a wide range of people from different backgrounds into politics. Isabel Hardman wrote a bestselling political book – and not many people do that – titled *Why We Get the Wrong Politicians*, which put flesh on the bones of this argument. She summed up her core argument in a *Spectator* column:

> Politics has become infected by a 'just war' mentality, where people on all sides believe it is acceptable to behave unconscionably to those they disagree with. They conflate fighting ideas with fighting a person physically, and

dehumanise their opponents to the extent that they end up 'deserving' the abuse because they are wrong. Urging people to 'just get on' isn't going to cut it: they often believe themselves to be peaceable because they are kind to those of a similar persuasion. Anyone who wants to ensure a good supply of 'normal' people coming into parliament is going to have to work out how to unpick the 'just war' mentality, otherwise we will lose far more from our politics than just individual MPs.

The phrase 'string 'em up' is used all too regularly on social media and elsewhere. It's a sentiment that is used to address any group of people or individuals who others find somewhat disobliging. I've heard it said about Extinction Rebellion protesters, for example. No one seriously believes that the accusers literally want them to be 'strung up', at least one would hope not.

I do find it slightly bizarre that, as a general rule – and there are of course exceptions – those who are most vociferous about the death penalty tend to take the Right to Life side of the argument over abortion. And those who scream about the barbarity of the death penalty tend to be those who apparently think little of terminating a 22-week-old foetus.

Ironic, isn't it? Either you believe in life or you don't. It's time people on either side of this argument looked at the consistency of their position.

Given that we all die eventually, and the fact that as we get older we start attending more funerals than weddings, it is remarkable how little we talk about the subject – either to each other or through the prism of the media. How many programmes on TV or radio can you think of that address the subject head on? Joan Bakewell's long-running Radio 4 series *We Need to Talk About Death* was cancelled, and the US funeral director-themed drama *Six Feet Under* lasted five series, but there are few others one could mention.

This is odd. When someone dies, we grieve. We shed tears. We recover, but extended grief can lead to all sorts of mental health problems. Some of the most moving hours that I've hosted on the radio have concerned grief.

My mother died on 9 June 2012. I had never lost anyone that close to me before. There is often a special bond between a son – especially, maybe, an eldest son – and a mother, and my mother and I had that in spades. I had never experienced that level of bereavement before. I didn't know how I should cope, or even whether I would. People who told me that it would get easier over time clearly meant well, but in the immediate aftermath there was not a day that went by without me analysing my feelings. When I went back to work a few days later, was I being heartless and betraying my mother's memory? I remember thinking that and telling myself not to be so stupid. But the thought was there. Part of me felt I should still be in pieces, that I shouldn't have been able to pick up my life again so quickly. Inwardly, I was still in pieces, of course, but I knew I had to get back behind the microphone.

I gave the eulogy at my mother's funeral. I felt I should have collapsed in tears halfway through, but I didn't. I had been more emotional doing the eulogy at other funerals, including the one a week previously of a schoolfriend, Barry Marsh. I felt proud that I had held it together, but guilty for doing so, too. That sounds ridiculous when I read it back to myself, but I hope it makes some sort of sense. In retrospect, I know why I managed to retain my composure. It was because I had practised reading the eulogy so many times that it took the emotion out of it. I also made sure I concentrated on someone at the back of the church and managed to avoid catching the eye of any of my nearest and dearest in the front pews. All I wanted was to do my mum proud. And I now know I did. But initially, I can't pretend that was how I felt. Grief plays havoc with your powers of logic and common sense.

Each of us has different ways of reacting to death and coping with the grieving process. Too often we bottle up everything and suffer the consequences. Do we get through it by talking about it, as Joan Bakewell suggests? If so, should it be with family or friends, or is it better to talk to strangers, who have no emotional investment in what we're going through? Somewhat bizarrely, I feel more comfortable talking about grief on the radio than I do to people close to me. What do you say to someone who has lost a husband, wife, son or daughter? My experience was that people would say the most inappropriate things – not because they were trying to hurt me, but because they didn't know what to say and had to fill a silence. Because my mother had been ill for some time, when she died one or two people told me I must be feeling relieved! Er, no. One of my close relations even told my sister that she must be feeling 'pleased'. She was open-mouthed at the insensitivity.

At times like this, I almost envy people of faith. Some religious people are able to bury their emotions in their faith and almost use it as an emotional crutch. They cling on to the belief that their loved one has 'gone to a better place' and that they are relishing the afterlife. I don't have that advantage, given I don't believe on heaven, hell or any form of life after death.

My mother hated to talk about death. She hated going to funerals, and generally didn't. I don't know if it was because her own mother had died at the youngish age of 61 (in 1953) or whether it was because of general squeamishness about the subject. I remember a conversation one of my sisters and I had with my parents that somehow moved on to talking about death and wills. Suddenly, my mother burst into tears and we never, ever, talked about the subject again.

I hosted a phone-in on grief a matter of days after my mother's funeral. My producers weren't sure this was a good idea given my tendency to become lachrymose at the most inconvenient moments. I wanted to do it because I'd received an anonymous letter from a listener:

Dear Mr Dale, I listen to LBC every evening. I'm so sorry about the loss of your mother. I lost my mother and I've been devastated without her. I lost my husband in 2011 under very unhappy circumstances. The stress is unbearable. Could you ask how others pick up the pieces of their life, being left alone for the first time? In 2010 my husband's brother committed suicide. I've just come out of mourning because I was told until I did, my loved ones would never rest. They say time is a great healer, but it's not true. The loneliness is so intense and the raison d'être is nil. My faith gives no answers except bear it. How? What have others done? I think I invented crying inside.

Everything was going swimmingly for the first 45 minutes and I held it together. That was until Dave in Dagenham phoned in. 'I can hear it in your voice, Iain,' he said. And off

I went. I couldn't speak for a few seconds, and when I did, my voice was wavering. Dave didn't mean to upset me. He was displaying basic human empathy.

Seven years on, have I 'got over' my mother's death? Nearly four years on, have I got over my father's passing? No. And I don't think I ever will. Am I supposed to have 'got over it' by now?

My mother and I were very tactile. We enjoyed a good hug. I'd tell her I loved her. In the eulogy I gave at her funeral I said:

> When someone close to you dies, there are usually huge regrets. You regret unkind things that were said. You regret those things you never said. The things you never had a chance to say, the things you were too embarrassed to say. We British leave a lot of things unsaid, trusting that unsaid things really don't need to be said. Well, we didn't leave anything unsaid. We didn't need to tell Mum we loved her; she knew. But we did, nonetheless. She left this earth in no doubt about the love we all had for her.

My relationship with my father was different. Close, but different. Only in the last years of his life did we hug each other. Before that, when I said goodbye we'd shake hands. I hate to tell you this, but as I type this sentence tears are streaming down my face. Why? Because I don't know if I ever told him I loved him. Isn't that a terrible thing?

50 Ways to Improve Public Discourse

*'Perfection is not attainable, but if we chase
perfection we can catch excellence.'*

Vince Lombardi

This book has sought to identify how and why our public discourse has declined. I am by nature an optimist and I don't think there is any reason why this continuing decline is inevitable. There is no silver bullet, but as individuals we can all act to ensure that the state of public discourse improves. It's not just down to each of us – media executives, politicians and governments all have a role to play. I've tried to draw up some recommendations for us all to adopt that would make a difference. None of us are perfect, and none of us will behave impeccably all the time, but here are some small ways we can all shout less and listen more. And get along.

SELF-IMPROVEMENT

1. Self-analyse the way you react to people who disagree with you and work out how you can argue better, more politely and more effectively.
2. Treat others how you would be wish to be treated yourself.
3. Be more forgiving for people's failures and failings.
4. Read long-form articles rather than short, tabloidy ones. Before you debate, inform yourself properly about the issue you're commenting on.
5. Switch your phone off. Reduce your screen time and avoid it interrupting you during conversations.
6. Avoid having the attention span of a flea – learn to engage more deeply with people.
7. If you feel the sap rising, think of what your mother would say.
8. Examine your friendship circle. Are they of the same race or ethnicity? Do they all vote the same way as you, or come from a similar background? If so, go and make new friends and you might learn something new.
9. Try to understand why people do and think things rather than rush to immediately contradict them.
10. Know yourself. If you're spoiling for a fight, don't go online.

DEBATE and ARGUMENT

1. For schools to start teaching children how to debate with each other better and more politely.

2. Teach children about civics, democracy and politics. and in particular enable teenagers to understand the concept of 'losers' consent' better.

3. Debate participants should understand that their opponents are not their enemies. They probably have the same aims, just a different way of achieving them.

4. Don't assume the worst about people who disagree with you.

5. You don't need to have an opinion on absolutely everything, let alone communicate it. Just because you live in a society where you can say anything, that doesn't mean that you should.

6. If someone disagrees with you, don't immediately rush to condemn them. Ask them why, and listen.

7. If you cite a fact, make sure it is just that, and not an exaggeration of something you think you heard somewhere. Facts matter.

8. Resist the temptation to shout down your interlocutor. It's not a good look.

9. Feel free to invoke John Stuart Mills' 'harm principle' ('the only purpose for which power can be rightfully exercised over any member of a civilized community, against his will, is to prevent harm to others') and intervene politely if you see someone invoking hate speech – but stay calm.

10. Make every effort to be the voice of sweet reason rather than the tyrant of the conversation.

MAINSTREAM MEDIA

1. Radio and TV broadcasters should think before they always go after the 'clip that will go viral'.
2. Political interviewers should understand that it's not about them. It's about enabling the viewers and listeners to understand politics better.
3. Editors and interviewers should avoid prioritising 'gotcha' moments.
4. Broadcasters should re-evaluate their obsession with short-form interviews and instead create programme formats in which long-form interviews can be held.
5. Broadcasters, especially the BBC, should make more effort to recruit producers from different backgrounds and from different worldviews.
6. Programmes like *Question Time* should retreat from the bearpit atmosphere that is encouraged at the moment.
7. Political programmes should be less about entertainment and more about informing and education, without losing the ability to engage.
8. Ofcom should update and modernise its 'due impartiality' rules and guidance on swear-words that are allowed on TV and radio.
9. Newspapers and broadcasters should be more willing to apologise properly (and prominently) for mistakes made.
10. Mainstream media channels should stop obsessing about youth, and cater just as much for the people who still read or watch them.

SOCIAL MEDIA

1. For Twitter, Facebook and YouTube to ban anonymous accounts and ensure all accounts are verified.
2. As a consumer of news, be careful where you're getting your news from. Ask yourself what agenda the news source might have and whether they are being entirely objective or impartial.
3. Facebook should change their algorithms to avoid people only being shown political adverts they are likely to agree with.
4. Social media companies need to do far more to regulate themselves in blocking harmful content.
5. Twitter, in particular, needs to rethink how it deals with people who deliberately stoke hatred and incite others to act illegally.
6. Twitter needs to address its 'blue tick' system and widen it to include anyone who can prove who they are.
7. Britain should emulate Germany's 'NetzDG' law, which forces any social media company with more than 2 million users to set up a transparent complaints system.
8. If governments can't find ways of regulating powerful social media companies, then they need to tax them into changing their ways to protect their users.
9. All the main social media companies (with two exceptions in China) are based in the United States. So it is the US government that needs to be lobbied to rein them in.
10. Encourage the social media companies – especially Facebook – to accept that they need to do more to counter 'fake news' without undermining free speech.

MIND YOUR LANGUAGE, IMPROVE YOUR BEHAVIOUR

1. In the field of mental health, avoid using terms like 'commit suicide' and 'nutter'.
2. Whatever you do, don't swear.
3. It's not 'woke' or 'politically correct' to want to avoid deliberately upsetting someone.
4. Don't attribute motives to someone you aren't 100 per cent sure they have.
5. Be careful of trying to be funny. Humour is a great ice-breaker and leveller, but it can also be exclusional and create walls.
6. If you have a large social media following, be aware that your words have impact. Avoid subliminally encouraging your followers to pile in on someone else, who may not be psychologically able to cope with it.
7. Retweeting may not be an endorsement, but is still seen to be so by many. Retweeting something that you think is highly amusing may not be seen as funny by others.
8. Never post a photo of someone without their permission.
9. Never post pictures of your food. No one is interested. Not even your mother.
10. Remember, everything you say, everything you post, everything you like, everything you share is a direct reflection on you.

Acknowledgements

While reading Emily Maitlis's excellent book *Airhead* last year, I had a lightbulb moment. It's a book based on thirty or forty of her experiences in journalism and interviewing, and I got a quarter of the way in when I suddenly thought to myself: 'This is the book I want to write.' So, as I read on, I started to jot down chapter headings of incidents I have been involved in during my broadcasting career and life involved in politics.

I phoned my literary agent, Martin Redfern at Northbank Talent Management, who had been discussing various book ideas with me for 12 months, and explained what I was thinking. Finally, I said, I've come up with an idea that excites me and a book I actually want to write.

He then told me he had been approached by Ed Faulkner at HarperCollins, who also had a book idea for me. 'It's all about the decline of public discourse and how we should disagree more politely,' he said.

We met with Ed and decided we should combine the two ideas into one book. You, dear reader, will be the judge and jury as to whether that has worked.

Thanks are very much due to Martin Redfern and Ed Faulkner for being joint midwives to this book. Thanks also to Isabel Prodger, Zoe Shine, Dawn Burnett and Joel Simons at HarperCollins, to my publicist Ruth Killick and to Nick Fawcett for his careful copyediting of the manuscript.

This book is a culmination of working in politics and the media over the last 35 years. I've had various jobs and learned so much from each of them. So in various ways, thank you to Patrick Thompson MP, Nicholas Finney, Evie Soames, David Gilbertson, Jo Phillips, Christine Captieux, David Davis, Lord Ashcroft, James Stephens, the dear departed Andy Wilson, Stephan Shakespeare, Gill Penlington and all the other magnificent people I have worked with in Parliament, at the British Ports Federation, Charles Barker, Lloyd's List, The Waterfront Partnership, Politico's, Oneword Radio, 18 Doughty Street, *Total Politics*, Biteback Publishing, CNN and Global Radio.

I'd like to pay a heartfelt tribute to all the producers at LBC who have had to put up with me over the last ten years. Each of them has taught me something, and I think we've made some very special radio together. Several of them have become lifelong friends: Matt Harris, Jagruti Dave, Laura Marshall, Jakub Szweda, Sophie Snelling, Victoria Gardiner, Rebekka Walker, Christian Mitchell, Henry Riley, Sandra Glab, Caroline Allen, Carl McQueen, Axel Kacoutié and my current producers Robbie Hawkins and Catriona Beck.

I hope the others won't mind if I pick out Matt Harris in particular. He produced me for my first year on LBC and then returned to me when I took over *Drive* in 2013, before eventually leaving LBC after ten years to go to *Newsnight*.

Matt has been by far the biggest single influence on my development as a presenter. He made me better than I really am. He got inside my brain in a way that sometimes frightened me. He spotted weaknesses in a politician's argument before I did and would whisper a killer question in my ear. I, of course, got the credit, but in reality, the credit was often his. We sometimes fought like cat and dog. Creative tension, I think it is called. Matt is a prince among producers and he still listens to the show when he can and gives me tips and advice.

Thank you also to the LBC management team who have been so supportive of me over the years and not only allowed me to do what I do, but taught me how to do it better. I know that from time to time I've caused them all sorts of headaches and irritations, but they have, without exception, supported me, encouraged me and on the odd occasion even had to stand by me.

James Rea, now Director of Broadcasting at Global Radio, was Managing Editor of LBC for eight of my first ten years on the station. Like me, he's a total radio geek and was instrumental in the recent success of LBC and its rise to prominence. Each time I went into a contract renegotiation with him I had convinced myself it would be 'Thanks, Iain, for all you've done, but it's time for a change'. But it never was.

Richard Park, James's predecessor as Director of Broadcasting, remains a big influence on me. He is one of those people who can truly be described as a legendary figure in the world of radio. He loves his politics and was a huge source of encouragement to me over the years. Ashley Tabor-King and Stephen Miron have been fantastic in their support for LBC, and me in particular, and I hope I've repaid their confidence.

James's successor as Managing Editor, Tom Cheal, served as his deputy for many years, and when I joined LBC was the station's political editor. I've hugely valued his wise advice and have enjoyed watching him grow into the job.

There are seven other people who have also had a huge impact on my radio career. Jo Phillips gave me my first break on the radio when she asked me to deputise on 5 Live's late lamented *Sunday Service*. She showed a confidence in me that no one had before.

Tommy Boyd, a legendary radio presenter in his own right, offered me the chance to present some shows on PlayTalk, a new internet radio station, and without having done those shows I doubt I'd have had the opportunity to join LBC.

Jonathan Richards was Managing Editor of LBC when I first joined, and he saw something in me that others had not. I'll never be able to repay him for giving me a chance and encouraging my development.

Chris Lowrie is an LBC institution and was a key part of the production and management team for 25 years before he left the station in 2015 to move to Spain. He took me under his wing, and his advice and encouragement, especially in those early days, were invaluable. His creativity in terms of imaging and making promos was incredible. I remember one day listening to one of his masterpieces and it moved me to tears!

And finally, Louise Birt, who was Deputy Managing Editor at LBC for an all-too-brief 18 months, but taught me a huge amount about how I could improve as a presenter. We made some very special radio together and I'll never forget her shouting at me before a programme to hit the ground with pace and verve. 'Big bollocks!' she'd shout into her microphone from behind the glass. I've still got no idea how she knew …

I've also got a lot to thank other radio presenters and broadcasters for. Peter Allen, Steve Allen, Christiane Amanpour, Anita Anand, Lisa Aziz, Richard Bacon, Duncan Barkes, Anna Botting, Adam Boulton, Clive Bull, Nicky Campbell, Jo Coburn, Ian Collins, Nick Conrad, Jon Craig, Evan Davis, Judith Dawson, Anne Diamond, Jonathan Dimbleby, Stephen Dixon, Lorna Dunkley, Nick Ferrari, Shelagh Fogarty, Max Foster, Sir David Frost, Kate Garraway, Jane Garvey, Fi Glover, Julia Hartley-Brewer, Brian Hayes, Petrie Hosken, Anna Jones, Iain Lee, Robin Lustig, Eddie Mair, Emily Maitlis, Olly Mann, Simon Marks, Andrew Marr, Chris Mason, James Max, Simon Mayo, Simon McCoy, Piers Morgan, Chris Moyles, Andrew Neil, Stephen Nolan, James O'Brien, Paddy O'Connell, Niall Paterson, David Prever, Mike Read, Susanna Reid, Steve Richards, Beth Rigby, Nick Robinson, Ben Shephard, Peter Sissons, Matt Stadlen, Martin Stanford, Tom Swarbrick, Jeremy Thompson, Hannah Vaughan-Jones, Jeremy Vine, Kirsty Wark, James Whale, Jim White and Steve Wright have all influenced me and taught me a lot about radio and radio presenting, even though they may not realise it.

Much of my life has been dedicated to the promotion of politics and political science as a worthy cause. Not just in what I do in the media, but also in the world of political bookselling and publishing. In all, I published more than six hundred books. Whether it was through Politico's Bookstore, Politico's Publishing, *Total Politics* magazine or Biteback Publishing, I like to think I've done something for the reputation of the body politic. I'd like to thank James

Stephens, Olivia Beattie, Jeremy Robson, Suzanne Sangster, Katy Scholes, Hollie Teague, Namkwan Cho, Antonello Sticca, Sam Carter, Shane Greer, Sarah Mackinlay, Ben Duckworth, Jeremy Halley, Amber de Botton, Emily Sutton, Joe Pike, Adam Lake, Asa Bennett, John Schwartz, Sean Magee, Mick Smith, Margaret Marchetti, Peter Just, Dean Williams, Nick Ostler and James Hatts for being such good colleagues and friends, without whose efforts none of those publications would have been possible.

There are many others without whose political inspiration, business advice and personal friendship and love I could not have achieved anything: Patricia Abbott, Yasmin Alibhai-Brown, Richard and Jonathan Archer, Simon Banks-Cooper, Audrey Barker, Helen and John Barrett, Donal Blaney, Paula Blay, Wendy and Chris Bond, Sir Graham Brady, Duncan Brack, Steve Bramall, Gyles and Michele Brandreth, Russell Brown, Daniel Bryce, Charlotte Bush, Alastair Campbell, David Canzini, James Carswell, John Chittenden, Peter and Juliet Clark, Michael Cockerell, Alison Collier, Alex Collinson, Eve Collishaw, Richard Collyer, Peter Cropper, Ashley Crossley, Tracey Crouch, Anthony Curwen, John Cushing, Gabriela and Felix Dasser-Fuchs, David Davis, Jenny Day, Nick de Bois, Corinne de Souza, Claire Dexter, Angela Entwistle, Judy Fletcher, Daniel Forrester, Mark Fox, Michael Fuerst, Mark Fullbrook, Jan George, Paul Goodman, Liam Halligan, Neil and Christine Hamilton, Cathy and Jordan Hardwick, Tom Harris, Ayesha Hazarika, Sir Michael Hintze, Ernie Horth, Lisa Jenkinson, Barney Jones, Simon Jones, Marci King, Jay-Louise Knight, Matt Lane, David Laws, Brandon and Justine Lewis, Marjorie Lloyd, Peter Lumsden, Sarah Mackinlay, Francesca Makins, Simon Marcus, Tracey

Meek, David Mills, Eleanor Mills, Mark and Jane Milosch, Tim Montgomerie, Simon Moore, Sandra Moy, Scott Mund, Anne Mylan, Jonathan Neale, Jan Neary, Alan Nicholl, Gloria Nicholl, Dennis, Marian, Alasdair and Suzanne Nicholls, Gerhard and Christa Niessner, Jochen and Mary Niessner, Christine and David Norman, John Parry, Andrew Pierce, Duncan Powell, Tim and Sharon Quint, Phyllis Reeve, Peter Riddell, Sheila Robinson, Bert and Sylvia Rose, Roger Rosewell, Liz, Paul, Alex and Amy Rosoman, James Seabright, Gillian and Tom Shephard, Jonathan Sheppard, Caroline and Tony Shingleton, Keith and Pepi Simpson, Roger Sizer, Deborah and Mike Slattery, Jacqui Smith, Deborah Towle, Grant Tucker, Gordon Turner, Theo Usherwood, Rena Valeh, Adam Vandermark, Simon Walters, Alan Webb, Dirk Weber, Ann Widdecombe, Tony Wishart, Tony Yallop, and Frances and Michael Yorke.

To quote the African proverb, 'It takes a village to raise a child.' My village was Ashdon and I wouldn't be who I am today without the friendship and influence in my younger years of the Bartlett family, the Bartrams, the Bidwells, the Bryces, the Chapmans, the Daveys, the Doubles, the Everitts, the Furzes, the Rev Walter Lane, the Lewises, the Sizers, the Swans, the Webbs and the Williamses.

I'd like to pay tribute to my teachers at Ashdon County Primary School, Arthur and Norrie Kemp, Dorothy Porter and Dorothy Homewood and Mary Swan, and those at Saffron Walden County High, Steve Boyle, Donald Cousins, Bob Crossan, Joyce De'Ath, Steve Earnshaw, Joe Findlay, Joyce Hammond, David Kuyper, David Lewis, Nick Pett, Eric Swan and Nigel Wills. At UEA, John Charmley, Richard Evans, Colin Good, Ken Lodge, Max Sebald and possibly the biggest influence on my university education, Gordon Turner.

My family have been an immense support to me, especially my parents Jane and Garry Dale, and the only grandparent I ever knew, my grandmother Constance. I would give anything to spend even just one more hour with them. Their constant encouragement and understanding meant the world to me. They never tried to push me in any particular direction but were always there for me. I know I am a constant source of annoyance and irritation to my sisters Tracey and Sheena, but that's what big brothers are for! I am very lucky to have three beautiful and talented nieces – Isabella, Ophelia and my god-daughter Zoe. Thank you also to my wider family – John and Esther Dale, their children and my cousins Caroline, Nicola and Richard, Molly and Percy Scotcher, my cousins Heather and Susan, Jean and Alan Watkins, my cousins Philip and Roy, my beloved godmother Eleanor Daniels, Jean Theobald, Mabel and Bill Smith, Norman and Margaret Smith, the Nordens and the Kiddys. I hope in some way I have made them all proud of me.

My final, and most important, thanks go to the person this book is dedicated to, my partner John Simmons. He has had to put up with an awful lot since we got together in the autumn of 1995. As this book is published we are about to celebrate 25 years together, 12 of them married. During much of that time we have both worked and lived together – a recipe for disaster in most relationships, yet somehow ours works. He understands me in ways that few ever have. His love for me is unconditional and mine for him. He's not a book person, but I hope he will read this one. I say that in the full knowledge that when he's read it, he'll say: 'I can't believe you said that. Can't you keep anything private?' John's parents, Enid and Roland, both sadly no longer with us, were wonderful in welcoming me into their family.

Since the hardback edition of this book was published in August 2020 I have been overwhelmed by the emails, tweets and messages from people who have bought it, read it and enjoyed it. I couldn't have asked for more. I'm very proud that it hasn't just appealed to my fellow political geeks – it's reached people who hadn't even heard of me before. My one sadness has been that I have been unable to meet readers in person at literary events and festivals up and down the country because of the coronavirus. Zoom talks and panel sessions are a poor substitute for basic human interaction. I've done a couple of live events but wasn't actually allowed to meet audience members. I'm hoping that this will change this summer and that lockdowns and social distancing will become distant memories. Do check out the Events page on my website at www.iaindale.com for details of where I will be appearing to discuss this and my other book *The Prime Ministers*.

I do hope you have enjoyed the book. If you have, please tell your friends and post about it on social media. The best form of marketing is word of mouth. Yours!

Iain Dale
Tunbridge Wells, March 2021